JEAN LANGLAIS

Jean Langlais. Photo by Jean-Louis Loriaut, courtesy of Jean Langlais.

JEAN LANGLAIS

A Bio-Bibliography

KATHLEEN THOMERSON

BIO-BIBLIOGRAPHIES IN MUSIC, NUMBER 10
Donald L. Hixon, Series Adviser

Greenwood Press
New York • Westport, Connecticut • London

Library of Congress Cataloging-in-Publication Data

Thomerson, Kathleen.
  Jean Langlais : a bio-bibliography / Kathleen Thomerson.
    p. cm.—(Bio-bibliographies in music, ISSN 0742-6968 ; no.
10)
  Discography: p.
  Bibliography: p.
  Includes indexes.
  ISBN 0-313-25547-4 (lib. bdg. : alk. paper)
  1. Langlais, Jean, 1907- —Bibliography. 2. Langlais, Jean,
1907- —Discography. 3. Music—France—Bio-bibliography.
4. Langlais, Jean, 1907- . 5. Composers—France—Biography.
I. Title. II. Series.
ML134.L18T5 1988
016.7865'092'4—dc19   87-37550

British Library Cataloguing in Publication Data is available.

Library of Congress Catalog Card Number: 87-37550
ISBN: 0-313-25547-4
ISSN: 0742-6968

First published in 1988

Greenwood Press, Inc.
88 Post Road West, Westport, Connecticut 06881

Printed in the United States of America

♾™

The paper used in this book complies with the
Permanent Paper Standard issued by the National
Information Standards Organization (Z39.48-1984).

10 9 8 7 6 5 4 3 2 1

Contents

Preface

Jean Langlais, French composer and organist, has had a brilliant career in both Europe and North America. His compositional style influenced contemporary music, particularly sacred music, on both continents, and his works are widely played. For example, *Organ Book*, ten pieces published by Elkan-Vogel of Philadelphia in 1957, has sold more than 20,000 copies. Many of his works remain unknown, however, and are worthy of study and performance. It is the author's hope that this book will lead to a broader appreciation of Langlais' musical contributions. Information is divided into five major sections: **Biography, Interviews, Works and Performances, Discography,** and **Bibliography**. There are one appendix and three indexes.

All facts in the **Biography** were checked with the composer during visits to France in 1986 and 1987. Unreferenced statements such as "he has no memory of sight" come from notes made by the author during the interviews or in her previous study with Langlais. She has known the composer since she auditioned for him in December 1954 at the Basilica of Sainte-Clotilde in Paris.

Works and Performances lists 240 compositions, classified by genre and arranged alphabetically by title. All manuscripts of published and unpublished works in the composer's possession are listed. Date of composition, time length stated by the composer on his copyright application, publisher where applicable, and premiere performances are included. Two premieres may be listed if it cannot be determined which was performed first. Each work is assigned a "W" number (W1, W2, etc.) for identification.

Compositions based on earlier works are noted. Langlais occasionally reuses, revises, or transcribes material, particularly from his unpublished or out-of-print works. An example is the unpublished vocal setting of *Psaume 123* [W61] of 1937, transcribed in 1972 for organ as the first movement of the *Cinq Méditations sur l'Apocalypse* [W146], and published by Bornemann in 1974.

Although Langlais has a large number of unpublished compositions, almost all have been performed. The **Bibliography** has five French reviews from 1938 of the *Psaume 123* mentioned above. Langlais himself has given many first performances of these unpublished works, often on the French radio. "Clarté dans la Nuit," a weekly broadcast of the ORTF (Office de la Radio-diffusion et Télévision Française, later RTF), is a showcase to promote the works of blind composers and performers. This program, usually thirty-five minutes, has been the vehicle for performances of many Langlais works. *Diptyque* [W213], is known to have premiered on "Clarté dans la Nuit." Other first notations for "premiere, radio," in the Langlais papers refer to this series and to organ recitals given by Langlais, Litaize, and others (*see* B97 for example of studio recital broadcast).

The **Discography** is cataloged by "D" numbers, arranged alphabetically by title and classified. Both commercially-produced and privately-released recordings are included. Solo voice and choir classifications are combined under the "Choral and Vocal" heading, since some works have been recorded in both ways. The author inventoried Langlais' personal collection of discs in 1986.

An annotated **Bibliography** of writings by and about Langlais covers the years 1926 to 1987, when he celebrated his eightieth birthday. Entries are prefaced by "B" numbers. Categories include general references, individual compositions, improvisation, reviews of recordings made by Langlais, nonprint sources, and archive information. All early articles were from French sources, and all from the 1930-1947 era available to the author are included. Approximately 75% of the American and European reviews read dating after 1950 were not cataloged here, as there was much duplication. Preference was given to signed, attributable articles which contained an interview, reported a premiere, or were good descriptions of reaction to Langlais' works and performances. A large selection of the included reviews, plus additional American reviews, recital programs, and correspondence, was deposited at Boston University in 1987 and is now available to researchers (*see* Archive Collections, B395).

The opus numbers assigned in the summer of 1987 by Marie-Louise Jaquet-Langlais are published here for the first time,   included   in   the chronological list of compositions, an **Appendix**. The index section is divided into **Index of Works, Index of Authors and Translators**, and **General Index**.

The compositions of Langlais are organized in three ways:
(1) alphabetically, by genre, in the **Works and Performances** section,
(2) chronologically, in the **Appendix**, and
(3) alphabetically, without genre grouping, in the **Index of Works**.

The author gratefully acknowledges the assistance of the following persons:

Jean Langlais and Marie-Louise Jaquet-Langlais, who answered many questions, provided hospitality at their homes in Paris and La Richardais, and allowed access to manuscripts, scrapbooks, music, recordings, and doctoral research materials;

Ann Labounsky, who shared her copies of Langlais' manuscripts and scores made during the course of her doctoral research, copies of Langlais' tour journals, Jeannette Langlais' catalog, and responded to numerous questions about chronology, premieres, and reviews;

Karen McFarlane, for reviews and recital tour information;

Stefan Kagl and Folkert Grondsma, who sent German and Dutch articles and discography entries;

Naji S. Hakim and Helga Schauerte, for French and German premiere and discography materials;

William Maul, for American premiere articles;

Margaret F. Stroud and Antoine Escudier, for French translations;

Michael Gray, J. F. Weber, and Eric Hughes, who answered discography questions;

Georgette Lano, Librarian of the Association Valentin Haüy, Paris, for access to the files of *Le Louis Braille*;

and Don Hixon, for encouragement for this project.

The author particularly appreciates the assistance and support of faculty members of the Music Department, Southern Illinois University at Edwardsville, Chairman William Claudson, and Professors Warren Joseph, Donald Loucks, Victor Markovich, and Joseph Pival. Therese Zoski, Humanities Librarian, Lovejoy Library, SIUE, aided in locating bibliographic resources. Periodicals, scores, and recordings of Langlais' music were examined at several libraries: Association Valentin Haüy, Illinois State University, Northwestern University, Rice University, St. Louis University, University of Illinois, University of Indiana, University of Nebraska, and Washington University, St. Louis. The assistance of the librarians and staff of these institutions is greatly appreciated.

JEAN LANGLAIS

Biography

The year was 1923 and the place was Paris, France. A sixteen-year-old student at the National Institute for the Young Blind decided to be a musician. Jean Langlais, that young student, then began to study and practice music for at least eleven hours daily. His musical training began rather late, at the age of ten, after he was sent to Paris. His Breton family was quite poor, and had no money for musical instruments or music lessons. The young man went on to have a brilliant international career, respected as composer and performer. This bio-bibliography is a record of the impact that Langlais' hard work, determination, and talent have had on the musical world. It is a fascinating story, not the usual one of musical gifts recognized early, or precocious talent carefully nurtured.

Jean-Marie-Hyacinthe Langlais was born on February 15, 1907, in a village in Brittany, La Fontenelle (Ille-et-Vilaine), 17 kilometers from Dol-de-Bretagne. His father Jean was a stonecutter, the family tradition. His mother Flavie Canto Langlais was a seamstress. As their first son, he was named Jean after his father. He was not born blind as has been often stated, but had some sight as an infant. Due to glaucoma his vision was gone by age three, and he has no memory of sight. His parents did not raise him as a protected handicapped child, but in the same way as his sighted sister Flavie (b. 1915) and brothers Louis (1920-1970) and Henri (1925-1972). The lullabies and folksongs his mother and grandmother sang to him are the first music he remembers. Years after, he put two of those Breton melodies in early works, the *Nativité* and *Suite armoricaine*.

Jean liked to climb trees. He was also good at rolling a hoop along by hitting it with a stick, and enjoyed playing games with other children. He learned to ride a bicycle, and stayed on the path by following the sound of a bicycle ridden ahead, or by linking arms with another rider. When his family went to the woods to pick up chestnuts, he found as many as the others did. The time to go to school came, and Jean went along with the other children his age. As he grew older, his uncle convinced his parents to send him to Paris to learn to read and write in braille at the Institution

Nationale des Jeunes Aveugles. This was a hard time for the young boy, aged ten. The big city, and the school with many young blind boys and girls, was a completely different environment than he had known in Brittany. The seacoast was far away. He had an example of courage, however, which was an inspiration to him. The previous year, in 1916, his grandmother learned to read for the first time at age 60 for the purpose of teaching Jean his catechism. His family was Catholic, which is usual in Brittany. The Catholic church has always been very important in his life.

Music was taught at the Institut, and Jean started violin with Rémy Clavers. Piano study with Maurice Blazy followed, and harmony with Albert Mahaut. The blind Mahaut had gained his *premier prix d'orgue* in César Franck's class at the Paris Conservatory in 1889. He was a very strict teacher who required the students to play each day's lesson from memory on a harmonium in front of the class. Eventually Langlais decided to give up the violin, realizing that he would always need an accompanist. He preferred to play an instrument where he could perform the literature by himself.

In the halls of the Institut he heard the sounds of the three Cavaillé-Coll organs as older students practiced. He wanted to become an organist, and to dedicate his life to a career in music. So at sixteen, he started organ study with the famous blind organist André Marchal, who also taught him counterpoint and composition at the Institut. Now he learned to harmonize Gregorian chant, and to improvise on chant themes. Plainsong, read in braille, became a great influence in his compositions. By 1927 he was giving organ recitals, and his organ *Prélude et fugue* won the Institut competition for compositions. It is based on original themes, with impressionistic harmonies. The joyful fugue's counterpoint is impressive.

Marcel Dupré headed the jury that awarded Langlais the first prize for his composition, "with the jury's compliments to the performer." In the fall of 1927 Langlais was admitted to his organ class at the Paris Conservatory. (The formal name for this school is the Conservatoire National Supérieur de Musique de Paris, but it is commonly called the Conservatoire de Paris. The school for young blind students is known both as the Institution Nationale des Jeunes Aveugles, or the Institut National des Jeunes Aveugles, often INJA.) In the class there were two graduates from the Institut, Langlais and Gaston Litaize. Dupré treated them exactly as the others, saying that there were not two kinds of students, sighted and blind, but only one kind, musicians.[1] An admirable concept, but in actual practice a support group is needed. At the Institut there was a library in braille, with many braille music scores. At the Paris Conservatory the assignments were not given in braille, nor could they be turned in without being copied into conventional notation. This was particularly important when Langlais studied counterpoint and fugue in the class of Noël Gallon. Langlais has always expressed thanks for the help and friendship given him by other students at the Conservatory, some in his classes, some older: Jehan Alain, René Malherbe, Maurice Duruflé, Olivier Messiaen, Noëlie Pierront, and

Henriette Roget, among others. He received a *premier prix d'orgue* in 1930.

Since 1927 he had been the assistant organist at the church of Saint-Antoine-des-Quinze-Vingts. Langlais' first published work, the choral *Deux Chansons* printed in 1933, was dedicated to the titular organist of that church, the Count Christian de Bertier.

Church organists in France have duties which are reflected by their titles. The titular organist plays the *grand orgue*, usually in a gallery. Another organist accompanies the choir on a small organ or harmonium located near the singers, often in another area of the church. There may be co-titulars (associates), and *suppléants*, the assistants or substitutes, who act as deputy or supply organists.

Langlais also taught at INJA, where he followed Adolph Marty as professor of organ and composition in 1930. He directed a choir, and shared the organ teaching with his former professor André Marchal, who performed Langlais' works on his recital tours, generously introducing his colleague's name abroad.

In 1930 Langlais studied improvisation for a year with the organist at Sainte-Clotilde, Charles Tournemire, who had a profound influence on him. Noted for his improvisations, Tournemire used the Gregorian chants of the day as themes each Sunday. The Basilica of Sainte-Clotilde is a mid-nineteenth-century Gothic revival church. Its beautiful organ, built by Aristide Cavaillé-Coll in 1859, was previously played by the titular organists César Franck (31 years, 1859-1890) and Gabriel Pierné (8 years, 1890-1898). Langlais coached with Tournemire to prepare for a competition held by Les Amis de l'Orgue in Paris in June 1931, which he won.

In December 1931 Langlais married Jeanne Sartre, a friend of one of his students. Jeannette, as she was called, was not a musician, but an amateur painter. After marriage she stopped painting in order to devote her time to the musical life and works of her husband. They moved into an apartment on rue Duroc where Langlais still lives in 1987, one block from the Association Valentin Haüy and the Institute. Shortly after his marriage, in 1932, he was named titular organist of Notre-Dame-de-la-Croix de Ménilmontant, and was also *suppléant* at Saint-Etienne-du-Mont. Although their first child did not survive birth, the young couple was later very happy to start their family with a baby girl, Janine, born in 1935.

One year earlier, Langlais made an important decision for the direction of his musical career. By 1934, he had composed the *Six Préludes, Poèmes Evangéliques*, three of the *Cinq Motets*, and had started on the *Vingt-quatre Piéces*. He requested admission to audit the Paris Conservatory composition class of Paul Dukas. When he showed Dukas his newly composed Gregorian Paraphrase *Mors et Resurrectio*, the professor said, "You are a born [natural] composer. I have nothing to teach you except orchestration." Dukas admitted him as a regular class member. There, Olivier Messaien helped him keep up with the classwork by dictating orchestral parts from works that were not available in braille score.

Langlais' orchestrations of two of his organ works won the second prize in Dukas' class of 1935, and were performed. Langlais greatly respected Dukas, and was planning to continue working with him. This did not happen, as Dukas died on May 17, 1935.

Some composers select a form, and write music to fit that structure. Dukas regarded form as having no value except as an appropriate vehicle for the creative ideas of the composer, and as a direct result of his creative impulse. Langlais agrees. Another of Dukas' ideas inspiring the young blind teacher was the concept of variety, that one should always write something new, not another version of previous work. One should sometimes play false to his own tradition, to what is expected of him.

> I have always tried to remember what Paul Dukas taught us, at a time when, may I remind you, he had four organists in succession as pupils – Duruflé, Messiaen, Alain and myself – Dukas often used to say, "A composer must belie his reputation." So if one compares the "Imploration", the last piece I've just spoken about, to the "Nativité" at the beginning, one will obviously say, "the same chap didn't write both!" But then *that* will give me very great pleasure![2]

After the death of his former piano professor Maurice Blazy, he became the titular organist of Saint-Pierre-de-Montrouge in 1935. On some Sunday mornings he listened to the twenty-minute improvisation which Tournemire played between the end of the 10:00 mass and the start of the one at 11:10.[3] Since he could not usually leave his own church position on Sunday mornings, he went to Vespers to hear the improvisations of Tournemire, or Vierne at Notre-Dame. He traveled about Paris by subway, or walked alone, with his wife, or a student. Sainte-Clotilde was a 10-minute walk from his apartment. He walked confidently and quickly, and remarked that Saint-Pierre was a 45-minute walk by himself, or 50 minutes with his wife.

He composed both large-scale and smaller works during 1935-1939, for various media: brass, 'cello, flute, organ, piano, violin, choir, vocal solo, orchestra, and chamber ensembles. The most important works were *Piece in Free Form* (organ or piano with strings), *Deux Psaumes* (choir and soloists with accompaniment for orchestra, also arranged for piano or organ), *Suite armoricaine* (piano), *Symphonie Concertante* (piano concerto), and *Thème, Variations et Final* (strings, brass, and organ). These were performed from manuscript, but only two works found publishers, and that would be twenty years in the future, with *Suite armoricaine* printed in France in 1958, and *Piece in Free Form* in America in 1960.

After having great success with his early organ pieces *Poèmes Evangéliques* [1932, published 1933], and *Trois Paraphrases grégoriennes* [1933-34, published 1935], Langlais sought to broaden his scope as a composer, inspired by his orchestration work with Dukas. At the same time, he wrote the small-scale *Vingt-quatre Pièces* for harmonium or organ during 1933-1939. The first volume was published in 1939, and the second in 1942. It soon became evident that his organ and choral works found publishers and were performed, so he turned more in this direction.

Now life became more difficult for Langlais. The war came, and Paris was occupied. INJA closed on June 10, 1940, and Langlais decided to move his family to the small Breton village of La Richardais, between Dinard and Saint-Malo. It was there that he wrote a *Tantum Ergo* for eight voices and organ on the day that the German forces occupied the village. He intended it to be sung by the chorale at INJA, and wrote for the time when the school would reopen. That soon came, in July of 1940, and Langlais and his family returned to the city. It was, of course, a very different Paris. In June 1941 he played in a recital series at the Palais de Chaillot. His program as scheduled included Vierne's *Carillon de Westminster*. This work was regarded by the censor as "pro-English," and he was forbidden to play it. He substituted, from the same *Pièces de Fantaisie*, the *Sur le Rhin*. At the close of the recital, his audience of French civilians and German soldiers demanded an encore, and they got the *Carillon de Westminster*.[4]

Tournemire died in 1939, and it was well known that he wished Langlais to follow him at the tribune of Sainte-Clotilde. The concours to fill the vacancy was scheduled for December 20, 1941, but the other candidates withdrew. The priest of the parish, the *curé*, wrote Langlais saying that he could not be appointed without a competition, and that there could not be a competition with only one candidate. On March 2, 1942 the *curé* wrote that the position was given to Tournemire's former pupil Joseph Ermend-Bonnal, director of the Ecole de Musique in Bayonne. Langlais was upset by this very irregular procedure. Ermend-Bonnal, the organist at Saint-André de Bayonne, was 62; Langlais at age 35 was deemed too young for such an important position, regardless of Tournemire's wishes.

A change of clergy led to less satisfactory working conditions at Saint-Pierre-de-Montrouge, where he had been very content for eight years as the titular organist. All this is reflected in the fact that Langlais now wrote fewer compositions, only two in 1940, both for voices. In 1941 he began a major organ work, completed the following year, his *Première Symphonie* of four movements, published in 1944. It is much more dissonant than his previous works, with more intricate rhythms. His turmoil and the many frustrations of that time are expressed. Inspired by César Franck and the symphonic sounds of the Cavaillé-Coll organ, this work also uses the forms of the French Romantic organ school. The first movement is a sonata-allegro, and the last-movement Final has cyclical influences.

Langlais' next organ work, one he wrote during 1942, is made up of short works quite unlike the *Symphonie*. This volume, *Neuf Pieces*, was published in 1945. It contains the beautiful *Chant de Paix (Song of Peace)*, which has become standard repertory for organists who possibly do not realize that it was written during wartime. There is also a work very dear to Langlais' heart, his tribute to the slain Jehan Alain, *Chant héroïque*, and memorials to his teachers Dukas and Tournemire. The following organ work of 1943, *Deux Offertoires pour tous les temps,* is dedicated to the memory of two others who died in the war years, Abel Decaux, former organist of Sacré-Coeur and professor at the Schola Cantorum, and Albert Mahaut, the harmony teacher from INJA. (Langlais continued the placement service for INJA organ students started by Mahaut.) Also in 1943, Langlais wrote a very beautiful and poignant choral work which remains one of his favorites, the first part of a work for Good Friday, *Mystère du Vendredi Saint.* Titled "Miserere Mei (Déploration)," it now is performed as "Déploration."

Langlais spent the war years in Paris, and at his wife's home in Escalquens, near Toulouse. Their son Claude was born on December 16, 1943. Ermend-Bonnal died in 1944, but no replacement was named. Many Parisian churches such as Sainte-Clotilde were closed because of the war and the extreme cold. The *curé* there announced that a competition would be held after the war.

By the end of 1945, life had improved. Paris was free, the war over, and Langlais named successor to Tournemire. He played his first service as titular organist at Sainte-Clotilde on November 4, 1945, exactly six years after the latter's death. His fame as a composer grew, and his first commission from the United States was received, resulting in the organ work *Fête.* Three suites followed which are still frequently played, and among his most popular works: *Suite brève* (1947), *Suite médiévale* (1947), and *Suite française* (1948). The radio commissioned orchestral works from French composers after the war, using them as stage music for drama programs. Langlais received three of these commissions, in 1946, 1947, and 1950, and wrote for large ensembles including orchestra, *Ondes Martenot,* and voices.

The American tours started in 1952, with his first trip so successful that he established the pattern of touring America almost every second year: 1952, 1954, 1956, 1959, 1962, 1964, 1967, 1969, and 1972. He taught two-week courses at the Liturgical Music Workshop during five summers in Boys Town, Nebraska, and made other American trips for special concerts and premieres of commissioned works. In all, he gave 297 recitals in North America, in addition to playing in fourteen European countries. While on tour he customarily gave a concert every other day, practicing three to four hours on each organ. He adapted quickly to the wide differences in the instruments he played, which impressed his audiences, as did his quiet stage manner, with no excess motion at the console, focusing attention on the music rather than on himself.

His personality was such that former students travelled many miles to see and hear him again. On the first tour, in 1952, his wife Jeannette mapped the organs for him. Later he only needed to be told what the stops were, and the location of the stopknob or tab. In fact, Langlais does not believe that it is more difficult for a blind person to play the organ than for a sighted person. His audiences thought otherwise, and marveled at his memory. Each tour seemed to add to his fame as a gifted improviser.

In his recital programs Langlais preferred to play French music and Bach. An early concert included compositions by J. S. Bach, Palestrina, Schumann, Dupré, Vierne, and Gigout.[5] Twenty years later, in 1946, his program at Aix-en-Provence was J. S. Bach, Franck, Tournemire, Dupré, Vierne, Langlais, and a concluding improvisation on "O filii et filiæ."[6] The press reviews of these concerts let us know how the composer performed his own works, and additionally there are recordings and videotapes of his playing and workshop teaching. Most importantly, Langlais kept detailed journals of the first five American tours, dictating them to his guides.

The enthusiasm of the Americans, and their drive to accomplish as much in each day as possible, led to a crowded schedule. Returning after the seventh tour, Langlais reported on a sample day, one in Columbus, Ohio:

7:00	arrival at the train station
8:00	invitation for breakfast
9:00	television interview
10:00	practice at the church for the recital
12:00	invitation for lunch
13:00	practice again at church
16:00	master class with students
19:00	invitation for dinner
20:00	concert
22:00	reception
24:00	leave from the train station for a trip of 23 hours[7]

Langlais tried to travel in America as he did in Europe, without flying. The upward motion of an elevated platform for an organ recital gave him vertigo once. He had not expected the organ to ascend, and found that this was not a good way to start concerts! He suspected that a plane trip would have the same effect. However, the vast distances to cover, and lack of train service in America forced him to start flying in 1967. Fortunately the vertigo did not recur.

Langlais was welcomed in universities and both Protestant and Catholic churches. In 1954 and 1959 Archbishop Cushing and the Music Commission of the Archdiocese of Boston sponsored his concerts in Boston Symphony Hall as Liturgical Music Festivals.

It is obvious that Langlais loves to compose. Many manuscripts are dated, and show that he works quickly; often during vacations which he takes at his second home in Brittany. Langlais composes on concert tours, on ships, on trains, anytime and anywhere. In a radio interview in Pittsburgh led by Jim Cunningham he commented on this:

JC: M. Langlais, how often do you compose, everyday?

JL: Oh, no. It depends upon my inspiration and my time. After teaching many hours, it is like a rest to compose; it is not tiring. Definitely, it is tiring; but I do not feel it.[8]

He works out a composition mentally, and then writes it in braille. Later he must name every note and its rhythmic value to a transcriber. He has dictated to his fellow students, colleagues, wife Jeannette, son Claude, and now to his wife Marie-Louise. He is able to compose quickly, showing the result of years of mental training. He has commented that he thought about his first mass, *Messe Solennelle* of 1949, for twelve years and composed and wrote it in thirteen days. A composer who writes in braille does not have the same work habits as one who looks at his manuscript, sees the harmonies lined up, and changes a few notes here and there with an eraser and pencil. Braille music is not written on a staff, but in horizontal lines of braille characters.

Toward the close of 1954 he received a request to compose a mass for the Christmas Eve Midnight service at the Cathedral of Notre-Dame de Paris. The service would be televised live and shown all over western Europe. It would be seen at the same time in Paris, Dublin, Berlin, Rome, and other cities. If the choirs and instrumentalists were to have the music to learn, it must be written immediately. Langlais decided to accept the project, and to reflect the medieval atmosphere and the spaces of the vast building, placing musical groups at the two far ends of the cathedral. A men's chorus, with organ and brass, was in the choir stalls; the gallery organ and brass spoke in dialogue from the other end of the building. In the center, the congregation sang three phrases in the Kyrie, again three plus an amen in the Gloria, twice in the Sanctus, and the *dona nobis pacem* of the Agnus Dei. Langlais drew inspiration from music of the twelfth to fourteenth centuries: Pérotin, Guillaume de Machaut, Dufay, and the Gregorian hymn *Salve Regina*, one of his favorite improvisation themes. This work, his *Missa Salve Regina*, was a tremendous success, with much comment in the press.

After a half-hour of patient waiting along with several thousand contemporaries of all nationalities, we entered the Cathedral at 10:30 P. M. to find standing room only. But soon even the cold was forgotten, and for three hours (rehearsal and performance) there prevailed a magical charm, an extra-ordinary impression of finding oneself in another world: the grandeur and simplicity of the music, the marvel-ous sonority of organs and brasses mingling with the medieval rudeness of the polyphonic chorus, the unusual contemplation of an attentive throng overwhelmed by such a work, and finally the building's unique reverberation--all contributed to make this 25th of December 1954 an unforgettable date.[9]

The *Missa Salve Regina* was recorded by Erato in one evening, February 18, 1955. The outstanding results were due to the work of the recording engineer André Charlin and the fortitude of the singers and instrumentalists in the frigid cathedral. Langlais played the *grand orgue* part.

French and foreign organ students came to study with the famous composer. He taught at the Schola Cantorum in Paris from 1961 until 1976, while continuing to teach organ, composition, and choral singing at INJA. After a two-manual organ was installed in his apartment, he had a studio in which to teach organ, improvisation, and chant harmonization to private students.

On three occasions he was asked to write the examination piece which is part of the Paris Conservatory concours d'orgue. Each year an organ work is commissioned, printed, and given to the advanced students, who have four weeks to learn it. In 1962 Langlais wrote *Essai* for the Conservatory. It was Langlais' "Trial" in atonal composition, and is technically difficult. The *Sonate en Trio* of 1967 is also atonal. *Imploration pour la Joie* was the concours piece in 1970, and contains a brilliant pedal solo.

Many Langlais works are written upon specific request. His large-scale *La Passion* was commissioned by Erato in 1957. It did not share the success of the *Missa Salve Regina*, and remains almost unknown today. A glance at the large body of unpublished, rarely-performed works shows that Langlais composes whether or not he is asked for a specific piece, although he has said many times that the piece he was writing would be his last one. The fine doctoral dissertation by Melvin West in 1959 notes that Langlais has written him that "he wishes to write a symphony for string orchestra and a lyrical work, and that these will be his last compositions."[10] Evidently West does not believe this, as he comments, "This, of course, is open to question as Langlais is still relatively young. Indeed, a new composition has just been made available, the *Tryptique* (1958)."[11] Almost thirty years later, Langlais has not stopped composing!

Langlais enjoys doing the unexpected. He plays and improvises toccatas, so we would expect written toccatas. And indeed he has, but they do not bear that title. His only *Toccata*, in the first volume of the *Vingt-quatre Pièces*, is a very short, slow piece in the style of a Frescobaldi *Toccata for the Elevation*.

It is also unexpected that Langlais could draw inspiration from misfortune. He does not use a guide dog, although he always has a dog at home, a great friend, whom he takes for daily walks. Since Langlais is adventuresome, an accident happens to him once in a while. In 1947 he broke his leg during vacation, as he was walking on an embankment near the edge of the sea, close to La Richardais. Since his leg did not heal perfectly straight, it had to be rebroken and reset in order not to interfere with his organplaying. During the nights when he was kept awake by his leg he finished the cantata written in honor of a Breton saint, Louis-Marie de Montfort. Later, for exercise and therapy, he wrote the pedal solo *Epilogue* to practice, and played the first performance in 1952. It became a famous piece, one of his audiences' favorite encores, and Langlais still loves to walk by the sea.

In 1963 his fingers got caught in a car door, with the result that he lost a fingernail and had to go six months without playing the organ with his right hand. He slipped during icy weather on Christmas Day of 1965 and broke his right arm, which affected his seventh American concert tour. In early 1973 there was a hospital stay of fifty days after his heart attack in January. He had a braille copy of the book of Revelation with him. Having read the book many times, he now reread five chapters over and over. He had difficulty sleeping at night. Lights were turned out, and all were to be quiet and rest. Langlais simply put his braille pages under the bed sheets, and read on. It was no inconvenience to him to have the lights out, and he always heard the nurses coming in time not to get caught. His own reactions and reflections at this time resulted in the large-scale *Cinq Méditations sur l'Apocalypse* for organ, a complex and violent piece, full of symbolism.

On July 1, 1984, Langlais had a stroke after playing the *grand-messe* in the Cathedral of Dol-de-Bretagne. As a result, he lost the ability to read language, due to brain damage in his left hemisphere. However, he retains the ability to read and write music in braille. A braille cell has six dots. Each braille character is made up of various arrangements of one or more raised dots punched in paper, and has multiple meanings. It can be a letter, or an abbreviation for an entire word. With a certain braille symbol preceeding it, it stands for a number. There is a highly developed, complex system for writing and reading music in braille.

Langlais' recovery, and ability to read music again, is of great interest to the medical profession. He clearly demonstrates that musical language is in a different part of the brain than spoken language, which was known, and that musical language memory stands independent of verbal memory. The connection between his formation of some words and their pronunciation was damaged, termed aphasia. He has no difficulty with the act of speaking, nor with memory, but the words to express thoughts sometimes cannot be found. Langlais' greatest damage was in the areas of proper names, and numbers.

His speech therapist Philippe Van Eeckhout believes that the best rehabilitation is to resume familiar activities. For Langlais, this meant playing the organ, even though he had frustrating memory slips. By early 1986, he played a recital at the Cathedral of Notre-Dame, with works by

Tournemire and his own compositions, concluding with an improvisation. To celebrate his eightieth birthday he recorded two long improvisations, straight through. He has commissions waiting from publishers, and his recent works have been well received.

The last twenty-five years have seen great alteration in the music of Catholic churches in Paris. Some of Langlais' best works, previously played and sung in the liturgy of the Mass, now are rarely heard except in concert. The organ mass, for which *Suite médiévale* was designed, became a casualty of the increased congregational participation. The beautiful solo voice (or unison choir) *Missa "in simplicitate"*, a setting in Latin, does not fit a service in the vernacular. The Second Vatican Council in 1962 allowed many changes in liturgical practice. Gregorian chant, and choral singing in Latin, is assuredly not forbidden, but is employed at the discretion of the clergy. The parish musician is rarely consulted as a policy-maker. At first Langlais wrote settings in French for the people or the choir to sing, and composed antiphons for the Gelineau Psalter. He had previously composed choral settings using both choir and congregation, such as the *Missa Salve Regina* of 1954, and he continued to do so in the three psalm settings of 1962-64. Gradually, however, he became disturbed by the quality of the new music used in French churches, and with the need to have his musical responses in French approved by church officials before they could be sung. Langlais' "popular" music is exemplified in the disc Studio SM 33 74, "Cantiques et Messe brève," issued in 1960.

He served on the organ subcommittee as a lay member of the Commission des Musiciens-Experts. With others, he signed a report directed to Monsignor Maurice Rigaud, president of the French Episcopal Committee on Sacred Music, expressing concern about the disappearance of Gregorian chant from the service, and the reduced use of the organ and organ music. They noted that music is not a "noise which one starts or stops by turning a handle," but is rather a language which makes no sense unless adequate preparation and development is given to it.[12]

In a 1968 interview, Langlais recounts how one of the clergy at Sainte-Clotilde cut the organ music off only ten seconds from the end of the Franck *Pastorale*. He grieves that the young, "revolutionary" vicars do not hear the beauties of sung Gregorian chant, nor do they appreciate classical organ works.[13] The *Pastorale* was just another piece of music that Sunday morning, not recognized as part of the heritage of the Basilica of Sainte-Clotilde, nor as a musical offering, a part of the liturgy. By 1971 Langlais refers to the usual Parisian Catholic music during Mass: "the congregation is supposed to sing very stupid music."[14] Questioned about this in 1987 by the writer, he responded that conditions have improved, and now the quality of music is higher. He continues to compose choral works in Latin and to use Gregorian chant themes (*Ubi Caritas*, 1986). He still uses French, English, and German texts, but presently writes more instrumental music than choral.

Langlais admires a wide range of music, from medieval to modern times. He has mentioned in interviews that he particularly likes Bartok, Beethoven, Fauré, Hindemith, Léonin, Machault, Messiaen, Palestrina, Pérotin, Ravel, Roussel, Satie, the electronic *musique concrète* of Pierre Schaeffer, Stravinsky, Breton airs, and of course, Gregorian chant. He has written musical hommages to Frescobaldi, Landino, Rameau, Stanley, and Webern. He also has the Breton love of folklore and of mystery. The flexible, rhapsodic quality of many of his compositions can be traced to his love for plainsong and its rhythmic freedom. He does not wish his music to sound predictable, though he does have a distinctive style, often with colorful harmonies. He agrees with the French traditions of organplaying, desiring clarity and poetry in music.

Sometimes Langlais creates musical themes for works by assigning letters to pitches. The octave placement varies in successive thematic statements. In *Deuxième Symphonie* (1977) the motifs DIEU and MARIE are indicated; in his memorial *Offrande à une âme* (1979), JEANNETTE is identified. Often there is no indication of the "name motif." *Mosaïque III* has themes constructed on the names of persons to whom pieces are dedicated. The musical pitches are chosen by the following pattern:

A	a	i	q	y
B flat	b	j	r	z[15]
C	c	k	s	
D	d	l	t	
E	e	m	u	
F	f	n	v	
G	g	o	w	
B natural	h	p	x	

Langlais and his music have gained official recognition many times. His *Salve Regina Mass* Erato recording won the Grand Prix du Disque and Madame René Coty Award in 1956. He received honorary doctorates from three American universities, Texas Christian University (1975), Duquesne University (1976), and the Catholic University of America (1982), is an Officer of the Legion d'Honneur, Officer of the Palmes Académiques (for excellence in teaching), Knight of the Order of St. Gregory the Great (from the Vatican), and was awarded the Boys Town Medal of St. Caecilia, the Prix François Duine 1964 (given to one born in Brittany who has honored his country), Bronze Medal of the City of Paris, Prix Rossini (for religious music) from the Académie des Beaux-Arts, and Prix d'Auberville: Commander of Arts and Letters. He serves on important examination juries in France and abroad, such as the concours d'orgue of the Paris Conservatory, and the Internation Organ Festival in Saint Albans, England. In 1985 he was one of the jurors for the selection of new organists for the Cathedral of

Notre-Dame de Paris.   In 1976 he became an honorary member of the American Guild of Organists, and on July 11, 1987 he was presented the diploma of Fellow (*Honoris causa*) of the Royal College of Organists in England.

In 1968 he retired from INJA after almost 40 years, and retired from the Schola Cantorum in 1976. He continued to play recitals, though American tours ceased after his heart attack in 1973.

Jeannette Langlais died of a heart attack In 1979, after two years of poor health which included several weeks in the hospital.   The life of a widower was very lonely, and soon Langlais remarried, on August 29, 1979. His second wife is Marie-Louise Jaquet, former organ student and guide, who is presently writing her doctoral dissertation in musicology at the Sorbonne. Her topic, not surprisingly, is the life and works of Jean Langlais. She has been active in performing his works during the past fifteen years, and has written many articles, plus a thesis, on them. Their daughter, Caroline, was born on May 25, 1980, so the apartment on rue Duroc in the 7th Arrondissement of Paris once again has a young child practicing the piano. Madame Langlais teaches organ at the Schola Cantorum and the Marseille Conservatory.

The usual way to refer to someone without visual sight is to say that he is blind. Langlais is blind, but he "sees" with other senses, particularly by touch and hearing. He mentions the immensity of a medieval Cathedral nave; a statue, the Piéta, in the Cathedral of Albi, which he "contemplates" with his hands whenever he gives a recital there.   Because he was blind, he received, completely without charge, an education and musical training from some of the best teachers in the world. Certainly it was a difficult life, but for Langlais, blindness gave him the opportunity to develop gifts he did not even know he had.

In his eightieth year, Langlais still gives lessons on the organ in his Paris apartment, and plays for services at Sainte-Clotilde. His wife and long-time colleague Pierre Cogen also play as co-titulars. He still enjoys walking the streets, but not alone. Numerous posts and signs on the sidewalk now make that very hazardous. He expresses satisfaction with his life, and happiness that his compositions continue to be performed. There are more available recordings of Langlais works now than at any time previously, and a growing number of European recordings. He is recognized internationally as a true artist. He has made his own way, that of a poet in music.

1.   Valmarin, "Après Franck, Pierné, Tournemire, un breton: Jean Langlais est organiste de la Basilique Ste. Clotilde," *Ouest-France,* December 20, 1948.
2.   François Carbou, trans. by Susan Landale, "Langlais joue Langlais," liner notes to Solstice 1, 1978.

3.   Bruce Gustafson, "Hommage à Dufourcq," *The Diapason* 70, no. 11 (October, 1979): 8.

4.   Marie-Louise Jaquet-Langlais, "La vie et l'œuvre de Jean Langlais," typescript of dissertation in progress, citing *Souvenirs,* band 2, face 4.

5.   J.-B. Le Comte, "Jean Langlais," *Les Artistes d'aujourdui,* May 1, 1926, n.p.

6.   Maurice Gay, "Récital d'orgue," *Terre de Provence* 3, no. 14 (April 7, 1946).

7.   Jean Langlais, "Mon 7e voyage aux Etats-Unis," *Le Louis Braille* 119 (September-October 1967): 2.

8.   David A. Billings, transcriber, "An interview with Jean Langlais," typescript from radio broadcast, station WQED-FM, Pittsburgh, September 21, 1981, 6.

9.   Seth Bingham, "The choral masses of Jean Langlais," *Caecilia* 86, no. 2 (Summer 1959): 81.

10.   Melvin West, "The organ works of Jean Langlais," D.M.A. diss., Boston University, 1959, 3.

11.   Ibid., 243.

12.   Raymond Anthony Kotek, "The French organ mass in the twentieth century," D.M.A. diss., University of Illinois, 1974, 126.

13.   René Mougeolle, *Le Journal de Nancy, L'Est Republicain,* May 8, 1968.

14.   Kotek, 130, personal communication from Jean Langlais dated February 25, 1971.

15.   Marie-Louise Jaquet, "Œuvres récentes de Jean Langlais," *Jeunesse et Orgue* 36 (Summer 1978): 7.

Two Interviews

I

Jean Langlais answered these questions in Paris on May 14, 1986. The transcription was read to him in La Richardais on July 24, 1987. Additional comments were added then to the answer about *Missa Salve Regina*, the third question.

KT: **Many of your reviews speak of you as a poet in music, and you yourself have said you look for poetry in musical sounds. Could you explain what this means to you?**
JL: J'aime tout ce qui est beau. I like everything that is beautiful.

--Until I started researching this book, I did not realize that you had been so involved with the early steps in setting music responses in French for the people. Is the music of this period still sung in the churches in France?
--Je ne m'en occupe plus. I'm no longer interested in that.

--*Missa Salve Regina* was a "succèss fou" in 1954-55. I believe I have heard you say that you wrote it very quickly, as you were requested to do so not long before it was to be sung. Do you recall how long a time you had to write this composition?
--Three weeks. Le Père Julien est venu fin Novembre me demander d'écrire une messe avec participation de la Foule. D'abord j'ai dit, "Non, c'est trop difficile." Il est revenu et j'ai fini par dire oui. Il y avait 9,000 personnes à Notre-Dame. Father Julien came at the end of November to ask me to write a mass with congregational participation. At first I said, "No, it is too difficult." He came again and I finally said yes. There were 9,000 persons at Notre-Dame.

--*La Passion*, written in 1957, and one of your longer works, has remained fairly unknown. Have there been any recent performances?   --Non. No.

--Your *Suite médiévale* of 1947, published in 1950, was a terrific success in America, and throughout the world. Obviously you could have made a lot of money by turning out several similar suites, yet you did not. The following *Suite française* and *Hommage à Frescobaldi* are quite different. Would you comment on that?

--Je ne m'occupe pas d'argent. Et j'ai toujours fait ce que je voulais sans m'occuper de rien d'autre. I'm not concerned with money. And I've always done that which I wanted without being concerned with anything else.

--What do you think will be the future of Gregorian chant in our culture?

--Aujourd'hui on ne s'en occupe pas beaucoup. Les prêtres ne le savent plus. Messiaen et moi trouvons cela terrible et nous sommes pessimistes. Today people aren't interested in that. The priests no longer know it. Messiaen and I find that terrible and we are pessimistic.

--Are you reading braille language now, or just music in braille, as you re-learned to do after your stroke?

--Seulement la musique. Only music.

--Are any of your braille scores in the INJA library (original manuscripts)?

--Non. Chez moi. No. At my home.

--I have read a newspaper clipping of the Daily Mail, Paris, February 5, 1952: "His 35-voice choir, which he has conducted before the President of the Republic, now appears in the film "La Nuit est mon Royaume." Was this your choir at the Institution Nationale de Jeunes Aveugles? How did it happen that you directed music for a film?

--Oui. Je suis allé au studio avec ma chorale de l'Institution des Jeunes Aveugles. Yes. I went to the studio with my chorale from the Young Blind Institute.

--Could you tell us about meeting Helen Keller, and playing for her?

--Elle était venue à Paris pour être décorée de la Légion d'Honneur et elle est venue me voir à l'INJA. Elle m'a demandé de lui jouer la *Toccata en ré mineur* de Bach. Elle a dit que c'était superbe et qu'elle avait senti des "vibrations on my face." She had come to Paris to be decorated with the Legion of Honor and she came to see me at INJA. She asked me to play the Toccata in d minor of Bach for her. She said that it was superb and that she felt the "vibrations on my face."

--You have said, "I became interested in music because I was blind. Other-wise I would have been a stonecutter like my father." What professions did your younger brothers Louis and Henri take up?

--Louis: conducteur de travaux   **works foreman, clerk of works**
  Henri: photographe   **photographer**

--How was it decided to send you away to school in Paris at age ten? Had you shown musical talent by that age?
--C'est mon oncle, le commandant Jules Langlais, qui a persuadé mes parents que le mieux pour moi était d'être éduqué à Paris à l'INJA et j'ai eu une bourse. Je ne savais rien en musique à l'époque. **It was my uncle, the commandant Jules Langlais, who persuaded my parents that it would be best for me to be educated in Paris at INJA and I had a scholarship. I didn't know music at that time.**

--Did it take a long time to make your French Franck recordings? (ARN 336 0008)
--Non: Tout en 3 soirs de 3 heures. **No: All in 3 evenings of 3 hours.**

--Janine Collard has sung first performances of many of your works. How did she become acquainted with your compositions, and has she encouraged you to write for the solo voice?
--Je l'ai connue à la Radio et sa voix était si belle que j'ai composé pour elle. Je l'accompagnais au piano. **I heard her on the Radio and her voice was so beautiful that I composed for her. I used to accompany her on the piano.**

--I've seen her voice described as contralto, mezzo-contralto, and mezzo-soprano. How would you classify it?
--Mezzo-soprano.

--Thank you for taking the time to answer these questions. If you'd like to add anything else, please feel free to do so.
--Dimanche 17 Mai prochain, pour célébrer mon Anniversaire, la Télévision Française va filmer en direct la Messe à Sainte-Clotilde (je vais improviser et la maîtrise d'Antony va chanter ma *Messe Solennelle,* comme à la Madeleine, avec les mèmes interprétes). Avant, on va faire passer une interview entre Messiaen et moi (filmée la semaine dernière) où nous parlons de nos carrières et de ce que nous pensons de l'évolution de la musique religieuse. Cela a été merveilleux et Messiaen a été formidable de gentillesse pour moi et mon œuvre. C'est ce qui a été le plus beau pour moi car c'est mon ami de toujours. **Next Sunday, May 17, to celebrate my birthday, the French Television is going to film live the Mass at Sainte-Clotilde (I will improvise and the choir of Sainte-Marie d'Antony will sing my *Messe Solennelle,* as at the Church of the Madeleine, with the same interpreters). Before, they're going to show an interview between Messiaen and me (filmed last week) where**

we talk of our careers and our thoughts on the evolution of religious music. It was marvellous and Messiaen was incredibly kind to me and my work. That's what was the most beautiful for me because he's my friend forever.

II

Interview with Marie-Louise Jaquet-Langlais in Paris, March 2, 1986.

KT: **Could we start out by your telling me about the book that you're writing?**
M-L J-L: It is a thesis, a dissertation for the doctorate in musicology at the Sorbonne. The subject is "La vie et l'œuvre de Jean Langlais." Maybe it will not be the definite title, I don't know, but it has to be 700 or 800 pages, and will cover the whole works and life. It will be in three sections: 1. biography, 2. philosophy, style, etc. of his music, and 3. analysis, work by work. So if I say 700 pages, maybe it will be 1,000; I don't know. Right now, on March 2, I have written 35 pages. I began in November, and I really worked. At this point, after 35 pages, he is 10 years old.

--**Since you have worked so thoroughly on his first 10 years, can you tell me about his father and grandfather who were stonecutters. Were they in the quarry cutting stones, or did they work in an atelier, shaping them?**
--They did everything: finding the stone in the ground, cutting it, and sanding it. They did stones for the bordure du trottoir [curbstones], gravestones, funeral monuments, and stones for the monuments which were put up all over France following the First World War.

--**Did they have their own business, or work for someone else?**
--No, they had a kind of cooperative. There were something like 140 stonecutters at the beginning of the century for a village of 800 inhabitants, because this place was famous in all of Brittany for the quality of the granite. In the village there were two categories of people, stonecutters and farmers, but poor farmers, very poor, 10 cows, no more.

--**To skip to the year 1954, the year that Langlais wrote the *Missa Salve Regina* for Christmas Eve at Notre-Dame, televised all over Europe, what have you heard him say about that?**
--He wrote it in one week. At first he didn't wish to write it. Le Père Julien came to him and said, "Would you be kind enough to compose a mass for congregation and organ?" And my husband said, "It is not possible for the people to learn a mass in one hour of rehearsal, just before the service. No, I do not wish to do this." Later, at the beginning of December, le Père Julien came again and said, "Yes, please try." And he talked more, and my

husband understood better what was proposed, so decided to try. And he composed it in one week.

--Was the performance of the *Missa Salve Regina* and its subsequent recording, which received the Grand Prix du Disque and Madame René Coty Award, the first time Langlais had a big success in France, and became generally known to the people of France?

--Yes, that was a big success. But, in fact, he was well known at that time. He has different periods. The first one was the period before the war, when he composed a lot for orchestra, solo instruments, and chamber music. At that time there were many societies performing works by young composers, so he wrote more. Then the war came, and he wrote much less. He wrote his *Symphonie*, but very few works because the conditions were terrible.

--Is it true that Sainte-Clotilde was closed part of the time during the war?

--Yes, because there was no heat and the organ did not work. In fact, the organist played on a harmonium.

At this time, Langlais was known as a good organist and composer. After the war, he became famous for his organ works. This was in his second period, when he wrote a lot of organ music. His two main publishers were Philippo, or Hérelle, and Bornemann. He was very successful. And then came his fifth mass, the *Salve Regina*, and then he composed more masses.

The third period was the American period, beginning in 1952, two years before his *Missa Salve Regina*. He had a huge success in the United States, and for me it is his third period. First period, after the conservatory, chamber music, organ, a lot of things; second one, organ, a lot of organ; third one, his American period, with many things, masses, less chamber music, less orchestral music, but more organ and vocal. From this time on, about 80% of his compositions were requested by editors or other persons; they were commissioned.

--So publishers would write and say, "Do you have an organ piece for us, or do you have a choral piece for us?"

--Exactly. 80%, at least. And, for me, his fourth period began when he had his first heart attack, in 1973. During this period he had a lot of difficulties: heart attack, '73; his wife died, '79; his stroke, '84. These 10 years were difficult for him personally, but he never stopped composing. In fact, these last years his style changed a little bit, and works (for me) like the *Apocalypse*, the *Cinq Soleils*, *B.A.C.H.*, are very original, very new, very important. So you cannot say, "Well, now he is old and he's not interesting."

--Not at all. I have read somewhere that, given the fact that Gregorian chant

is not so often used in church these days, Maître had stopped composing for the voice. I think that he is now writing vocal works again. Is that correct?

--I don't think he ever stopped. He did stop composing small cantiques for the church, yes. There was an ecclesiastical commission who had to judge those musical settings for the church. They selected what could be printed and used. He just hated that idea.

--In November of 1985, he celebrated his 40th year as titular organist at Sainte-Clotilde with two organ recitals of his compositions at the Basilica.

--Yes, there were two programs, one by Pierre Cogen, and the other by three people. It was difficult to decide. It was my husband who organized that. I think he could have selected a lot of people to play. He wished to have Pierre and me because we are organists at Sainte-Clotilde with him, and Naji Hakim and Marie-Bernadette Dufourcet-Hakim as representing his pupils. Naji is the organist at the Basilique Sacré-Coeur in Montmartre now, and he won a lot of prizes all over the world. And Naji's wife is as brilliant as he is. I think that Naji and Olivier Latry will be the big organists here in ten years. My husband selected the pieces played, except the *Te Deum*. He did not wish Pierre to play the *Te Deum*, because he hates that piece, and Pierre insisted, and said, "Yes, I want to play that."

--He hates it because he's heard it so many times?

--Yes, exactly. Pierre played his *Première Symphonie* marvelously, really marvelously. Messiaen was present at the second recital. He was standing by Langlais. I gave the music to him because he did not know this *Symphonie*. He was very interested.

--They were together in the composition class of Dukas at the Paris Conservatory in 1934-35. Was Duruflé also in that class?

--No, Duruflé was not in the class. He was older. Sometimes he would come and show his works, but he was not there regularly.

--On the same recital with the *Première Symphonie*, Pierre Cogen played the first performance of *Talitha Koum*.

--Yes. The title is Aramaic, and means, little girl, wake up. It is a resurrection. Langlais was very struck by these words of Jesus in the biblical account of a miracle. It was about a year after his stroke when he heard the minister in La Richardais deliver a sermon around this text, "Talitha Koum." He decided to make a collection, a book with that title.

--The pieces in this collection use plainsong themes. What do you think is the future for Gregorian chant?

--I think it will come back. For the moment it is difficult, and the young people ignore Gregorian chant, but I am sure there will be a restoration.

Works and Performances

"B" references, *e.g.*, Review: B85, identify citations in the "Bibliography" section. "D" citations refer to the "Discography" section. The duration of a composition given is that reported by the composer on his copyright application. If two timings are given, the first is the copyright and the second is the one printed on the score.

ORCHESTRA

W1. CLOCHES (1935). Unpublished.
Symphonic poem listed in *Portraits de trente musiciens français* (*see* : B171) and *Baker's Biographical Dictionary of Musicians* (*see* : B225). Manuscript of 24 measures exists, title *Cloches de deuil (Funeral Bells)*, followed by *Minuet* of 27 measures with indicated repeat. Scored for flutes, oboe, clarinet, bassoon, and strings. No performance noted.

W2. DANSES, TROIS (1944). 14'. Unpublished. 3 movements, 46 pages.
Woodwinds, piano, and percussion: English horn, 2 clarinets, 2 bassoons, 3 trumpets, 3 trombones, snare drum, cymbals, tam-tam, and piano.
Premiere March 6, 1949, Salle du Conservatoire National de Musique, Paris, l'Orchestre Oubradous, Fernand Oubradous, conductor, Ida Périn, piano. Also: Radiodiffusion française. (Reviews: B264 a-c)

W3. DIABLE QUI N'EST A PERSONNE, LE (1946). (The Devil who belongs to Nobody). 25'. "Musique de scène," stage music, commissioned by Radiodiffusion française, for a radio drama, play by Jean Cayrol. 49 pages. Unpublished. Full orchestra and *Ondes Martenot*. English horn theme in the first dance of *Trois Danses* used again; also later arranged for organ solo as *Plainte* (5'30") of *Suite brève.* (*See*: W2, W192)
Premiere February 14, 1947, Radiodiffusion française. Actors: Berthe Bovy, Pierre Renoir, Jean Vilar. (Review: B265)

W4. ESSAI SUR L'EVANGILE DE NOEL (1935). Unpublished.
Arrangement for orchestra and organ of the organ solo *La Nativité* from *Poèmes Evangeliques* (1932); orchestration done while Langlais was studying with Paul Dukas.

Premiere February 1936, Concerts Classiques de Lyon, Lyon, France, Jean Langlais, organ, Witkowski, conductor. (Review: B266-67c) Also: November 16, 1938, Concerts du Conservatoire de Nancy, France, Jean Langlais, organ; Alfred Bachelet, conductor. (Reviews: B266-67a-b)

W5. HYMNE D'ACTION DE GRACES (1935). Unpublished.

Arrangement for orchestra and organ of the organ solo *Te Deum*, from *Trois Paraphrases grégoriennes*; orchestration done while Langlais was studying with Paul Dukas.
Premiere Performed with *Essai*. (*See*: W4).

W6. LEGENDE DE ST. JULIEN L'HOSPITALIER (1947). Unpublished.

Stage music, commissioned by Radiodiffusion française, for a radio drama based on works of Gustave Flaubert. 49 pages.
Orchestra: 2 flutes, 2 bassoons, 2 trumpets, 2 trombones, harp, *Ondes Martenot,* percussion, strings.
Premiere March 8, 1948, Radiodiffusion française.

W7. PIECE SYMPHONIQUE (1937). Unpublished in this version.

Three movements: The first, an arrangement for string orchestra and organ of *Quintette* (1935), which was later issued separately as *Piece in Free Form (Pièce en forme libre)*. Second movement, an arrangement for brass and organ of the *Toccata,* #10 from *24 Pièces* (1933). Third movement, *Thème et Variations*, for brass, strings, and organ, is the *Thème, Variations et Final* (1937), and was used again in *Deuxième Concerto* (1961) for organ and string orchestra.

W8. REMINISCENCES (February 1980). 12' 15". Unpublished.

String orchestra, 2 flutes or 2 trumpets, harpsichord, and timpani. Title indicates references to the end of *Piece in Free Form* and the fugue from *Troisième Concerto*.
Première August 6, 1980, Ensemble Instrumental de Basse Bretagne, Semaines Musicales de Quimper. The E.I.B.B. is a group of Breton chamber musicians organized in 1978 in Brest: Xavier J. LaFerriere, Charles Canier, François Goic, Katell Guillemot, violins; Françoise Gneri, viola; Patrick Lehoux, Etienne Larat, violoncelli; Christiant Riche, clavecin; Jean Luc Menet, Yvon Quenea, flutes; Philippe Roy, René Guillameau, oboes. (Review: B268b) Also performed by the Atelier de Musique de Ville d'Avray, November 18, 1981, Ville d'Avray.

W9. SOLEIL SE LEVE SUR ASSISE, LE (1950). 45'. Unpublished.

Stage music commissioned by Henri Dutilleux of Radiodiffusion française for a radio drama by Albert Vidalie. Drama text based on the life of St. Francis.
Orchestra: large orchestra, small orchestra, 3 *Ondes Martenot*, 3 women's voices, 3 men's voices.
Premiere December 30, 1950, Radiodiffusion française. Louis de Froment, conductor. (Reviews: B269a, d)

W10. SUITE CONCERTANTE (1936). 25'. Violoncello and orchestra. Unpublished. Manuscript marked opus 13. Reduction of orchestra part for piano, 4 hands, also exists.
I. Adagio sostenuto   II. Introduction et vivace
III. Vivace, staccato et leggiero   IV. Allegro appassionata
Written for M. Maréchal.
Note: Not the same work as *Suite concertante* (1943) for violin and 'cello duet, published 1974, U.C.P. Publications, W234.

W11. SYMPHONIE CONCERTANTE (1936). 10'. Piano and orchestra. Unpublished.
    I. Adagio sostenuto   II. Introduction et vivace
    Title in Jeannette Langlais' catalog: *Concerto pour piano et orchestre*. Arrangement of the first two movements of the 'cello and orchestra work *Suite concertante* (1936). (*See*: W10)

W12. THEME, VARIATIONS ET FINAL (1937). 15'. Unpublished.
    Organ, string orchestra, trumpets, and trombones. Originally written from October 18-December 14, 1937. (*See*: W7, *Pièce symphonique*) Award: Deuxième Prix, Concours de Composition des Amis de l'Orgue, 1938. (Review: B270)
    Premiere June, 1938, Paris, Concert of Les Amis de l'Orgue.

    Revised in late 1970s, as *Theme and Variations for Organ, Brass and Strings*.
    Premiere April 21, 1978, William Maul, organ, Stephen Simon, conductor, St. Raymond's Church, the Bronx, New York. (Review: B71)

See also: **Concertos 1, 2, 3**, in Organ and Instruments section, W209-211.

CHOIR

W13. ADVENT THE PROMISE (1952). Unpublished. 4 mixed voices.

W14. A LA CLAIRE FONTAINE (August 1961). French-Canadian melody.
    Editions Philippo-Combre, 1971. 6 mixed voices *a cappella*, dedicated to the vocal ensemble Contrepoint.

W15. ANTIENNES (1955). Antiphons for Gelineau Psalm Settings.
    In: Gelineau, Joseph. *265 Antiennes/53 Psaumes et quatre cantiques*. Paris: Les Editions du Cerf, 1958. Texts from the Psalter of the Jerusalem Bible. Antiphon settings by 14 composers. 4 mixed voices, optional unison voices. Langlais wrote antiphons for Psalms 25, 26, 44, 68, 79, 80, 85, 96, 97, 102, 109, 112, 117, 131, 137.
    Later edition: Gelineau, Joseph, and Paul Cneude. *Refrains Psalmiques pour les 150 Psaumes et les 18 cantiques bibliques*. Paris: Les Editions du Cerf, 1963.
    Psalm 102 is #24 in the hymnal *Cantate Domino* (World Council of Churches, full score edition, Oxford University Press, 1980.)

W16. AVE MARIS STELLA (1961). Unpublished. 3 equal voices.

W17. CANTATE A SAINT VINCENT DE PAUL (1946). 9'. Unpublished, manuscript lost. Choir with string orchestra or organ.
    Premiere 1946, Centennial Celebration of l'Ecole Saint-Vincent, Rennes.
    Also: February 10, 1952, Chorale du collège, M. l'abbé Royer, director, l'Ecole Saint-Vincent, Rennes, at the dedication of the new organ in the Chapel. (Review: B272)

W18. CANTATE DE NOEL (1951). Unpublished. Text: Loÿs Masson.
    1. Prélude   2. Fuite en Egypte   3. Massacre des Innocents
    Flute, oboe, 2 clarinets, bassoon, trumpets, 2 horns, percussion, piano, celesta, harp, choirs, and soloists.

Premiere Radiodiffusion française, December 25, 1951. Names of soloists written on conductor's score: Perron, tenor; J. Collard, mezzo; Béronita, soprano; Mollet, bass.

W19. CANTATE EN L'HONNEUR DE SAINT LOUIS-MARIE DE MONTFORT (1947).
Unpublished. 3 treble voices, organ, 3 trumpets *ad lib.*
15 page manuscript, written for a school in Larnay, near Poitiers.
Premiere Nantes

W20. CANTATE "EN OVALE COMME UN JET D'EAU" (Composed March 30-June 5, 1958). 31'. Text: Edmond Lequien. Presses Ile de France, 1958.
Premiere 1959, Choralies de Vaisons la Romaine.

W21. CANTATE "LE PRINCE DE LA PAIX" (December 1970). 3' 45".
Unpublished. 4 mixed voices and organ.
Premiere Christmas Eve 1970, Parish Choir, Basilica of Ste.-Clotilde, François Tricot, director.

W22. CANTICLE OF THE SUN, THE (September 10-20, 1965). 10' 40".
Elkan-Vogel. Text: English. Prelude and 7 sections. 3 equal (treble) voices, two versions for the accompaniment: a. organ or piano, b. string quintette (string orchestra), with organ or piano, arranged by Theodore Marier. Commissioned by Texas Boy Choir, Fort Worth.
Premiere March 7, 1967, St. Monica Boys' Choir, Anselmo Inforzato, director, John Tuttle, organ, Cathedral of Saints Peter and Paul, Philadelphia.

Cantiques dans GLOIRE AU SEIGNEUR *See*: W84, unison voices.

W23. CANTIQUES BIBLIQUES, DOUZE (12) (1962).
Biblical text paraphrases by Daniel Hameline. Editions musicales Fleurus, 1962, unison version. Editions musicales Fleurus, 1963, 1965, 4 mixed voices SATB version, optional organ or harmonium accompaniment which doubles the voice parts.
1. Cantique de David "Nous acclamons, Seigneur"
2. Cantique d'Isaïe "Chantez les hauts faits de Dieu"
3. Cantique de Tobie "Béni soit Dieu"
4. Cantique d'Ezechias "Ni la mort, ni la vie"
5. Cantique de Judith "Seigneur, Maître de la vie"
6. Cantique d'Anne "De riche qu'il était"
7. Cantique de Jérémie "Tu nous as comblés"
8. Cantique d'Isaïe "Un jour viendra"
9. Cantique de Moïse "C'est toi, Seigneur"
10. Cantique universaliste "A votre Église Sainte"
11. Cantique de Moïse "Dieu de bienveillance"
12. Cantique d'Habacuc "Qui sera contre nous"

W24. CARITAS CHRISTI (1953). Editions Schola Cantorum, 1953.
4 mixed voices, organ accompaniment. Arranged from W17, *Cantate à Saint Vincent de Paul* (1946), now lost.

W25. CHANSONS DE CLEMENT MAROT, DEUX (1931). 4'. Hérelle, 1933.
Langlais' first published composition, printed as opus 1.
4 mixed voices *a cappella.*
1. Je suis aymé de la plus belle
2. Aux damoyselles paresseuses d'escrire à leurs amys
Premiere June 10, 1931, Association Valentin Haüy, Paris.

Chansons Folkloriques Françaises, Neuf *See*: W82.

W26. CHANSONS POPULAIRES BRETONNES, TROIS (1954). Henry Lemoine, 1955.
4 equal voices, or three treble parts and tenor, *a cappella*.
1. Dessus les sables de la mer   2. Lamentations   3. Le Lin

W27. CHANSONS POPULAIRES DE HAUTE-BRETAGNE, DEUX (1961). Editions
Philippo-Combre, 1971. SSATTB 4 or 6 mixed voices *a cappella*.
1. Rennes – La fille entêtée
2. Saint-Briac – L'amoureux de Thomine

W28. CHANT D'ENTREE POUR LA FETE DE SAINT-VINCENT (1965). Unpublished.
Unison with 4 mixed voices (or unison) *ad libitum*.
Premiere Canon Delehedde-Viviers.

W29. CHANTS CHORAL, DEUX (December 1982). Europart-Music, 1983.
4 mixed voices and organ *ad libitum*.
1. Dans ma faiblesse   2. L'aube se levera

W30. CORPUS CHRISTI (September–October, December 25, 1979).   13' 30".
UCP Publications, 1982/Combre, 1987. Text: Latin. 4 equal voices
(SSAA) and organ. Commissioned by the Portsmouth Boys' Choir
(England) in 1979.
1. Introït «Cibavit» 2. Graduel «Oculi» 3. Alleluia «Caro mea»
4. Offertoire «Sacerdotes»   5. Communion «Quotiescumque»
6. Panis Angelicus
Premiere August 29, 1982, Kammerchor Schmallenberg, Ulrich
Schauerte, Director, Helga Schauerte, organ, Festival "Wormbacher
Sommerkonzerte," Wormbach, Germany.

W31. DIEU, NOUS AVONS VU TA GLOIRE (1956). Philippo, 1957.
Hymn text: Didler Rimaud, S.J., 9 stanzas and refrain.
Stanzas for 4 mixed voices, refrain for unison congregation,
accompaniment in two versions: small organ or harmonium, and
large organ with octave doublings.
Reprinted in various hymnals. Two English translations are:
"Lord, your glory in Christ we have seen," 5 stanzas and refrain,
translated Anthony G. Petti,*145, *New Catholic Hymnal*, London:
Faber Music Ltd., 1971; and
"God, your glory we have seen in your Son," 5 stanzas translated
Brian Wren 1964, refrain (antiphon) translated Ronald Johnson
1964, * H-11, *More Hymns & Spiritual Songs*, The Joint
Commission on Church Music of the Episcopal Church, New York:
Walton Music Corporation, 1972.

Other hymnals include:
*395, *The Australian Hymn Book with Catholic Supplement*
(harmony edition, Sydney: Wm. Collins Publishers, 1977);
*96, *Cantate Domino* (World Council of Churches, full score
edition, Oxford University Press, 1980) 5 stanzas, English and
French texts;
*469, *The Church Hymnary, Third Edition* (London: Oxford Univ.
Press, 1973);
Dunblane Praises (Scotland); and
*36, *New Church Praise* (Supplement, United Reformed Church,
England, 1975).
Premiere July, 1957, Strasbourg Cathedral, service of Vigils
during the Congress of the Centre de Pastorale Liturgique, 3,000
congress attendants as choir.   Written specifically for this
Congress meeting. Premiere recorded. (*See*: D7)

W32. FESTIVAL ALLELUIA (1969).   8' 40". Elkan-Vogel, 1971.
4 mixed voices and organ.
Premiere October 1970, Chant sacré, Madeleine Will, director, Marie-Louise Jaquet, organ, Mulhouse, France.

W33. GLOIRE A TOI MARIE (arr. 1975). Procure Romande de Musique Sacrée,1975. Arrangements for 4 mixed voices, or 3 treble voices, of song from **Gloire au Seigneur** unison voices. (*See*: W84)

W34. HYMNE DU SOIR (April 1984). 2' 2". Harmonization of an anonymous motif from Kiev. Unpublished. 4 part male choir, TTBB.
Premiere   May   14,   1984,   Quatuor   Rachmaninoff.

W35. HYMN OF PRAISE "TE DEUM LAUDAMUS" (1973). 5' 30". Commissioned by and published 1974, Composers Forum for Catholic Worship (USA); for 4 mixed voices, unison congregation, and organ, with trumpets and timpani *ad libitum*.   Two text versions: a. English, as published, b. Latin, arr. by Pierre Cogen, unpublished.
Premiere 1974, Pittsburgh.

W36. LAUDA JERUSALEM DOMINUM (1955). Edition Schola Cantorum, 1957; also published in *Musique et Liturgie* 53 (September–October 1956). 4 mixed voices, unison congregation, organ, optional trumpets and trombones; composed for the Congrès Eucharistique de Rennes; In three sections: 1) a congregational antiphon 2) 9 psalm verses, sung by the choir   3) a doxology.
Premiere July 1956, Congrès Eucharistique de Rennes.

Le Prince de la Paix (1970) *See*: Cantate, W21.

W37. LIBERA ME, DOMINE (December 7, 1948). 3' 56".   La Procure du Clergé. 3 mixed voices (STB) and organ. Dedicated "à la mémoire de Louis Braille."   **Premiere** INJA choir, Paris.

W38. MASS "GRANT US THY PEACE" (completed March 24, 1979).
13' with cuts, 16' complete. Optional cuts marked in printed score. Basil Ramsey, 1981. English text. 4 mixed voices.
Kyrie - Gloria - Sanctus - Benedictus - Agnus Dei
Premiere August 22, 1981, sung by Worcester Cathedral Choir, Donald Hunt, director, at the opening Eucharist, Three Choirs Festival, Worcester Cathedral, England.
American premiere September 20, 1981, The National Shrine of The Immaculate Conception, Washington, D. C.,   Choir of the National Shrine, Robert Shafer, director, Robert Grogan, organ, Carolyn Walker, soprano, Stanley Cornett, tenor.

W39. MASS IN ANCIENT STYLE (June 5-8, 1952, on board the *Ile de France*). 15'. McLaughlin and Reilly, 1952. 4 mixed voices *a cappella*, optional organ doubling the voice parts. Text: Latin.
Kyrie - Gloria - Sanctus - Benedictus - Agnus Dei
Reprinted Combre, 1985, as *Messe en style ancien*.
Premiere Boston Oratorio Society, Theodore Marier, director, St. Paul's Church, Cambridge, Mass.

Mass "Orbis Factor"   *See*: Solemn Mass, W69.

W40. MESSE "DIEU, PRENDS PITIE" (1965). 9' 15".   Musique et Liturgie, 1965. Text: French. 4 part or unison choir and congregation, organ.
Kyrie - Gloria - Credo - Sanctus - Agnus Dei

W41.   MESSE POUR 2 UOIX et harmonium   (Summer 1935). Unpublished.
Premiere   September 1935, Parish choir, Escalquens, Jean Langlais, harmonium.

Messe Salve Regina   *See*: Missa, W44.

W42. MESSE SOLENNELLE (Nov. 9-22, 1949).   20'. Editions Schola Cantorum, 1952. 4 mixed voices, congregation, and two organs; also version with brass and one organ.
Kyrie - Gloria - Sanctus/Benedictus - Agnus Dei
Premiere October 15, 1950, Grand-Messe at Sainte-Clotilde with Jean Langlais and Pierre Denis, Student choir from INJA, Gaussens, conductor.
American premiere   March 19, 1951, Hugh Giles, conductor, Central Presbyterian Church, New York City. (Review: B278a)

W43.   MISSA MISERICORDIA DOMINI   (September 15-18, 1958).   16'. Commissioned by the Gregorian Institute of America, published 1959. Text: Latin. Three mixed voices (no alto line), with organ.
Kyrie - Gloria - Credo - Sanctus/Benedictus - Agnus Dei
Premiere August 1959, High Mass, Boys Town Liturgical Music Workshop, Boys Town Choir. (Review: B280)

W44. MISSA SALUE REGINA   (1954). 17-19 mins. Editions Costellat, 1955, two printed versions: a. men's three-part choir, people's unison chorus, three trumpets, five trombones and two organs, 64 pages; b. reduction for men's choir, people's unison chorus, and accompaniment of one organ, 39 pages. Text: Latin.
Premiere December 24, 1954, Christmas Eve Midnight Mass, Cathedral of Notre-Dame de Paris, Schola des Pères du Saint-Esprit du Grand Scholasticat de Chevilly, R. P. Lucien Deiss C.S. Sp., director; Abbé David Julien, director of the chorus of the congregation; Jean Langlais, great organ; Jean Dattas, choir organ. (Reviews: B281e, j)
American Premiere   January 7, 1956, Sacred Heart Church, Roslindale, Mass., St. John Seminary Choir, Russel Davis, director, Paul St. George, director of the congregation, Jean Langlais and William Stetson, organists. Sponsored by the Music Commission, Archdiocese of Boston. (Reviews: B281c, r)
New York Premiere   Feb. 26, 1956, Church of the Heavenly Rest, Charles Dodsley Walker, director.

W45. MORNING HYMN, A (August 1985). Text: Frederick Pratt Green. Unison or 4 mixed voices, organ or piano accompaniment.   Commissioned by the San Francisco Chapter, American Guild of Organists, for their 1986 "Winter Organ Weekend" at Stanford University. Printed in *The American Organist* 20, no. 6 (June 1986): 93.
Premiere January 12, 1986, Saint Ignatius Church, San Francisco.

W46. MOTET POUR UN TEMPS DE PENITENCE   (1960). Unpublished.
Propers for Ash Wednesday. 4 mixed voices *a cappella*.
Introit, "Misereris omnium Domine"
Trait, "Domine non secundum"
Offertoire, "Exaltabo te Domine"
Communion, "Qui meditabitur in lege, Domini"
Premiere February 15, 1961, St. Roch, Paris, Messe des Artistes.

W47. MOTETS, CINQ   (1932-42). Hérelle et Cie., 1933, 1944, now Combre.
1. O Salutaris Hostia (printed Opus 3, No. 1) 2. Ave mundi gloria

3. Tantum Ergo   4. O Bone Jesu   5. Chant Litanique
2 equal voices, organ. #1-3 composed 1932, #4 1941, #5 1942.
Premiere #1-3 May 29, 1933, Jean Langlais, St. Antoine des
Quinze-Vingts, Paris.

Motets, Trois *See*: Oremus pro Pontifice, and W106.

W48. MYSTERE DU CHRIST, LE (1957). 21'. Unpublished. Narrator, soloists,
choirs and orchestra. **Premiere** Radiodiffusion française, 1958.

W49. MYSTERE DU VENDREDI SAINT (1943). Editions Costallat, 1956,
section I only, with title Déploration. Original titles:
I. Miserere Mei (Déploration) (4 part mixed choir and organ) 4'.
II. O crux Ave (mixed choir, orchestra, and organ) 3'.
Premiere #1 Good Friday service, 1943, La Chorale de
Saint-Pierre-de-Montrouge, G. Helbig, conductor, Antoine Reboulot,
organ.

W50. NOELS, TROIS (1959). 7'. 4 mixed voices *a cappella*, also arranged
for 4 voice male choir. Unpublished. Text: French.
1. Entre le boeuf et l'âne gris (not same setting as Noëls
   populaires anciens, W51.)
2. Noël provençal (Guillaume, Antoine, et Pierre)
3. Michaut veillait

W51. NOELS POPULAIRES ANCIENS (1960) 21'. Philippo, 1960. Organ or
piano accompaniment. Text: French.
1. Nous étions trois bergerettes   2. A la venue de Noël
3. Entre le bœuf et l'âne gris   4. Allons bergers, allons tous
5. Joseph est bien marié   6. C'était à l'heure de minuit
7. Boutons noute habit le pus biau
Written for the choir at the Institute for the Young Blind, Paris.

W52. OFFERTOIRE POUR L'OFFICE DE SAINTE CLAIRE (1962). 2'. Unpublished.
3 equal voices, *a cappella*

W53. O GOD, OUR FATHER (1961). 2' 45". Unpublished.
4 mixed voices and organ.

W54. O SALUTARIS (August 8, 1941). Unpublished. 2 voices and organ.

OREMUS PRO PONTIFICE Third motet from *Trois Motets* (1943).
Unpublished. Version for two voices and organ, arranged from one
voice setting. (*See*: W106)

W55. PASSION, LA (July-October 1957). Original length, 62'; after
premiere, revised with cuts to 53'. Chorus parts published by
Editions Costallat, 1957. Comissioned by Erato, not recorded.
French text: Loÿs Masson, also translated into English by Theodore
Marier (not published). Choirs, full orchestra, 8 soloists, and
narrator. Solo parts: Mary, contralto; Pilate, tenor; Peter, baritone;
Jesus, baritone; Judas, bass, two unnamed women, one unnamed man.
Premiere Maundy Thursday, March 27, 1958, Radiodiffusion
française. Manuel Rosenthal, conductor, National Orchestra, R.T.F.
Choir, with soloists Janine Collard (Mary), Claudine Verneuil
(woman 1), Flore Wendt (woman 2), Joseph Peyron (Pilate), Bernard
Demigny (Jesus), L.-J. Rondeleux (Peter), Xavier Depraz (Judas),
Jean Giraudeau (man), and the actor Alain Cuny (narrator). Concert
given in the Champs-Élysées Theater. (Reviews: B285 a-j)

Praise the Lord, Psalm 150 (1961) *See*: W57.

Prière pour les Marins, La (1979) *See*: W240.

Prince de la Paix, Le (1970) *See*: W21.

W56. PRELUDE, FUGUE ET CHACONNE (January 1956). Unpublished. 4 mixed voices, no text. Not transcribed; inspired by Buxtehude organ work.

W57. PSALM 150 "PRAISE YE THE LORD" (1958). 3' 30". McLaughlin and Reilly, 1958. Text: English. 3 male voices (TTB) and organ. In 1961, arranged for 4 part mixed choir and brass as *Praise the Lord*. **Premiere** January 10, 1959, Boston Symphony Hall.

W58. PSAUME 111 "BEATUS VIR QUI TIMET DOMINUM" (1977). 5' 18". Editions Schola Cantorum, 1985. Text: Latin. 4 mixed voices and organ.
Premiere April 28, 1978, Boston Boys Choir, Schola Cantorum of Men, Theodore Marier, director, St. Paul's Church, Cambridge, Mass.

W59. PSAUME 116 "LAUDATE DOMINUM OMNES GENTES" (December 12, 1976). 8' 30". Unpublished. Text: Latin. 6 mixed voices, 3 trumpets, organ.

W60. PSAUME 120 "DES MONTEES" (1968). Unpublished. Text: French. 4 mixed voices and organ.
Premiere Christmas 1968, Parish choir, Basilique Sainte-Clotilde, François Tricot, director.

Psaume 58, Psaume 123 *See*: Psaumes, Deux, W61.

W61. PSAUMES, DEUX (1937). Unpublished.
1. CXXIII "Je lève les yeux vers toi" for soprano and tenor soloists (as cantors), 4 mixed voices, accompaniment *ad libitum* for orchestra, or piano/organ. Manuscript marked opus 17, no. 1. Arranged for organ solo in 1973 as the first movement of *Cinq Méditations sur l'Apocalypse*.
2. LVIII "Contre les juges iniques" 4 mixed voices, organ or piano.
Premiere March 19, 1938, Societé Nationale de Musique, Paris, Chorale "La Campanile", Joseph Noyon, director, Jean Langlais, piano, Mlle. Parodi, soprano, M. Guiez, tenor. (Reviews: B288a-e)

W62. PSAUME SOLENNEL 1 (December 2-23, 1962). 15' 30". Editions Schola Cantorum, 1963. Text: Psalm 150 in Latin, "Laudate Dominum in Sanctis ejus." Unison choir, 4 mixed voice choir, organ accompaniment, optional brass: 2 trumpets, 2 trombones, timpani.
Premiere August 30, 1963, choir and instruments directed by Roger Wagner, Claude Langlais, organ, sung as the recessional of the Solemn Pontifical Mass, 11th Annual Liturgical Music Workshop, Boys Town, Nebraska. Also: 1967, New York; August 31, 1972, Providence, Rhode Island, C. Alexander Peloquin, director.

W63. PSAUME SOLENNEL 2 (1963). 23'. Editions Schola Cantorum, 1965. Text: Psalm 50 in Latin, "Miserere mei Deus." Unison choir, 4 mixed voice choir, organ accompaniment, optional brass: 2 trumpets, 2 trombones, timpani. Commissioned by the Asylum Hill Congregational Church, Hartford, Connecticut in recognition of its centennial year.

Premiere   March 7, 1965, Asylum Hill Oratorio Choir, Albert Russell, organist-choirmaster, and St. Joseph's Cathedral Choir, Edward Diemente, director. Also: August 31, 1972, C. Alexander Peloquin, director, Providence, Rhode Island.

W64. PSAUME SOLENNEL 3 (1964). 9'. Editions Schola Cantorum, 1965.
Text: Psalm 148 in Latin, "Laudate Dominum de caelis." Unison choir, 4 mixed voice choir, organ accompaniment, optional brass: 2 trumpets, 2 trombones, timpani. Commissioned by the Asylum Hill Congregational Church, Hartford, Connecticut in recognition of its centennial year.
Premiere   March 7, 1965, Asylum Hill Oratorio Choir, Albert Russell, organist-choirmaster, and St. Joseph's Cathedral Choir, Edward Diemente, director. Also: February 19, 1975, Texas Christian University, during "Langlais Week." (Review: B226)

W65. REGINA CAELI (Feb. 15, 1958, London). 3'. World Library of Sacred Music, 1961. 2 treble voices and organ.

W66. REPONS LITURGIQUES PROTESTANTS   (1974). 7'. Musique et Chant, 1975. With organ accompaniment.
Prelude, Psaume, Introït, Louange, Gloria, Communion, Rèponse à l'Epiclèse, Bénédiction.

W67. REPONS POUR UNE MESSE DE FUNERAILLES (1967). Editions du Levain, 1968. Commission diocésaine de Musique sacrée d'Amiens.
3 mixed voices, soprano, tenor, and bass, with organ or harmonium accompaniment; or unison voices.
Venez, saints du ciel; Jusqu'en Paradis; Je crois que mon Sauveur; Toi qui as brisé.

W68. SHORT ANTHEMS, THREE (1978-79). Hinshaw Music, 1980.
1. Beloved, Let Us Love One Another (Unison, organ, 1'40")
   Text: 1st John 4: 7-8, 10.
2. Grace To You (4 mixed voices *a cappella*, 1'20")
   Text: Revelation 1: 4-6.
3. At The Name Of Jesus   (4 mixed voices *a cappella*, 55")
   Text: Philippians 2: 10-11.
Premiere June 17, 1979, First Presbyterian Church Choir, Burlington, N. C., Robert Burns King, director, commissioned for the centennial celebration of the church.

Soleil se lève sur Assise, Le   *See*: W9.

W69. SOLEMN MASS (1969). 16' 38"-15'. Elkan-Vogel, 1969. English text.
4 mixed voices, congregation, organ; brass *ad libitum*.
Kyrie - Gloria - Sanctus - Agnus Dei.
Written in honor of the tenth anniversary of the dedication of the Main Church, The National Shrine of the Immaculate Conception. Often called *Solemn Mass in English* or *Solemn Mass "Orbis Factor"* to distinguish it from *Messe Solennelle.*
Premiere November 1, 1969, the National Shrine Chorale, Joseph Michaud, Music Director; 350 singers including Catholic University Chorus, and massed military choirs: United States Air Force Academy Catholic Choir, United States Naval Academy Catholic Chapel Choir, Holy Trinity Chapel Choir of West Point; Brass choirs from Catholic University School of Music; Jean Langlais, organ, the National Shrine of the Immaculate Conception, Washington D.C. The military choirs sang the part of the congregation. (Review: B289a)

W70. TANTUM ERGO (1930). Procure du Clergé. 3 voices and organ.

W71. TANTUM ERGO (1940). 3'. Unpublished.   8 mixed voices, SSAATTBB, and organ.
Premiere   June 25, 1942, INJA choir, Jean Langlais, director, Gaston Litaize, organ, Salle Valentin Haüy, Paris.

W72. THREEFOLD TRUTH, THE (1985). Text: Frederick Pratt Green. Hymntune commissioned by Star of the Sea Catholic Church, distributed in computer-form printout.
Premiere   Easter Day 1986; Star of the Sea Catholic Church, San Francisco, Layten Heckman, director.

W73. UBI CARITAS (1986). FitzSimons, 1986. Latin text from the Office of Mandatum, Maundy Thursday. Based on a 4th mode plainsong.
4 mixed voices and organ.
Premiere   October 12, 1986, Edith Ho, director, James David Christie, organ, The Church of the Advent, Boston.

W74. VENITE ET AUDITE (1958). 3'. Editions Schola Cantorum, 1961.
Complete title: "Motet en l'honneur de la Sainte Vierge/Venite et audite." Dedicated to Marie Bigot, the 52nd miracle of Lourdes.
4 mixed voices, *a cappella.*

W75. LA VILLE D'IS, LA (1945). Hèrelle, 1947. Sometimes printed as **D'YS**.
Text: French. Breton folksong, harmonized for 4 mixed voices.
Premiere December 18, 1948, INJA Choir, Jean Langlais, director.

W76. VOIX DU VENT, LA (HYMNE) (1934). 10'. Unpublished. French text: G. Carimalho.   Choir, soprano solo and orchestra.
Premiere   Nov. 15, 1934, Eglise St. Germain, Rennes,   Jean Langlais, director.
American premiere   October 20, 1976, Mija Novich, soprano; Duquesne University Concert Choir, Marshall Hill, conductor; Duquesne University Orchestra, Bernard Z. Goldberg, conductor; Duquesne University Chapel, Pittsburgh.

SOLO VOICE OR UNISON CHOIR

W77. A LA VIERGE MARIE (1981). 3'. Unpublished. French text: Jean Langlais.
Organ or piano accompaniment.   Following a recital given September 27, 1981 at the Museum, Langlais decided to dedicate a song to his hosts in Cleveland.
Premiere December 13, 1981, Noriko Fujii, voice, Karel Paukert, organ, Gartner Auditorium, Cleveland Museum of Art.

W78. ALLELUIA-AMEN (October 1982). 4'. Unpublished.
Premiere March 27, 1983, Eglise des Invalides, Paris, Maria Posa, voice, Pierre Gazin, organ.

W79. ARMOR (September 22, 1952). Unpublished. Text: Tristan Corbière.
Piano accompaniment.

W80. AU PIED DU CALVAIRE (1947). 2'. Unpublished. Text: M. Lafragette.
Piano accompaniment.

W81. AVE MARIA (n.d.) Voice, organ, violin, and violoncello. Unpublished.

W82. CANTIQUE EN L'HONNEUR D'ANNE DE BRETAGNE (1976). 4'. Unpublished.
Text: Yves Cosson. Organ *ad libitum*.
Premiere December 1, 1977, Nantes.

W83. CANTIQUE EUCHARISTIQUE (1956). "Accourrez au passage du Seigneur."
Musique et Liturgie, 1956. Text: P. de la Tour du Pin.
Premiere July 1956, Congrès eucharistique, Rennes.

W84. CANTIQUES dans GLOIRE AU SEIGNEUR (1948-1952).
Gloire au Seigneur/Chants nouveaux pour les Sacrements,
Editions du Seuil, Paris. A three volume collection with French
texts, music by several composers. Langlais' contributions:
Vol. 1, **Amis, nous partons** (text: Paul-Louis Bernard)
    Seigneur Jésus, ne sois pas rebuté (Paul-Louis Bernard)
      also printed in *Musique et Liturgie* 4-5 (July-October
      1948): 24, music supplement: 3.
Vol. 2, **L'étable au bord du talus** (J. C. Renard)
    Il y eut des couronnes (J. Cayrol)
    Je suis pauvre, je suis nu (J. Cayrol)
    Comme cherche le soir (Louis Aragon)
    Gloire à toi Marie (L.A. and B. G.)
    Heureux celui (Luc Estang)
Vol. 3, **Au paradis** (Bernard Geoffroy)

Cantiques Bibliques, Douze (12), (unison or SATB) *See*: W23.

W85. CHANSONS FOLKLORIQUES FRANÇAISES, NEUF (Sept. 7-25, 1960).
Philippo, 1961. Unison choir with piano accompaniment, optional
contralto and baritone soloists.
1. J'ai pris la clef de mon jardin   2. La nuit passée
3. Où allez-vous, la Belle?   4. Rossignol du bois sauvage
5. Là-haut dessus ces côtes   6. Si tu parl' encore
7. C'était p'tit-Jean r'venant du bois
8. Quand le marin revient de guerre 9. Tout auprès de Pont-Scorff
Recorded for Erato under the title *Neuf chansons populaires.*

Chant d'entrèe pour la fête de Saint-Vincent (1965) *See*: W28.

W86. CHANTS POUR LA MESSE (December 1953). French text. Organ or
harmonium accompaniment. Editions du Levain, 1954, 1956.
Kyrie - Gloria - Sanctus - Agnus Dei
Also published with Credo. (See *Je Crois en Dieu,* also W103)
Revised in 1961 as **Messe "Joie sur terre,"** W103.

W87. CHANTS POUR LA PENTECOTE (1963). **"Ouvrons nos cœurs à l'Esprit."**
Editions Schola Cantorum, 1964. Musique et Liturgie 98 (April-
June 1964): 21-25. French text: J. Beaude.   Organ or harmonium.
Chant d'entrée, Inviatoire, "Ouvrons nos cœurs à l'Esprit"
Chant de méditation sur l'Epitre, Alleluia, "Source jaillissante"
Annonce de l'Evangile, "Qui m'aime garde ma parole"
Chant de Communion, "Esprit du Christ"
Chant final, "Esprit, le monde espère"

W88. CHANTS POUR LES DIMANCHES DE L'AVENT (1964). Organ or harmonium.
Four settings of J. Beaude's French texts for the Sundays in Advent.
Advent 1, "Le Seigneur est délivrance"
Advent 2, "Peuple de Dieu"
Advent 3, "Que la joie règne"
Advent 4, "Que la terre s'ouvre"

The first three are published in *Musique et Liturgie* 99 (July-September 1964), the fourth in *Musique et Liturgie* 100 (October-December 1964); also published separately. Each set has four or five parts: Chant d'entrée, Chant de méditation sur l'Epitre, Annonce de l'Evangile, Chant de Communion, Chant final.

W89. DENTELLE S'ABOLIT, UNE (June 1934). Unpublished. Text: Stéphane Mallarmé. Piano accompaniment.

W90. ERRANTE, L' (December 7-8, 1959). Unpublished. Text: Minou Drouet. Piano accompaniment.

W91. EUROPA (1961). Hymn for voice. Text: Edmond Lequien. Unpublished.

W92. HOMMAGE A LOUIS BRAILLE (December 23, 1951-January 2, 1952). Unpublished. French text: Firmin Le Guével. Piano accompaniment.
1. Coupvray ("Petit bourg calme")
2. Lux et Tenebris ("Ses seize ans ont trouvé")
3. Serve Bone et Fidelis ("C'est que, tandis que jeune")
Premiere January 29, 1952, Janine Collard, voice, Jean Langlais, piano, Association Valentin Haüy.

W93. HOMMAGE A LOUIS BRAILLE (March 1975). Unpublished. French text: Jean Langlais. Piano accompaniment. **Premiere** May 22, 1975, Janine Collard, voice, Jean Langlais, piano, Institution Nationale des Jeunes Aveugles, Paris. Premiere recorded. (*See*: D8)

W94. HUMILIS (1935). 8'. Unpublished. Text: Pierre-Jean Jouve. Piano accompaniment. Six songs, no titles: I. II. III. IV. V. VI.
Premieres Private: December 5, 1935, Simone Blin, voice, Jean Langlais, piano. Public: Societé Nationale, 1936, Mme. Marchal, voice, Jean Langlais, piano.

Je crois en Dieu Editions du Levain. From *Chants pour la Messe* (1953), published separately. Choir and Congregation, with organ or harmonium accompaniment. (*See*: W86)

W95. MACKENZIE (1962). Chanson de marin. Unpublished. Piano accomp.

W96. MASS "GOD HAVE MERCY" (1964). 11'. McLaughlin and Reilly, 1965. Text: English. Unison choir, unison congregation, with organ.
Kyrie - Gloria - Credo - Sanctus - Agnus Dei

W97. MASS "ON EARTH PEACE" (1965). 8'. Benziger Brothers, 1966. English text. Organ accompaniment.
Kyrie - Gloria - Creed - Sanctus - Agnus Dei

W98. MELODIES (1936-38). Unpublished, copyright March 3, 1953. Piano accompaniment.
1. Epitaphe (Text: Gauthier-Ferriéres) 2. L'arbre (André Romane) 3. Le rien du tout (H. Pouplain) ms. marked opus 14, 28 Sept. 1936 4. La Concierge (Firmin Le Guével)

W99. MELODIES, CINQ (1954). Texts: Ronsard et J.-A. de Baillif. 10'. Philippo. Piano accompaniment. Sometimes titled *Cinq mélodies sur des poémes de Ronsard*
1. A Francine 2. Je veux mourir 3. Marie, qui voudrait votre nom
4. Demandes-tu, chère Marie 5. Marie, levez-vous
Revised, with additions, 1974 as *5 Pièces pour flûte*.

W100. MELODIES, DEUX (1963).   Text: M. J. Durry.   Unpublished.   Piano accompaniment.
1. Mon ombre   3'.   2. Soleils de sable   3'. 15".
Premiere June 16, 1965.

W101. MELODIES, QUATRE (1940). Unpublished. Text: Clément Marot.   Piano accompaniment.
1. Frére Lubin   [manuscript exists]   copyright March 9, 1953.
2. A une damoyselle malade   [manuscript lost]
3. Huitain   [manuscript lost]
4. A une damoyselle   [manuscript lost]

W102. MELODIES, TROIS   (1949). Unpublished. Text: Alain Messiaen, in *Bestiaire Mystique*, 21 poems, published 1948.
1. Le Mariage raté du Paon
2. Le Porcelet de l'Anachorète
3. [manuscript lost]

W103. MESSE "JOIE SUR TERRE" (1965).   6' 30". Editions du Levain, Paris, 1965. Text: French. Accompaniment for organ or harmonium.
Seigneur, prends pitié – Gloire à Dieu – Je crois en un seul Dieu – Saint, le Seigneur – Agneau de Dieu
Revision of *Chants Pour La Messe* (1953),   some melodic adaptation due to text changes. "Seigneur, ayez pitié de nous" becomes "Seigneur, prends pitié."

W104. MISSA DONA NOBIS PACEM (April–July 1962).   H. W. Gray, 1964?
Text: English.   Organ accompaniment.
Kyrie – Gloria – Sanctus – Agnus Dei

W105. MISSA "IN SIMPLICITATE" (July 18–10 August 1952). 16'.   Editions Musicales de la Schola Cantorum, 1953.
Kyrie – Gloria – Credo – Sanctus – Agnus Dei   Text: Latin.
Two accompaniment versions: a. organ, b. strings.
Vocal part (no accompaniment) also published in *Musique et liturgie* 32 (March–April 1953) music supplement no. 1.
Premieres Radiodiffusion française, Janine Collard, voice, Jean Langlais, organ. 1953, INJA, Janine Collard, voice, string orchestra from the radio, Pierre Capdeville, conductor.

Morning Hymn, A (August 1985). Unison or 4 part   *See*: W45.

W106. MOTETS, TROIS (1943).   Unpublished, all three motets copyrighted June 22, 1945. Orchestra accompaniment: strings, flutes, oboe, clarinets,   bassoons,   handbells;   also   arranged   for   organ accompaniment.   1. O Salutaris   2. Salve Regina   6'.
3. Oremus pro Pontifice (version b. for 2 voices and organ)
Premiere #2   1944, Concerts Colonne, Irène Joachim, soprano.
American   premiere #2 October 20, 1976, Julia May, mezzo-soprano; Duquesne University Orchestra, Bernard Z. Goldberg, conductor; Duquesne University Chapel, Pittsburgh.

W107. MY HEART'S IN THE HIGHLANDS (1951). Unpublished.   Text: Robert Burns. Soprano with piano accompaniment.
Premiere June 22, 1952, Association Valentin Haüy, Janet Hayes, soprano, Jean Langlais, piano.

W108. NOUUEAUX CHANTS FRANÇAIS POUR LA MESSE   (February 1961). Editions du Levain, 1961. Text: Dom H. Van Erck.

Kyrie (Trisagion byzantin) "O Dieu Saint, pitié pour nous"
Gloria (D'après une doxologie byzantine) "Gloire à Dieu"
Sanctus "Saint, infiniment Saint"
Fraction du pain "Agneau de Dieu"
Premiere March 1961.

W109. ORAISONS, TROIS (1973). 9' 25". U.C.P. Publications, 1974/Combre, 1987. Solo voice or unison choir, with organ and flute or violin.
1. Salve Regina   2. Jam sol recedit igneus
3. Jesu dulcis memoria
Premiere August 13, 1973, Eglise de Cancale; Claude Dubois-Guyot, vocal, Pierre Guyot, flute, Jean Langlais, organ. (Review: B283)

W110. PARFUMS (1938). Unpublished. Text: Michel Poissenot. With piano.

W111. PAROLES (1946). 13'. Unpublished. Texts: Jacques Prévert, Edmond Lequien (Paroles de rechange). Piano accompaniment.
1. Déjeuner du matin (Inventaire)   2. Chanson [manuscript lost]
3. Pour toi, mon amour (Enfantillages)
4. Quartier libre (Poisson d'Avril)
5. Le jardin (Une rose)   6. Paris at night (Emerveillement)
7. Sables mouvants [manuscript lost]
8. Conversation (Existentialisme)
9. Les belles familles (Emploi du temps)
Premiere May 10, 1946, Societé Nationale de Musique, Paris; Mlle. A. M. de Barbentane, voice, Jean Langlais, piano. (Review: B284)

W112. PASSE-TEMPS DE L'HOMME ET DES OISEAUX (1948). 8'. Unpublished, copyright October 20, 1950. Text: Jean Cayrol. Piano accompaniment.
1. J'ai chanté   2. A bas la Feville
3. Oiseaux fatigués de m'entendre   4. Il y a des hommes
Premiere October 4, 1951, Ginette Guillamat, soprano, Jean Langlais, piano, Societé Nationale, Paris, also Radiodiffusion française.

W113. PATER NOSTER (1965). Unpublished. Text: French.

W114. PIE JESU (1943) Unpublished. Two versions: a. Soprano or tenor solo, 2 violins, violoncello, organ, with harp *ad libitum*, b. mixed choir, soloist, instruments. Written to be sung at funeral services (messe de funérailles), therefore the instruments usually used for these masses were designated, with provision for substitutes. West's dissertation (*see*: B258) cites this work as being composed in 1945, with accompaniment of organ, two 'cellos, and harp.

W115. POUR CECILE (December 1, 1946). Unpublished. Text: Jean Langlais. Piano accompaniment.

W116. PRIERES, TROIS (1949). 5' 35". Bornemann, 1949.
1. Ave Verum (French text)   2. Ave Maris Stella (French text)
3. Tantum ergo (French and Latin texts)
For medium voice/unison choir, with organ (harmonium or piano).

Répons pour une Messe de Funérailles (1967).
Unison or 3 mixed voices, soprano, tenor, bass. (*See*: W67)

W117. SACERDOS ET PONTIFEX, "TU ES PETRUS" (1959). 3'. World Library of Sacred Music, 1961. Unison choir, organ, 2 trumpets *ad libitum*. **Premiere** August 1959, Solemn Pontifical Mass, Workshop Choir, Roger Wagner, conductor, Kathleen Thomerson, organ, 7th Annual Liturgical Music Workshop, Boys Town, Nebraska.

W118. SAINT CLEMENT (August 1954). Unpublished. Text: Alain Messiaen. Piano accompaniment.

Short Anthems, Three (1978-79). Hinshaw Music, 1980. (*See*: W68)
   1. Beloved, Let Us Love One Another (Unison, organ, 1' 40".)

W119. VOCALISE (November 19, 1974). 2' 25". UCP Publications, 1975/Combre 1987. Text: none, sung on "Ah." Piano accompaniment. **Premiere** 1975, Janine Collard, Examination for Music Teaching Certification (Certificat d'Aptitude à l'Enseignement Musical), Paris.

I N S T R U M E N T A L

O R G A N

W120. ADORATION (August 30, 1968). 4' 30". Editions Eulenburg, 1970, in the volume *Zeitgenössische Orgelmusik im Gottesdienst* (*Contemporary Organ Music for Liturgical Use*.) **Premiere** March 1969, Jean Langlais, Eglise St. Etienne, Mulhouse. (Review: B291)

W121. ADORATION DES BERGERS (1929). 3'.
   The only surviving work from a set of *Six Préludes* composed in 1929. First published in the Revue de la Schola Cantorum (Petite Maîtrise, September-October 1938); republished in 1982 under the title "Chant des bergers" in *Das neue Orgelalbum*, Universal Edition. See review of 1930 performance under *Six Préludes*. **Premiere** 1930, Jean Langlais, Paris; August 10, 1930, l'église du Sacré-Cœur, Toulouse. (Review: B312a) **Premiere of complete set** 1931, Gaston Litaize, Saint-François-Xavier, Paris.

W122. AMERICAN FOLK-HYMN SETTINGS (completed February 12, 1986). FitzSimons, 1986. Manuscript order and titles: Six American Hymntune Settings, When I Can Read My Title Clear, How Happy Every Child of Grace, On Jordan's Stormy Banks I Stand, Amazing Grace! How Sweet the Sound, How Firm a Foundation, Mine Eyes Have Seen the Glory.   Printed order (changed by publisher):
   1. Amazing Grace! How Sweet the Sound
   2. Battle Hymn of the Republic
   3. How Firm a Foundation
   4. There is a Fountain Filled with Blood
   5. When I Can Read My Title Clear
   6. On Jordan's Stormy Banks I Stand
Premiere June 8, 1986, Kathleen Thomerson, Peters Memorial Presbyterian Church, St. Louis.

W123. AMERICAN SUITE (1959-60). 45'. H. W. Gray, 1961. Out of print, seven movements reprinted in 1977 and 1980.
   1. Big Texas (March 19-May 9, 1959); reprinted by Universal as the first movement, "Introduction," of *Troisième Symphonie*.

2. New York on a Sunday Morning (June 1-3, 1959); reprinted by Universal as the fourth movement, "Un dimanche matin à New York," of *Troisième Symphonie*.
3. Californian Evocation (July 25-August 13, 1959); revised when reprinted by Universal as the second movement, "Cantabile," of *Troisième Symphonie*.
4. Confirmation in Chicago (August 8-September 5, 1959).
5. At Buffalo Bill's Grave (August 8, 1959); reprinted by Combre in *Mosaïque, Vol. 1*.
6. Scherzo-Cats (October 27, 1959), later published separately by H. W. Gray in Saint Cecilia Series; reprinted by Universal as the third movement, "Intermezzo," in *Troisième Symphonie* (with the fifth removed from the final chord).
7. Boys Town, Place of Peace (January 10, 1960); reprinted by Combre in *Mosaïque, Vol. 1*.
8. Storm in Florida (October 17-20, 1959); reprinted in a shorter version (three cuts) by Universal as the fifth movement, "Orage," of *Troisième Symphonie*.

Premiere no record of first complete performance; New York, 1970; August 29, 1971, Heinz-Georges; May 29, 1973, Marie-Louise Jaquet.
Premieres of individual movements
#4. August 29, 1961, Jean Langlais, National Convention, Royal Canadian College of Organists, John Knox Presbyterian Church, St. Catharines, Ontario. (Review B292b)
#5. July 18, 1961, Kathleen Thomerson, Regional Convention, American Guild of Organists, First Congregational Church, Boulder, Colorado.

W124. AVE MARIS STELLA, CHORAL pour orgue (1977). 1'20". Unpublished, copyrighted November 2, 1977.

W125. B.A.C.H. (August-September 1985). 13'37". Bornemann, 1985.
Six pièces pour orgue composées pour le tricentenaire de la naissance de Jean Sébastien Bach (composed for the tricentennial of the birth of Johann Sebastian Bach.)
Premiere December 21, 1985, Helga Schauerte, Eglise Evangélique Allemande, Paris. **American premiere** February 19, 1986, Ann Labounsky, Parkwood Presbyterian Church, Allison Park, PA.

W126. CELEBRATION (January 14, 1975). 4'. Unpublished.
Dedicated to Frank Cunkle, a tribute following his retirement from the American organ journal *The Diapason*

Chant des bergers, *see* W118.

W127. CHANTS DE BRETAGNE, HUIT (September-November 1974). 27' 15". Bornemann, 1975. Titles in French, Breton/Celtic, and English.
1. Le Paradis (Ar Baradoz) (Paradise)   2. Disons le Chapelet (Lavaromp ar Chapeled) (Let us say the Rosary)   3. Angélus   4. Noël Breton (Nouel Breizonek) (Carol of Brittany)
5. Jésus, mon Sauveur béni (Jezuz, va Zalver benniget) (Jesus, my blessed Lord)   6. Jésus nous dit de prier (Jezuz lavar d'eomp pedi) (Jesus tells us to pray)   7. Aux lys avec leurs feuilles argentées (Itron varia rumengol) (To the Fleurs-de-lys with their silvery leaves)   8. Pensez à l'éternité (Sonjit den faziet) (Meditate on eternity)
Premiere November 30, 1975, Jean Langlais, Cathedral of Notre-Dame de Paris.

American premiere January 22, 1976, Ann Labounsky, Duquesne University Chapel, Pittsburgh.

W128. CHARACTERISTIC PIECES, THREE (February 28–March 1, 1957). Novello, 1957. Homage to John Stanley.
1. Pastoral–Prelude   2. Interlude   3. Bells
Langlais' foreword is dated May 1957, Paris.   (*See*: W201)

W129. CHORALS, CINQ (September 4–9 and November 9–12, 1971). Bärenreiter, 1975, in volume IV of *Choralvorspiele für den Gottesdienstlichen Gebrauch*, edited by Adolf Graf. These 96 chorale preludes and intonations include five Langlais works.
1. Gesegn uns, Herr, die Gaben dein   2. Jauchzt, alle Lande, Gott zu Ehren   3. O daß doch bald dein Feuer brennte   4. Wie lieblich schön, Herr Zebaoth   5. Wir wollen singn ein' Lobgesang.

Concerti, Organ   *See*: W209–211.

Deo Gratias   *See*: Organ Postlude, W161.

Deuxième Symphonie   *See*: Symphonie, Deuxième, "alla Webern," W196.

Diptyque, organ solo   *See*: Offrande à une âme, W159.

W130. DOMINICA IN PALMIS (In die palmarum) (October 21, 1954). 5'.
L'Organiste Liturgique 8/Passion, Editions Schola Cantorum, 1954, 21–24. Also published separately, Editions Schola Cantorum, 1980, and in *Music/the AGO-RCCO Magazine* 11, no. 3 (March 1977): 31–34.
Premiere 1955, François Tricot, Sainte-Clotilde.

15 Elevations   *See*: W206.

W131. ESQUISSES GOTHIQUES, TROIS (1975). 17' 55". Bornemann, 1977.
For two organs, second organ ad lib. Plainchant themes are:
1. Veni Créator – Séquence de la Messe pour St. Denis, Exultet ecclesia (12–16 July)
2. Virgo Dei Genitrix – Inviolata   (October 23)
3. Séquence pour la fête de la Dédicace – Salve Regina (October 23–26)
Commissioned in 1975 by the French Ministry of Cultural Affairs.
Premiere October 29, 1976, Ann Labounsky and Robert Grogan, the National Shrine of the Immaculate Conception, Washington, D.C.
European premiere   Jean Langlais and Marie-Louise Jaquet, Notre-Dame de Paris, November 13, 1977.
Premiere #1.   November 29, 1975, Robert Sutherland Lord, First Presbyterian Church, Sharon, Pennsylvania, Wedding Processional, Marriage of Elizabeth Strock and Douglas Himes.   (*See*: B298c)

W132. ESQUISSES ROMANES, TROIS (1975). 32' 02". Bornemann, 1976.
For two organs, second organ ad lib. Plainchant themes are:
1. Séquence Hac Clara Die – Tu Autem (August 9–13)
2. Kyrie Rex Splendens (July 29–August 2)
3. Jerusalem mirabilis (August 8–September 14) [Theme and nine variations, depicting the eleventh to the twentieth centuries]
Commissioned in 1974 by the French Ministry of Cultural Affairs to be premiered in the Cathedral of Angoulême.
Premiere 1974, Jean Langlais, P. Brunet, Angoulême Cathedral.
American premiere October 29, 1976. Ann Labounsky and Robert

Grogan, the National Shrine of the Immaculate Conception, Washington, D. C.

W133. ESSAI (TRIAL) (November 10-11, 1962). 9'30". Bornemann, 1962.
Commissioned by the National Conservatory for the examination for advanced organ students.
Premiere May, 1962, Concours d'Orgue du Conservatoire National Supérieur de Musique, Paris.   (Review: B300b)

W134. ETUDES DE CONCERT, SEPT pour pédale seule (June 1983). 22' 50".
Universal, 1984.
1. Chromatique   2. Countrepoint 1 (Kyrie, Missa "Orbis factor")
3. Alternances   4. Contrepoint 2
5. Staccato   6. Trilles
7. Alleluia (based on "O filii et filiæ")
Premiere August 14, 1985, Bruno Mathieu, Ingolstadt.
American premiere November 12, 1985, Ann Labounsky, Duquesne University, Pittsburgh.

W135. FANTASY ON TWO SCOTTISH THEMES (1986).   In press, Novello.
Commissioned by Marjorie Bruce and the Scottish Arts Council in recognition of the composer's eightieth birthday.
Premiere June 10, 1987, Marjorie Bruce, St. Stephen's Church, Edinburgh, during the Edinburgh Organ Week.

W136. FETE (1946). 7'. H. W. Gray, 1949, in *Modern Anthology,* edited by David McK. Williams; later published separately in Saint Cecilia Series, no. 884-885. First American commission.

W137. FOLKLORIC SUITE (1952). 24'. FitzSimons, 1954.
1. Fugue on *"O Filii"*   2. Legende de Saint Nicolas (1937)
3. Cantique   4. Canzona   5. Rhapsodie sur deux Noëls
Premiere Jean Langlais. Sections of this work were played by the composer in 1954 on tour in America.

W138. HOMAGE TO JEAN-PHILIPPE RAMEAU (1962-64). 31'-33'. Elkan-Vogel, 1965. Movements 3, 4, 6 reprinted by Bornemann, 1987 as *Hommage à Rameau* [1. Ostinato 2. Meditation 3. Evocation].
Commissioned by the French Minister of Fine Arts, M. André Malraux, on the occasion of the 200th anniversary of the death of Rameau. First written in 5 movements: Ouverture sur le nom de Rameau, Chant Pastoral, Invocation, Interlude, Fugue. Printed as:
1. Remembrance [In the Style of Rameau] (August 16, 1962)
2. Allegretto (August 6-7, 1962)
3. Meditation (August 24-25, 1962)
4. Evocation (July 16-30, 1964)
5. As a fugue (September 6-9, 1963, on board ship to France)
6. United themes (August 16-20, 1964) [Title changed to
        Ostinato when reprinted.]
Premiere July 20, 1965, William Teague, Riverside Church, New York City. Also August 20, 1965, Ann Labounsky, Dowd Memorial Chapel, Boys Town, Nebraska.
European premiere November 10, 1965, Jean-Claude Raynaud, Sainte-Clotilde, recital sponsored by the "Amis de l'Orgue."
Premiere #1, #4, March 28, 1965, Ann Labounsky, Church of the Heavenly Rest, New York City.

W139. HOMMAGE A FRESCOBALDI (1951). 28'. Bornemann, 1954.
1. Prélude au Kyrie   2. Offertoire   3. Elévation   4. Communion
5. Fantaisie   6. Antienne   7. Thème et variations   8. Epilogue
The first five pieces constitute an organ mass.
Premiere 1952, Jean Langlais, Paris.

W140. IMPLORATIONS, TROIS (1970). 10' 40". Bornemann, 1970.
1. Pour la Joie
Commissioned by the National Conservatory for the 1970
examination for advanced organ students.
Premiere May, 1970, Concours d'Orgue du Conservatoire National
Supérieur de Musique, Paris.
2. Pour l'indulgence   3. Pour la Croyance   (March 24-27)
Premiere March 1971, Jean Langlais, Radio ORTF, Paris.

W141. INCANTATION POUR UN JOUR SAINT (February 14-20, 1949). 5' 10". In
Orgue et Liturgie I/ Pâques, Editions Schola Cantorum, Paris,
1950. Printed separately, Editions Schola Cantorum, 1980.
Premiere 1950, Jean Langlais, Radio, Paris.

W142. IN MEMORIAM (1986). Combre, 1987. Dedication: « A la mémoire de
mon maître, Charles Tournemire »
Premiere   February 13, 1987, Naji Hakim, St. Joseph Church,
Bonn-Beuel, Germany, in recital as part of the "Bonner
Langlais-Tage."   **American premiere**   June 23, 1987, Ann
Labounsky, Region III Convention, American Guild of Organists, Mt.
Lebanon United Methodist Church, Pittsburgh.

Légende de St. Nicolas (1937).   4'.   Originally an improvisation on a
folksong theme given Langlais by Radio Strasbourg for a broadcast
there. In 1952, made part of *Folkloric Suite*, W137.

**W143. LEICHTE STÜCKE FÜR ORGEL, DREI   (Trois pièces faciles pour
orgue/Three easy pieces for organ)** (1985). Pro Organo, 1986.
1. Libre   2. Recitativ   3. Allegro
Premiere   March 14, 1987, Stefan Kagl, Kaiser-Wilhelm-
Gedächtnis-Kirche, Berlin.

W144. LIVRE ŒCUMENIQUE (January 28-February 19, 1968).   40' 35".
Bornemann, 1968.
1. Sacris Solemnis   2. Du fond de ma détresse   3. Verbum
Supernum   4. Notre Dieu est une puissance forteresse   5. Ave
Maris Stella   6. Mon âme exalte le Seigneur   7. Pater Noster
8. Notre Père qui es aux Cieux 9. Kyrie (orbis factor) 10. Kyrie,
Dieu, Père Eternel 11. Gloria (orbis factor)   12. Gloire à Dieu au
plus haut des Cieux. Six pieces based on Gregorian themes, six on
chorale melodies used by J. S. Bach.
Premiere June 19, 1968, Jean Langlais, St. Merry, Paris. (Review:
B308a) Two pieces premiered at Nancy, France, on May 7, 1968.

W145. MARIENSTATT CHORALS (December 24, 1979-June 20, 1980). Breitkopf
& Härtel, in volumes of the *Marienstatter Orgelbüchlein*, edited
by the Rev. Fr. Gabriel Hammer. Each hymntune is set as an organ
chorale prelude, and as a chorale reharmonization for unison voices
with organ accompaniment: *choralvorspiele und orgelsätze*.
1. Lobpreiset all zu dieser Zeit (*22, vol. 1, published 1982)
2. Erfreue dich, Himmel (*3, vol. 3, published 1987)
3. Freu dich, du Himmels Königin   4. Pange Lingua
Premiere Gabriel Hammer, Marienstatt Abbey, Germany.

W146. MEDITATIONS SUR L'APOCALYPSE, CINQ (1972-73). 48' 23".
Bornemann, 1974.
1. Celui qui a des oreilles, qu'il écoute
   Transcription of the choral work *Psaume 123*, which the
   ms. shows as opus 17, no. 1 (1937). The soprano/tenor psalm-
   ordiants' part becomes the pedal line; the SATB choir (no text,
   on "Ah") becomes the manual part.
2. Il était, Il est et Il vient (December 26-28, 1972)
3. Visions prophétiques (March 15-25, 1973)
4. Oh oui, viens Seigneur Jésus (March 24-25, 1973)
5. La Cinquième trompette (December 1-17, 1972)
Premiere April 11, 1974, Jean Langlais, Notre-Dame de Paris.
Premiere #2 July 12, 1973, 11th International Festival of Organ
Music, Magadino, Gambarogno, Switzerland, Marie-Louise Jaquet.
American premiere of complete work: August 4, 1974, Ann
Labounsky, Cathedral of St. John the Divine, New York City.

W147. MEDITATIONS SUR LA SAINTE TRINITE, TROIS (1962).   10' 45".
Philippo, 1962.
1. Première Personne: Le Père
2. Deuxième Personne: Le Fils
3. Troisième Personne: Le Saint Esprit
Premiere 1962, Jean Langlais, Paris.

W148. METHODE D'ORGUE (1984). Combre, 1984.
In collaboration with Marie-Louise Jaquet-Langlais.   French,
English, and German text. 50 pages.

W149. MINIATURE (1958, modified from 1935).   7'.   H. W. Gray, 1960.
Commissioned and edited by Marilyn Mason.
Premiere December 30, 1958, Marilyn Mason, St. Paul's Chapel of
Trinity Parish, New York City, recital for the American Guild of
Organists' Midwinter Conclave. (Review: B312)

W150. MINIATURE II (March 1984). Combre, 1984.
Collection « La Pléiade », new series of instrumental pieces
expressly for contests, examinations, and auditions of
conservatories and music schools, Michel Mériot, editor.   Grade
level: Elementaire. 2.
Premiere May 13, 1984, Helga Schauerte, Kirchhundem, Germany.

W151. MOSAIQUE, Volume 1 (1959,1975-76). Combre, 1977.
1. Stèle pour Gabriel Fauré   (3') Based on the motet *Ave mundi
   gloria*, composed in 1932   (*See*: W47)
2. Sur la tombe de Buffalo Bill
   (At Buffalo Bill's Grave, August 1959, *American Suite*)
3. Double Fantaisie pour deux organistes   (9' 40")
   [December 7-21, 1976 is date given in catalog; since premiere
   and recording were earlier in 1976; mentioned in 1976 article
   by Jaquet (*see*: B313b); probably composed December 1975.]
Premiere Ellen and Kenneth Landis, Duquesne University Chapel,
Pittsburgh, October 21, 1976. **European premiere** Marie-Louise
Jaquet and Anne-Catherine Plasse, Temple St. Jean, Mulhouse.
4. Boys town, lieu de paix
   (Boys town, place of peace, January 1960, *American Suite*)

W152. MOSAIQUE, Volume II (1976). 30' 25". Combre, 1977.
1. Gable   2. Images   3. Trio
4. Complainte de Pontkalleg (Gwerz Maro Pontkalleg)

5.   Salve Regina **Premiere #5**.   Jean Langlais, East Liberty Presbyterian Church,   Pittsburgh, October 17, 1976.
Premiere of complete work   September 15, 1977, Ann Labounsky, Duquesne University Chapel, Pittsburgh.

W153. MOSAIQUE, Uolume III (1977). 35' 45". Combre, 1978.
1. Lumière 2. Parfum 3. Printemps 4. Thèmes 5. Pax
6. Double Fantaisie #2
Premiere of complete work April 25, 1978, Ann Labounsky, Heinz Chapel, University of Pittsburgh, with Pierre Whalon on *Double Fantaisie*, in the program "In Hommage to Jean Langlais."
European premiere#6 Marie-Louise Jaquet and Viviane Damiani.

W154. NOELS AUEC UARIATIONS (June–September 1979). 21'. Universal, 1981.
1.   Noël 1 (Noël provençal) **Premiere** August 19, 1979, Karen Hastings, Notre-Dame de Paris.
2. Noël II (II est né le Divin Enfant)
3. Noël III (Ihr Hirten, erwacht – Noël pour l'amour de Marie)
Premiere of complete work December 30, 1979, Pierre Cogen, Saint-Louis des Invalides, Paris.

W155. OFFERTOIRES POUR TOUS LES TEMPS, DEUH (1943). 4'. Durand, 1943.
1. Paraphrase de la messe "*Stelliferi conditor orbis*"
2. Paraphrase de la messe "*Magnæ Deus potentiæ*"
Premiere#2   June 24, 1943, Antoine Reboulot, Association Valentin Haüy.

W156. OFFICE DE LA FETE DE LA SAINTE TRINITE (1957–58). *Organum in Missa Cantata* Vol. 2, Christophorus-Verlag Herder, 1961.
In Festo SS. Trinitatis
Prélude à l'Introit – Offertoire – Communion – Final
The "Final" is based on the antiphon *Te Deum* from the Second Vespers on Trinity Sunday.
Premiere Noëlie Pierront, Paris, 1959.

W157. OFFICE POUR LA SAINTE FAMILLE (July 1957). 12'. *Organum in Missa Cantata* Vol. 1, Christophorus-Verlag Herder (Freiburg, Germany), 1959.   *Sanctae Familiae, Jesu, Mariae, Joseph*
Prélude – Offertoire – Communion – Sortie
The "Sortie" is based on the antiphon *Jacob autem* from the First Vespers on the feast of the Holy Family. *Organum in Missa Cantata* is a three volume collection of short organ masses by contemporary European composers, for Sundays and feast days.
Premiere 1958, Noëlie Pierront, Paris.

W158. OFFRANDE A MARIE (1971). 32' 10". Philippo, 1972.
1. Mater admirabilis	2. Consolatrix afflictorum
3. Régina Angelorum	4. Régina Pacis
5. Mater Christi	6. Maria Mater Gratiæ
Premiere August 20, 1972, Jean Langlais, The National Shrine of The Immaculate Conception, Washington, D. C.; August 23, 1972, Jean Langlais, Church of the Heavenly Rest, New York City. Not complete work. (Review: B315)

W159. OFFRANDE A UNE AME, DIPTYQUE (August 8–October 21, 1979).
22' 30". Bornemann, 1980.   Composed in memory of his wife Jeannette, who died in June, 1979. Dedication: « à ma très chère épouse Jeannette rappelée à Dieu, in memoriam » **(To my very dear**

wife, Jeannette, called back to God, in memoriam.)
1. Vers la Lumière (**Toward the Light**) 2. Dans la Lumière (**In the Light**)
Premiere March 29, 1980, Jean Langlais, Notre-Dame de Paris.
American premiere March 8, 1981, Ann Labounsky, Heinz Chapel, University of Pittsburgh.

W160. ORGAN BOOK (10 Pieces) (1956). Elkan-Vogel, 1957.
1. Prelude 2. Pastoral Song 3. Choral in E Minor 4. Flutes
5. Musette 6. Choral in F Major 7. Scherzando 8. Andantino
9. Epithalamium 10. Pasticcio
Premiere unknown. Jean Langlais' programs for his 1958/59 American tour list the Scherzando and Pasticcio as "First performance in the U. S.", but this is doubtful, as they had been in print in America since 1957. (Reviews: B259, B317b)

Organ Method *See*: Méthode d'Orgue, W148.

W161. ORGAN POSTLUDE ON THE *DEO GRATIAS* of Gregorian Mass 16/18 (1958). 3'. World Library of Sacred Music (Cincinnati), 1960. Pages 56-57 in the volume "Organ Postludes on All the Deo Gratias's/by Just as Many Composers."

W162. PARAPHRASES GREGORIENNES, TROIS (1933-34). 15'. Hérelle, 1935.
Printed order: 1. Ave Maria, Ave maris stella   2. Mors et Resurrectio 3. Hymne d'actions de grâce "Te Deum"
Order of composition: 1. Mors et Resurrectio 2. Ave Maria, Ave maris stella 3. Hymne d'actions de grâce "Te Deum"
Premiere 28 June 1934, Jean Langlais, Paris, orgue de Mme. Flersheim. (Review of later performance in 1934: B6)
Langlais' second published organ work, printed as opus 5.

W163. PETITES PIECES, DOUZE (12) organ or harmonium (1960,1962). Editions Schola Cantorum, 1962. **Dix versets dans les modes grégoriens** (1962) and **Deux petites pièces dans le style médiéval** (1960).

W164. PETITES PIECES, SIX (March 6-7, 1976). 10' 15". Unpublished.
Very short exercises (about 15 measures each) written at the request of American organist Allen Hobbs for his *Method of Organ Playing.*
1. Trio 2. Repeated notes 3. Legato 4. Staccato 5. Chords
6. Rhythms

W165. PIECES, NEUF, pour orgue (1942-43). 38' 29". Bornemann, 1945.
1. Chant de peine   2. Chant de joie   3. Chant de paix   4. Chant héroïque 5. Dans une douce joie 6. De profundis 7. Mon âme cherche une fin paisible 8. Prélude sur une antienne (from 1929)
9. Rhapsodie grégorienne (revised March 1980)
Premiere 1944, Jean Langlais, Paris.   **#9.** Noëlie Pierront, Palais de Chaillot.

W166. PIECES, VINGT-QUATRE, pour harmonium ou orgue (1933-39). Hérelle, 1939 and 1942. (Sometimes "pour orgue ou harmonium.")
Volume 1: 1. Prélude modal 2. Hommage 3. Arabesque
4. Fugue 5. Paraphrase sur "*Salve Regina*" 6. Noël, avec variations 7. Choral 8. Ricercare 9. Scherzetto 10. Toccata
11. Prière pour les morts 12. Hommage à Fr. Landino. Volume 2:
13. Homo quidam 14. Allegro 15. Prière 16. Choral orné 17. Pour une Sainte de Légende 18. Fantaisie sur un thème Norvégien

19. Prélude et Fuguette   20. Fuguette   21. Fantaisie   22. Chant élégiaque   23. Point d'Orgue   24. Impromptu
Premiere 1939, Jean Langlais, Paris. (1933 Review: B319a)
Premiere #9 January 29, 1935, Olivier Messiaen, St. Antoine des Quinze-Vingts.

W167. PIECES BREVES, DEUX   (June 1983). 4' 10". Combre, 1983.
Brève I.   Brève 2.
Collection « La Pléiade », new series of instrumental pieces expressly for contests, examinations, and auditions of conservatories and music schools, Michel Mériot, editor. Grade level: Elementaire.1.2.

Pièces faciles, Trois, pour orgue   *See*: Leichte Stücke für Orgel, Drei, W143.

W168. PIECES MODALES, HUIT (1956). Philippo, 1957.
1. Mode de ré (January 31)   2. Mode de la (March 8)
3. Mode de mi (February 6)   4. Mode de si (February 10)
5. Mode de fa (March 12)   6. Mode de do (April 3)
7. Mode de sol (June 6)   8. Mode de sol (May 12)
Premiere 1956, Xavier Dufresse, Paris. Langlais included "Mode de ré" on his 1958-59 American tour programs. (Review: B259)

W169. PIECES pour la *Méthode d'Orgue* of Noëlie Pierront and Jean Bonfils, *Nouvelle Méthode de Clavier* **(harmonium ou orgue)**, Editions Schola Cantorum, 1961. 3 volumes.
Deux petites pièces dans le style médiéval (1960) are on pages 123-124 of volume II, with the note that they were composed especially for this organ method. **Deux versets du 7e ton** (1960) are on pages 153-154 of volume III. The four pieces are found as part of **Douze petites pièces**. (*See*: W163)

W170. PLEIN JEU A LA FRANÇAISE   (1974). 2' 20". Musical Supplement, Revue de Musique Sacrée, La Procure du Clergé (Paris), 1974.

W171. POEMES EVANGELIQUES d'après les textes sacrés (1932). 15' 35".
Hérèlle, 1933. (Title sometimes spelled *Poèms;* or *Trois Poèms Evangéliques.*)
1. L'Annonciation   2. La Nativité   3. Les Rameaux (Entrée de Jésus à Jérusalem)   First published organ work of Langlais, printed as opus 2.
Premiere of complete work May 29, 1932, Jean Langlais, St. Antoine des Quinze-Vingts. **Premiere #3** February 22, 1932, Jean Langlais, St. Merry, Paris.
American premiere #2 La Nativité, André Marchal, tour 1932.

W172. POEM OF HAPPINESS (1966). Elkan-Vogel, 1967.
Premiere Not known; May 17, 1969, Jean Langlais, Basilica of Ste. Clotilde, Paris, marriage of Monique Bourreau and Claude Langlais.

W173. POEM OF LIFE (1965). 20' 10".   Elkan-Vogel, 1966. Second part composed January 26-31; first part, February 1- April 5.
Premiere 1965, Jean Langlais, Radiodiffusion française.

W174. POEM OF PEACE (1966). 6' 30". Elkan-Vogel, 1967.
Premiere   January 16, 1967, Jean Langlais, Union Methodist Church, Washington, D. C., first concert of seventh American tour. (Review: B220)

W175. POSTLUDES FOR ORGAN, FOUR (1950). McLaughlin & Reilly, 1951.
    1. Postlude I   **Brillante e vivo**   (composed May 10-11)
    2. Postlude II   **Presto e leggiero** (July 20-23)
    3. Postlude III   **Vivace**   (July 29-31)
    4. Postlude IV   **Allegro energico** (September 1-3)

W176. PRELUDE A LA MESSE "*ORBIS FACTOR*" (Kyrie XI) (1956).
    Music supplement to the journal *De Præstant* (Tongerlo, Belgium),
    October 1956. [Title sometimes appears as *Prélude au
    Kyrie Orbis Factor (Messe XI)*.]

W177. PRELUDE DANS LE STYLE ANCIEN (1968). 3' 30". Editions Eulenburg,
    1970, in the volume *Zeitgenössische Orgelmusik im Gottes-
    dienst   (Contemporary Organ Music for Liturgical Use)*.
    Premiere 1969, Jean Langlais, St. Etienne, Mulhouse, France.

W178. PRELUDE ET ALLEGRO (completed July 1, 1982). 19' 50"-14'.
    Universal, 1985.   Commissioned by the Welsh Arts Council,
    dedicated to Nicholas Jackson, organist of St. David's Cathedral.
    Premiere May 28, 1983, St. David's Festival, Wales.

W179. PRELUDE ET FUGUE (1927). Composition prize, Institut National des
    Jeunes Aveugles, 1928. 7'. Universal Edition, 1982.
    Premiere July 1927, Jean Langlais, INJA examination, Paris. He
    was awarded first prize "with the jury's compliments to the
    performer." **Premiere, printed score** August 8, 1982, Masevaux,
    Marie-Agnes Grall-Menet.

W180. PRELUDE GREGORIEN (August 5, 1979). 4'. Unpublished.
    Composed for the dedication of the Schudi tracker organ at the
    Catholic University of America; first performed at the program
    where President Pellegrino conferred the degree Doctor of Music,
    honoris causa, to Langlais.
    Premiere   September 19, 1979, George C. Baker, St. Vincent's
    Chapel, Catholic University of America, Washington, D.C.

W181. PRELUDE ON *CORONATION* (March 1, 1963). Oxford University Press,
    1964, in the collection *Modern Organ Music, Book 2.*
    Premiere 1963, Beatrice Collins.

W182. PRELUDES, HUIT (December 27, 1983-January 16, 1984). 20' 37".
    Bornemann, 1984.
    1. Une voix 2. Duo 3. Trio 4. 4 voix 5. 5 voix 6. 6 voix
    7. 7 voix 8. 8 voix, Troisième fantaisie pour 2 organistes
    Premiere   September 9, 1984,   Ann Labounsky, Church of the
    Assumption, Pittsburgh.

W183. PRELUDES, QUATRE (1975).   **Premiere** October 24, 1975, Holland.

W184. PRELUDES, SIX (1929). Manuscript lost. One section published, see
    Adoration des Bergers, W121. Titles of three other preludes, taken
    from reviews: *Lamentation, Images, Chant héraldique.*
    Premiere 1930, Jean Langlais, Paris; August 10, 1930, l'Eglise du
    Sacré-Cœur, Toulouse. (Reviews: B328a, b)
    Premiere of complete set 1931, Gaston Litaize, Saint-
    François-Xavier, Paris.

Première Symphonie   *See*: Symphonie, Première, W197.

W185. PRIERE DES MAGES (1971, 1981). 3'. Universal, 1982, in the collection *Das neue Orgelalbum*. Originally written for strings and organ as part of the Third Organ Concerto, deleted when the concerto was revised for publication. (*See*: W211)

W186. PROGRESSION (1978). 27' 15". Bornemann, 1979.
1. Monodie (October 14-19)   2. Duo (October 19)
3. Larmes [Trio] (October 18)   4. Offering (September 16-19)
5. Fugue et Continuo (December 23-26)
Première May 21, 1979, Ann Labounsky, Basilica of Ste. Clotilde, Paris; also May 23, 1979, Association Valentin Haüy, Paris; Sept. 30, 1979, Heinz Chapel, University of Pittsburgh.

Quatre Postludes   *See*: Postludes, Four, W175.

W187. RHAPSODIE SAVOYARDE (June 11-12, 1960). Unpublished. Premiere title reported as *Rhapsodie sur des airs savoyards*, using themes of four 16th century Noëls of Nicolas Martin.
Première August 1960, Jean Langlais, Megève. (Review: B40)

W188. ROSACE (Rose Window) (April 22-June 21, 1980). 26' 10". Combre, 1981. 1. Pour une célébration   2. Introduction et Marche
          3. Croquis (Sketch)   4. Feux d'Artifice (Fireworks)
Première June 7,1982, Marie-Louise Jaquet-Langlais, Association Valentin Haüy, Paris.
Première #1 October 1980, Lester Berenbroick, Jubilee Service, Presbyterian Church of Madison, New Jersey. Commissioned by the church and choir as his 25th anniversary gift.
Première #4 Marie-Louise Jaquet-Langlais, February 22, 1981, The Riverside Church, New York City.

Six American Hymntune Settings   *See*: American Folk-Hymn, W122.

W189. SOLEILS, CINQ (1983). 33' 40". Combre, 1983. Commissioned by Pierre Lacroix, Director of the 1983 Festival of Comminges [Cathédrale de Saint Bertrand de Comminges].
1. Soleil du Matin 2. Soleil de Midi 3. Soleil du Soir 4. Soleil des Etoiles 5. Soleil de France
Premieres #1-3: August 13, 1983, Makiko Hayashima, Festival de Saint Bertrand de Comminges. **#4-5**: July 24, 1984, Naji Hakim, Festival de Saint Bertrand de Comminges.

W190. SONATE EN TRIO (1967). Bornemann, 1968. Commissioned by the National Conservatory for the 1968 examination for advanced organ students.   Allegro - Andante - Final
Première May 1968, Concours du Conservatoire National Supérieur de Musique, Paris. (Review: B331a)

W191. SUITE BAROQUE (1973). 16' 51". Philippo & Combre, 1973.
1. Plein Jeu 2. Trémolo en Taille 3. Dialogue 4. Flûtes
5. Dialogues entre le Hautbois, le Boudon et le Nazard
6. Voix humaine 7. Grand Jeu
Première Dec. 2, 1973, Jean Langlais, Temple de St. Jean, Mulhouse, France. (Review: B332a)

W192. SUITE BREVE (1947). 16' 17". Bornemann, 1947.
1. Grands jeux (first theme previously used in W3)   2. Cantilène
3. Plainte (*See*: W2, W3)   4. Dialogue sur les mixtures
Première Jean Langlais, Radiodiffusion française.

W193. SUITE FRANÇAISE (1948) 37' 20". Bornemann, 1949.
1. Prélude sur les grands jeux 2. Nasard 3. Contrepoint sur les jeux d'anches   4. Française   5. Choral sur la voix humaine 6. Arabesque sur les flûtes   7. Méditation sur les jeux de fonds 8. Trio   9. Voix céleste   10. Final rhapsodique
Premieres 1949, Alexandre Kraskievitch, Paris; May 8, 1949, Jean Langlais, Radio-Lorraine.

W194. SUITE MEDIEVALE EN FORME DE MESSE BASSE (1947). 19'. Editions Salabert, (Rouart et Lerolle) 1950.
1. Prélude (Entrée) 2. Tiento (Offertoire)   3. Improvisation (Elévation) 4. Méditation (Communion) 5. Acclamations (sur le texte des acclamations carolingiennes)
Premiere 1948, André Marchal, Saint-Eustache, Paris.

W195. SUPPLICATION (January 20, 1972). 2' 10". Stichting Internatonaal Orgelcentrum, Haarlem, Holland, 1972.

W196. SYMPHONIE, DEUXIEME, "ALLA WEBERN" (December 19-20, 1976- January 11, 1977). 5' 10". Combre, 1977.
1. Prélude   2. Lude   3. Interlude   4. Postlude
Premiere April 3, 1977, Kathleen Thomerson, The Principia College, Elsah, Illinois; **European premiere** April 18, 1977, Marie-Louise Jaquet, Würzburg.

W197. SYMPHONIE, PREMIERE (1941-42). 31' 30". Hérelle, 1944.
1. Allegro   2. Eglogue   3. Choral   4. Final
Premiere June 1943, Jean Langlais, Paris, Palais de Chaillot.
(Reviews: B336a, b)

W198. SYMPHONIE, TROISIEME (1959, revised 1979). 25'. Universal, 1980.
1. Introduction 2. Cantabile 3. Intermezzo 4. Un dimanche matin à New York 5. Orage
The out-of-print *American Suite,* W123, with Cantabile and Orage revised.
Premiere May 31, 1982, Marie-Louise Jaquet-Langlais, Notre-Dame de Paris.

W199. TALITHA KOUM (Résurrection) (May 28-June 10, 1985). 25' 20". Combre, 1985. The title is a scripture reference, Mark 5:41.
1. Salve Regina
2. Regina Caeli (in three sections: O Clemens, O Pia, Dulcis; may be played together or separately)
3. Alme Pater (Messe X: Aux Fêtes de la Sainte-Vierge) Kyrie - Gloria - Sanctus - Agnus Dei
4. 1-7-8 (Alleluia)
Premiere November 18, 1985, Pierre Cogen, Ste-Clotilde.

W200. THEME LIBRE (summer 1929). Unpublished.
Theme assigned by Marcel Dupré for his organ class.

W201. TRIPTYQUE (November-December 1956). Novello, 1958.
1. Melody   2. Trio   3. Final
Written at the publisher's request for their service music series "Novello's Organ Music Club." When submitted to them, it was judged to be more difficult than expected, so Langlais wrote an easier work for that series, *Three Characteristic Pieces,* published in 1957. (*See*: W128) Novello then decided to publish

Triptyque in their series "International Series of Contemporary Organ Music."
Premiere   February 1958, English recital tour, Jean Langlais, Royal Festival Hall, London (Review: B337b), or Leeds. He also included this work on two of the three programs prepared for his 1958-59 American tour, as "First performance in the U. S."

W202. TRIPTYQUE GREGORIEN (1978). 17' 50". Universal, 1979.
1. Rosa mystica   2. In Paradisum   3. Alléluia
Premiere   September 14, 1978, Ann Labounsky, Pittsburgh, Duquesne University Chapel.

W203. TRUMPET TUNE (completed March 13, 1987). FitzSimons, in press.
Commissioned for the state trumpet at the Cathedral of St. John the Divine, New York City.
Premiere   Jonathan Dimmock, Cathedral of St. John the Divine.

Trois Poèmes Evangéliques   *See*: Poèmes Evangéliques, W171.

Troisième Symphonie   *See*: Symphonie 3, W198.

W204. VERSETS, DOUZE (12) (September-October 1986). Bornemann, 1987.
Numbered 1-12, no titles.

W205. VOLUNTARIES, THREE (July 20-August 10, 1969). FitzSimons, 1970.
1. Voluntary Saint Jacques le Majeur (12')
2. Voluntary Sainte Marie-Madeleine (11' 30")
3. Voluntary Sainte Trinité (14' 08")
Premiere   November 9, 1971, Michelle Leclerc, Basilique Sainte-Clotilde for Les Amis de l'Orgue.

IN PRESS:

W206.   Original title, **15 ELEVATIONS**, (November-December 1986) is to be changed.   Probable new title: **EXPRESSIONS**. FitzSimons, 1987 or 1988. Each short piece of 20 to 24 measures is designed to fit on 2 printed pages. The key relationships are such that an organist may continue from one piece to the next to form a piece of needed length. Naji Hakim has written 15 pieces of the same nature; thus the volume will have 30 pieces by the two composers.

ORGAN AND INSTRUMENTS

W207. CHORAL MEDIEVAL (1937, 1938). 3'. Unpublished. 3 trumpets, 3 trombones, and organ. Two versions: a. Transcription in 1937 of the Toccata, #10 of the *24 Pièces* (1933, W170), listed in catalog as the second movement of *Piece symphonique.*
b. Toccata expanded with additional material in 1938, including ending with *Victimae paschali* , plainsong sequence for Easter Day. *Choral Médiéval* title assigned at time of premiere.
Premiere   1945, Jean Langlais, organ, Jacques Chailley, conductor, Radiodiffusion française.

W208. CORTEGE (1969). Unpublished.
2 organs, 8 brass, and timpani. Written at the request of William Self, St. Thomas Church, New York City.

Premiere June 24, 1971, Claire Coci. **European premiere** May 27, 1976, Marie-Louise Jaquet, organ, brass ensemble (6 trumpets, 2 French horns) of the Collegium musicum, University of Marburg, Germany, concert at Bitschwiller-lès-Thann, France. (*See*: B340) Also: October 22, 1976, Ann Labounsky, Duquesne University Chapel, Solemn High Mass, Sacred Music Convocation.

W209. CONCERTO, DEUXIEME pour orgue (1961). 28' 40". Manuscript copies distributed through Universal Edition for performance.
Thème et variations – Interlude – Final.
Organ and string orchestra. Revision of *Thème, variations et final* (1937), with short Interlude for organ solo added. The music of *Plainte (Suite brève)* is also used.
Premiere May 11, 1962, Fourth Annual May Festival of Contemporary Music, Fenner Douglass, organ, members of the Cleveland Orchestra, Walter Blodgett, conductor, St. Paul's Church, Cleveland Heights, Ohio. Commissioned for the Festival by Walter Blodgett.
Also: March 23, 1970, University of Pittsburgh, Heinz Chapel, Dr. Robert Sutherland Lord, organ; instrumentalists from the Univ. of Pittsburgh, Bernard Z. Goldberg, conductor.

W210. CONCERTO, PREMIER pour orgue ou clavecin et orchestre (October 1, 1948–July 23, 1949). 13'. Manuscript copies available through Universal Edition.   Allegro – Andante – Final.
Strings (5), 2 flutes, 2 oboes, 2 clarinets, 2 bassoons.
Premiere Jeanne Demessieux, organ; Radiodiffusion, l'Orchestre Radio symphonique de Paris, E. Bigot, conductor; also Berne, Switzerland, and Radio Suisse.

W211. CONCERTO, TROISIEME : REACTION (December 28, 1970–April 9,1971). 23'. Published version 18'. Universal Edition, 1980. Miniature score with preface and formal analysis in English, French, and German, 55 pages, Philharmonia Partituren no. 504, Universal Edition, 1980. Organ, string orchestra, and timpani.
Introduction – Vif – Fugue – Cadence – Conclusion.
Original version recorded on ABC Records (*see*: D78) in 1981. String music deleted (when revised for publication) was arranged for organ solo and published as *Prière des Mages*, W180. Commissioned by the Crane School of Music, State University College, Potsdam, New York, to be performed at the opening of the Crane Music Center. Due to delays in construction of the new organ, the official premiere was not given until 1978.
Official Premiere March 2, 1978, William Maul, organist, John Jadlos, conductor, Crane Symphony Orchestra Strings, Richard Holly, timpani, Helen M. Hosmer Hall, Crane School of Music, Potsdam, New York. (Review: B71)
Previous performance October 19, 1976, Ann Labounsky, organ, John Carnahan, timpani, Duquesne University String Orchestra, Richard Goldner, conductor, Duquesne University Chapel, Pittsburgh.

W212. PIECE IN FREE FORM (1935). 10'. H. W. Gray, 1960; then Combre, 1984 under French title *Pièce en forme libre*. String quartet (or string orchestra) and organ. In 1937, designated as the first movement of *Pièce symphonique*. (*See*: W7)
Adagio – Maestoso energico – Adagio.
Premieres a. (organ version, original title *Quintette*) January 28, 1936, Noëllie Pierront, Saint-Pierre du Gros-Caillou, Paris, Les

Amis de l'Orgue; b. (piano version, title *Fantaisie*) February 6, 1937, Jean Langlais, piano, string quartet: Mme. Primans-Bach, Mlle. Monique Jeanne, Mmes. Combrisson and Yvonne Thibout. Société Nationale de Musique, Paris. (Reviews: B341c, B342a, b)

Trumpet and Organ   *See* : W224-28.

PIANO AND ORGAN

W213. DIPTYQUE (1974). 8' 50". Combre, 1983.
In two movements , titled "1er Mouvement," "2eme Mouvement." The second is an arrangement of the *Mouvement perpetuel* for piano (1936).
Premiere February 11, 1976; Rolande Falcinelli and Marie-José Chasseguet, Radio ORTF in program "Clarté dans la nuit."

PIANO

PIANO QUINTET

Fantaisie/Pièce en Forme Libre (piano version of *Piece in Free Form*, 1935). 10'. Unpublished (organ version published). String quartet (or orchestra) and piano. (*See* : W212)

PIANO SOLO

W214. HISTOIRE URAIE POUR UNE MON (May 5, 1941). Unpublished. Original version for piano, arranged in 1942 for flute and piano. (*See* : W239)

W215. MOUVEMENT PERPETUEL (1936). 4'. U.C.P. Publications, 1976. Arranged in 1974 for piano and organ. (*See* : W213)
Premiere May 3, 1939, Ida Périn, Salle Erard, Paris.

W216. NOEL BRETON (April 1987). Unpublished as of September 1987.
Premiere June 3, 1987, Caroline Langlais, Schola Cantorum examination, Paris.

W217. PETITE SUITE (December 1985-June 1986). Combre, 1987. Four easy pieces.
1. Danse Bretonne   2. Il est né, le Divin Enfant
3. Ah! Vous Dirai-Je Maman   4. J'ai du bon tabac
Premiere #1   June 1986, Caroline Langlais, Schola Cantorum examination, Paris.

W218. PRELUDE ET FUGUE (1937). 5'. Unpublished, manuscript lost.
Premiere December 1937, Jean Langlais, Association Valentin Haüy, Paris.

W219. SUITE (1934). 9'. Piano, four hands. Unpublished, manuscript lost. Revised in 1947, primo part simplified.

W220. SUITE ARMORICAINE (1938).   8'.   Printed as opus 20, Editions du Clavier, Paris, 1958. Original title, *Suite celtique pour piano*.
I. Epitaphe pour les marins qui n'ont pas eu de tombe

II. Le vieux pêcheur au large   III. Baigneuses
IV. Coquillage solitaire   V. Conciliabule chez les mouettes
Premiere May 3, 1938, Ida Périn, piano, Societé Nationale, Ecole Normale, Paris. (Review: B343b)

HARPSICHORD

W221. SUITE POUR CLAVECIN (1944). 12'. Unpublished.
  1. Introduction   2. Allegro   3. Choral orné
  4. Prélude   5. Fuguette   6. Fantaisie sur un thème norvegien
All movements except the Introduction are arranged from *24 Pièces* (1933-39). **Premiere** Marcelle Delacour.
Revised in 1978 with order of movements:
  1. Introduction   2. Allegro   3. Choral orné
  4. Choral (et variations)   5. Prelude et fuguette
  6. Scherzetto   7. Fantaisie sur un thème norvegien
Premiere June 28, 1986, Stefan Kagl, harpsichord, Villa Stuck, Munich, Germany.

HANDBELLS [CLOCHES]

W222. CARILLONS (1967). 8 pages. H. W. Gray, 1968. Two versions, for 37 or 52 handbells.
Commissioned by the Westminster Bell-Ringers Guild of Westminster Presbyterian Church, Lincoln, Nebraska.
Premiere June 30, 1968, National Convention, American Guild of Organists, Westminster Bell-Ringers Guild, Dale Fleck, director, Immaculate Conception Cathedral, Denver.

BRASS

BRASS CHOIR

Choral Médiéval (1938) *See:* W207.

Cortège (1969) *See:* W208.

W223. SONNERIE (INTRADA) (February 21-22, 1961). 4' 30". Unpublished.
4 trumpets, 4 trombones. **Premiere** 1961, Contrepoint Sorbonne.

TWO TRUMPETS AND ORGAN

W224. PASTORALE ET RONDO (1982). 9'. Elkan-Vogel, 1983.
The theme of *Pastorale*, a Breton folksong, is found in the second movement of *Sonatine pour trompette* and as #6 of the organ *Huit Chants de Bretagne*. *Rondo* is based on *Pasticcio* from *Organ Book*. Both have new material. Written at the request of Wolfgang G. Haas for the Ensemble "Trumpet und Orgel Köln."
Premiere September 30, 1982, Edward H. Tarr and Wolfgang G. Hass, trumpets; Paul Wisskirchen, organ; Altenberg Cathedral, Germany, in concert of "International Orgel Series."
American premiere June 11, 1983, Roger Sherman, Charles

Litette, trumpets; Ann Labounsky, organ; St. Paul of the Cross
Monastery, Pittsburgh.

TRUMPET SOLO

W225. CHORALS, SEPT (April 9-15, 1972). 22' 30". Philippo, 1972.
Title: *7 Chorals pour trompette (ou hautbois ou flute)*
avec accompagnement d'orgue, de piano ou de clavecin.
Chorale titles not given in score, numbered I-VII.
   I. DE PROFUNDIS/AUS TIEFER NOT (DU FOND DE LA MISERE)
   II. EIN FESTE BURG (DIEU EST LE REMPART DE NOTRE VIE)
   III. VATER UNSER (NOTRE PERE AU ROYAUME DES CIEUX)
   IV. COMMANDMENTS/O DASS DOCH BALD DEIN FEUER BRENNTE
      (LORSQUE NOUS SOMMES DANS LES PLUS GRANDES DETRESSES)
   V. IN DULCI JUBILO
   VI. JESU, MEINE FREUDE
   VII. LOBE DEN HERREN
   Premiere February 21 and 28, 1974, André Bernard, trumpet,
   Marie-Louise Jaquet, organ, Radio ORTF.

W226. PIECE (October 15-19, 1971). 14' 25". Philippo, 1972.
Title: *Pièce pour trompette (ou hautbois, ou flûte) avec*
accompagnement d'orgue, de piano ou de clavecin.
Premiere April 26, 1972, Charles Hois, trumpet, Ann Labounsky,
organ, Brentwood Presbyterian Church, Pittsburgh, PA.
European Premiere André Bernard, trumpet, Edgar Krapp, organ,
Eglise Evangélique Allemande, Paris.

W227. PIECES POUR TROMPETTE ET ORGUE OU PIANO, NEUF
(July-August 1986). Combre, 1987. Numbered 1 to 9, no titles.

W228. SONATINE (1976). 12' 40". Combre & Philippo, 1976.
Title: *Sonatine pour trompette avec accompagnement de*
piano, clavecin ou orgue (sans mixtures).
1. Allegro   2. Andantino   3. Movement perpétuel
Premiere April 25, 1978, Alan Suska, trumpet, Ann Labounsky,
organ, Heinz Chapel, University of Pittsburgh, in the program "In
Hommage to Jean Langlais." **European premiere** Maurice André,
trumpet, André Luy, Lausanne, Switzerland. (*See*: D83b)

CHAMBER MUSIC

W229. ELEGIE (1965). 12'. Unpublished. for 10 instruments: flute, oboe,
clarinet, French horn, bassoon, string quintet.
Premiere March 21, 1966, Rennes, Groupe Instrumental Musica
Æterna, Odette Ramon, Director.

Réminiscences *See*: W8.

W230. TRIO POUR FLUTE, VIOLON, ALTO (1935). 12'. Unpublished.
(Flute, violin, viola.) *Also called "Suite brève."*
1. Prélude blanc   2. Guirlandes
3. Fuguette (transcription of #20 of Vol. II, *24 Pièces,* W170)
4. Gigue (transcription of #9, Vol. I, *24 Pièces,* W170)
Premiere February 9, 1935, Societé Nationale, Paris.

STRINGS

W231. SUITE BRETONNE pour cordes (1938). Unpublished. String ensemble.
I. Epitaphe pour les marins qui n'ont pas eu de tombe (transcribed from the *Suite armoricaine* for piano)
II. Minuet de cour
III. Danse de village (only contrebasse part exists)
Premiere December 21, 1938, Institut National des Jeunes Aveugles, Jean Langlais, conductor.

W232. LIGNE (July 16, 1937). 3'. U.C.P. Publications, 1975/Combre, 1987.
Printed for solo violoncello; the original 1937 version has optional piano accompaniment.
Premiere Julien Bertault, La Boite à Musique, Nantes.

W233. PIECES pour violon et piano (1951). Contract signed with Les Editions Noël, but not published.
Originally two pieces for violin and piano, manuscript lost, one title known, *Ronde*. **Premiere** Radiodiffusion française.

W234. SUITE CONCERTANTE (August-September 1943). 12'. U.C.P. Publications, 1974/Combre, 1987. Violin and violoncello duet, no accompaniment.
1. Danse rustique   2. Cantilène
3. Chasse et Danse   4. Final
Original title: **Duo pour violon et violoncelle**. **Premiere** 1943, concert sponsored by the chamber music society Le Tryptique; M. Maréchal and F. Pollain, soloists, Salle Rossini, Paris.

WOODWINDS

CLARINET

W235. PIECE POUR CLARINETTE ET PIANO (July-August 1987). Commissioned by Claude Langlais.
Premiere Scheduled for 1988 in Roumazières.

FLUTE

W236. MOUVEMENT POUR FLUTE (ou hautbois ou violon) ET CLAVIER (April, 1987). Pro Organo Musikverlag, 1987.
"A la memoire de mes ancêtres Bretons à la Fontenelle"
Premiere October 6, 1987, Wendy Kumer, flute; Ann Labounsky, organ; Duquesne University, Pittsburgh.

W237. PETITE RHAPSODIE (June 1983). 2' 40". Gérard Billaudot, 1984.
Piano accompaniment.

W238. PIECES, CINQ (1974, based on 1954 vocal work *Cinq Mélodies*).
10'15". Editions M. Combre & Philippo, Paris, 1976.
Complete title published as *5 Pièces pour flûte (ou violon) avec accompagnement de piano ou clavecin ou orgue*.
Premiere February 9, 1975, Harvey Boatright, flute; Jo Boatright, piano; Ed Landreth Auditorium, Texas Christian University, Fort Worth, Texas. (*See*: B226)

W239. PIECES, DEUX (1942). 7 pages. Unpublished. Piano accompaniment.
  1. Histoire vraie pour une Môn (transcription of piano solo, W214)
  2. Rondel dans le style médiéval

ADDENDUM

W240. LA PRIERE POUR LES MARINS (1979). Unpublished. Text: Madeleine Kieffer.
  16th century melody, harmonized for choir. Manuscript not in Langlais archives, research in progress. Recorded in 1981. (*See*: D21)

Discography

All "D" citations refer to listings in this Discography section. Numbers listed as "also on disc" are "D" numbers. Improvisations and works of other composers recorded by Jean Langlais follow the composition section.

CHORAL and VOCAL

D1. ANTIENNES. (1955) Antiphons for Gelineau Psalm Settings.

> **Psalm 102, Bénis le Seigneur, ô mon âme**
> Studio SM 45-24.
> **Psalm 109, Oracle du Seigneur**
> **Psalm 112, Louez, serviteurs du Seigneur**
> Studio SM 33-09.
> **Psalm 117, Rendez grâce au Seigneur.** Studio SM. --

D2. CANTIQUE EUCHARISTIQUE (Accourez au passage du Seigneur) (1956)

> Studio SM 33-74. 25 cm. 1960. *Cantiques et Messe Brève*. Chorale Stéphane Caillat, Stéphane Caillat, director; Jean Langlais, organ. Also on disc: **D4a, 13**.

D3. CANTIQUES BIBLIQUES, DOUZE (1962)

> Disques Pastorale et Musique PM 17038 LD. 17 cm.
> *Six cantiques bibliques a l'usage des paroisses*.
> Les petits chanteurs de Saint-Laurent, Abbé Zurfluh, director.
> **A votre Eglise sainte; Béni soit Dieu; Chantez les hauts faits de Dieu; Ni la mort, ni la vie; Nous acclamons, Seigneur; Un jour viendra.**

D4. CANTIQUES from **GLOIRE AU SEIGNEUR (1948-52)**

> **D4a.** Studio SM 33-74. 25 cm. 1960. *Cantiques et Messe Brève*. Chorale Stéphane Caillat, Stéphane Caillat, director; Jean Langlais, organ.
> Songs: **Amis nous partons, Au paradis, Comme cherche le soir, Gloire à toi Marie, Il y eut des couronnes, Je suis pauvre.**
> Also on disc: D2, 13.

D4b. 455.654. 45 rpm. *Louange a Dieu (No. 3).* Choeur des Séminaristes de Strasbourg, P. Kirchhoffer, director; M. Chapuis, organ. Song: **Seigneur Jésus, ne sois pas rebuté.**

D5. CHANSONS FOLKLORIQUES FRANÇAIS, NEUF (1960)

D5a. Erato EFM 42081 (mono), STE 60011 (stereo). 25 cm. 1962. *9 Chansons Populaires pour contralto, baryton et piano.* Janine Collard, contralto; Camille Maurane, baritone; Sylvanie Billier, piano; Ensemble Vocal Stéphane Caillat, Stéphane Caillat, director; Daniel Madeleine, sound engineer.

D5b. Studio SM 3011.87, Cassette K204 SM 37. 1982. *Noëls Populaires/Chansons Folkloriques Françaises pour chœur et piano.* Ensemble choral "A Cœur Joie de Vincennes," M. Martzolf, D. Reis, directors; Gerard Glatigny, piano. Also on disc: D19b.

CHANTS POUR LA MESSE *See*: D13.

D6. CORPUS CHRISTI (1979)

Coronata COR 5001. 1985. *Jean Langlais vokalwerk I.* Marlies Schauerte, soprano; Helga Schauerte, organ; Kammerchor Schmallenberg, Ulrich Schauerte, director; Ansgar Ballhorn, producer. Recorded in the Cathedral of Altenberg, Germany, April, 1985 (*sic* 1983). Also on disc: **D9, 15d, 18b, 18d, 22a, 23, 26b.**

D7. DIEU, NOUS AVONS VU TA GLOIRE (1956)

Studio S.M. 33-50. 30 cm., 33 rpm. 1957/8. S.M. 433-50. 17 cm., 45 rpm. 1957/8. *Bible et Liturgie/Vigile du 7e Dimanche apres la Pentecote.* Recorded in Strasbourg Cathedral during the Congress of the Centre de Pastorale Liturgique, July 25-28, 1957, with 3,000 congress attendants singing.

GLOIRE AU SEIGNEUR *See*: D4.

D8. HOMMAGE A LOUIS BRAILLE (1975)

FY P1. L'Association Valentin Haüy, Paris. *Concert donné le 22 Mai 1975 en la Chapelle de l'Institut National des Jeunes Aveugles à Paris.* Janine Collard, mezzo-soprano; Jean Langlais, piano. A concert given May 22, 1975 in the Chapel of the National Institute for the Young Blind, Paris, during the International Congress for the 150th Anniversary of the Braille System. Also on disc: **D12.**

HYMN OF PRAISE "TE DEUM LAUDAMUS" (1973) *See*: D128.

D9. LIBERA ME, DOMINE (1948)

Coronata COR 5001. 1985. *Jean Langlais vokalwerk I.* Marlies Schauerte, soprano; Helga Schauerte, organ; Kammerchor Schmallenberg, Ulrich Schauerte, director; Ansgar Ballhorn, producer. Recorded in the Cathedral of Altenberg, Germany, April, 1985 (*sic* 1983). Also on disc: **D6, 15d, 18b, 18d, 22a, 23, 26b.**

D10. MASS "GRANT US THY PEACE" (1979)

Alpha Records ACA 533. 1984. *Music for Worcester Cathedral.*
First performance at 1981 Three Choirs Festival.
First recording at Worcester Cathedral, March 13, 14, 15, 1984.
Worcester Cathedral Choir, Donald Hunt, director; Adrian
Partington, organ.

D11. MASS IN ANCIENT STYLE (1952)

Cambridge Records CRS 407 (mono) CRS-1407X (stereo).
Choral and organ music by Jean Langlais.
Cecilia Society of Boston Chamber Singers, Theodore Marier,
conductor; The Joseph Pastor String Quartet: Joseph Pastor and
Robert Brunt, violins, Barbara Kroll, viola, Alex Mark, 'cello;
Recorded in Gasson Hall, Boston College. Also on disc: **D15c, 40f.**

See also: **D128.**

D12. MELODIES SUR DES POEMES DE RONSARD, CINQ (1954)

FY P1. L'Association Valentin Haüy, Paris. *Concert donné le
22 Mai 1975 en la Chapelle de l'Institut National des
Jeunes Aveugles à Paris.* Janine Collard, mezzo-soprano; Jean
Langlais, piano. A concert given May 22, 1975 in the Chapel of the
National Institute for the Young Blind, Paris, during the
International Congress for the 150th Anniversary of the Braille
System. Also on disc: **D8.**

D13. MESSE BREVE (CHANTS POUR LA MESSE EN FRANÇAIS, 1953)

Studio SM 33-74. 25 cm. 1960. *Cantiques et Messe Brève.*
Chorale Stéphane Caillat; Stéphane Caillat, director; Jean
Langlais, organ. Also on disc: **D2, 4a.**

D14. MESSE "DIEU, PRENDS PITIE" (1965)

Disques Pastorale et Musique, PM 17053 M. 17 cm. 45 rpm.
Les Chœurs Massillon, R. P. François Picard, director; Jean
Langlais, organ. Recorded in l'Eglise St-Roch, Paris, France.

MESSE SALVE REGINA *See:* **MISSA SALVE REGINA**, D17.

D15. MESSE SOLENNELLE (1949)

D15a. Argo ZRG 662. 1971.
O Sacrum Convivium/Modern French church music.
Andrew Brunt, Solo treble; Choir of St. John's College, Cambridge;
George Guest, conductor; Stephen Cleobury, organ.

D15b. BIS LP-289; CD-289 (compact disc). 1985.
Täby Church Choir; Orpheus Chamber Ensemble; Kerstin Ek,
conductor; Peter Bengston, organ; Ulf Rosenberg, Håkan Sjögren,
producers.

D15c. Cambridge Records CRS-407 (mono) CRS-1407X (stereo).
Choral and organ music by Jean Langlais.
Cecilia Society of Boston, Theodore Marier, conductor; Willem

Frank, organ; H. Vose Greenough, Jr., engineer; Church of the Advent, Boston. Also on disc: **D11, 40f.**

D15d. Coronata COR 5001. 1985. *Jean Langlais vokalwerk I.* Marlies Schauerte, soprano; Helga Schauerte, organ; Kammerchor Schmallenberg, Ulrich Schauerte, director; Ansgar Ballhorn, producer. Recorded in the Cathedral of Altenberg, Germany, April, 1985 (*sic* 1983). Also on disc: **D6, 9, 18b, 18d, 22a, 23, 26b.**

D16. MISSA "IN SIMPLICITATE" (1952)

D16a. Capella Verlag Speyer CVS Spi 2111XD. *Vivaldi/Langlais.* Frauke Hahne, soprano; Fritz Sander, organ.

D16b. Ducretet-Thomson 270 C 003. 25 cm. 1954. *Messiaen/Langlais.* Janine Collard, mezzo-soprano; Jean Langlais, organ; Basilica of Sainte-Clotilde, Paris. The first recording made by Langlais, the second recording of one of his works. Also on disc: **D121.**

D16c. Eclipse ECS 700. 1973. *The choir of Winchester Cathedral.* The boys of Winchester Cathedral Choir, Alwyn Surplice, director; Clement McWilliam, organ.

D16d. Erato STU 70358. 1967. *Musique de notre temps.* Janine Collard, contralto; Jean Langlais, organ; Cathedral of Notre-Dame de Paris. Also on disc: **D17c, 22b.**

D16e. Eurosound 313-20, Nijmegen, Holland. 1979. Elisabeth Cooymans, mezzo-soprano; Albert De Klerk, organ; St. Joseph Church, Haarlem, Holland.

D16f. MD & G 1093. *Orgelpunkte Dom zu Braunsweig.* Ingebord Hischer, soprano; Helmut Kruse, organ.

D16g. Musical Heritage Society MHS 3745. 1978. *Jean Langlais/Missa "Salve Regina"/Missa "In Simplicitate"/Three Prayers.* American release of Erato STU 70358. (*See*: **D16d**) Also on disc: **D17e, 22c.**

D16h. Musikproduktion Ambitus Amb 63 807; FSM 63807. *Alt und Orgel.* Cornelia Dietrich, contralto; Rolf Schönstedt, organ.

MISSA MISERICORDIA DOMINI (1958) *See*: D128.

D17. MISSA SALVE REGINA (1954)

D17a. Argo 596 017 (ZRG 938). 1981. *Langlais Messe 'Salve Regina'/Duruflé Messe 'Cum Jubilo'.* Recorded in 1980 in St. Alban's Church, Holborn, England. The Richard Hickox Singers; Philip Jones Brass Ensemble; Wooburn Singers; Richard Hickox, director; Ian Watson, organ; Chris Hazell, producer, Stan Goodall, recording engineer.

D17b. Erato LDE 3023. 1955. *Missa « Salve Regina ».* Awarded Grand Prix du Disque in 1956. (Prix Madame René Coty, Académie du Disque Français.) Recorded in the Cathedral of Notre-Dame de Paris, Feb. 18, 1955. Schola des Pères du Saint-Esprit du Grand Scholasticat de

Chevilly, R. P. Lucien Deiss C.S. Sp., director; Abbé David Julien, director of the chorus of the congregation; Jean Langlais, great organ; Jean Dattas, choir organ; Brass Ensemble; André Charlin, recording engineer. (*See*: D17c, e)

D17c. Erato STU 70358. 1967. *Musique de notre temps.*
Recorded in the Cathedral of Notre-Dame de Paris, Feb. 18, 1955, previously issued on LDE 3023. (*See*: D17b) American release, 1978: MHS 3745. (*See*: D17e) Also on disc: D16d, 22b.

D17d. Haydn Society HS 9008. *Langlais: Missa Salve Regina/Dufay: Missa Sine Nomine.* American release of Erato LDE 3023.

D17e. Musical Heritage Society MHS 3745. 1978. *Jean Langlais/Missa "Salve Regina"/Missa "In Simplicitate"/Three Prayers.*
American release of Erato STU 70358. Also on disc: D16g, 22c.

D17f. Solstice SOL 14. 1980. *Jean Langlais à Notre-Dame de Paris.*
Recorded under the direction of the composer, Dec. 10 and 11, 1979. Patrick Girard, conductor; Pierre Cochereau, great organ; Georges Bessonnet, choir organ; La Maîtrise de Notre-Dame de Paris, Jehan Revert, director; Les Petits Chanteurs de Sainte-Marie d'Antony, Patrick Giraud, director; La Maîtrise de la Résurrection, Francis Bardot, director; L'Ensemble de Cuivres Roger Delmotte; le Quatuor de Trombones de Paris. Also on disc: D24, 80h.

D18. MOTETS, CINQ (1932-42)

complete work

D18a. Studio SM 45-87. 17 cm. 1962. *O Bone Jesu/Cinq motets de Jean Langlais.* Chorale Stèphane Caillat; Jean Langlais, organ.

1. O SALUTARIS HOSTIA

D18b. Coronata COR 5001. 1985.　*Jean Langlais vokalwerk I.*
Marlies Schauerte, soprano; Helga Schauerte, organ; Kammerchor Schmallenberg, Ulrich Schauerte, director; Ansgar Ballhorn, producer. Recorded in the Cathedral of Altenberg, Germany, April, 1985 (*sic* 1983). Also on disc: D6, 9, 15d, 18d, 22a, 23, 26b.

2. AVE MUNDI GLORIA

D18c. Columbia LFX 923. 78 rpm. 1950.　*Fête de l'Immaculée Conception.* Les Petits Chanteurs de Fourvières, M. l'Abbé Jean Vuaillat, director; M. le Chanoine Joubert, organ.
First recorded Langlais work.

D18d. Coronata COR 5001. 1985.　*Jean Langlais vokalwerk I.*
Marlies Schauerte, soprano; Helga Schauerte, organ; Kammerchor Schmallenberg, Ulrich Schauerte, director; Ansgar Ballhorn, producer. Recorded in the Cathedral of Altenberg, Germany, April, 1985 (*sic* 1983). Also on disc: D6, 9, 15d, 18b, 22a, 23, 26b.

D18e. FY 107. 1983. *Les plus beaux chants à la Vierge à Notre-Dame de Chartres.* Maîtrise de la Cathédrale de Chartres et de la Résurrection, Francis Bardot, director; Philippe Lefebvre, organ; François Carbou, recording engineer.
Recorded Chartres, France, November-December 1982.

D18f.   Proprius PROP 7816. 1979. *Mariakören sjunger om Maria.*
Mariakören, Bror Samuelson, director; Gunnar Nordenfors, organ;
Karl-Göran Lanzander, producer. Dingtuna Kyrka, Västerås, Sweden.

D19. NOELS POPULAIRES ANCIENS (1960)

D19a.   Erato LDEV 2024. 25 cm.   circa 1960.
*La Chorale de L'Institution Nationale des Jeunes Aveugles
chante Noël.*   Choir of the National Institute for the Young Blind,
Paris; Jean Langlais, organ.

D19b.   Studio SM 3011.87, Cassette K204 SM 37. 1982.
*Noëls Populaires/Chansons Folkloriques Françaises pour
chœur et piano.* Ensemble choral "A Cœur Joie de Vincennes,"
M. Martzolf, D. Reis, directors; Gérard Glatigny, piano. Also on
disc: **D5b**.

3. ENTRE LE BŒUF ET L'ANE GRIS

D19c.   K. Lyc. Janson.   circa 1960. [Belgium]

D20. ORAISONS, TROIS, for flute, soprano and organ (1973)

1. SALVE REGINA

Abbey Recording Co. Ltd. APR 301. 1979. *St. David's Cathedral
Choir.* Phillip Raymond, soprano; Nicholas Jackson, organ;   Sue
Hardscombe, flute.

D21. PRIERE POUR LES MARINS, LA (1979)

Inter-Loisirs Disc 1015. 45 rpm. 1981.
La Prière pour les Marins.
Les Petits Chanteurs à la Croix de Bois, Bernard Houdy, director.

D22. PRIERES, TROIS (1949)

D22a.   Coronata COR 5001. 1985.   *Jean Langlais Vokalwerk I.*
Marlies Schauerte, soprano; Helga Schauerte, organ; Kammerchor
Schmallenberg, Ulrich Schauerte, director; Ansgar Ballhorn,
producer. Also on disc: **D6, 9, 15d, 18b, 18d, 23, 26b**.

D22b.   Erato STU 70358.   1967.   *Musique de notre temps.* Janine
Collard, contralto; Jean Langlais, organ. Recorded in the Cathedral
of Notre-Dame de Paris.   American release: Musical Heritage
Society 3745, 1978. Also on disc: **D16c, 17c**.

D22c.   Musical Heritage Society MHS 3745. 1978. *Jean Langlais/Missa
"Salve Regina"/Missa "In Simplicitate"/Three Prayers.*
American release of Erato STU 70358 (*See*: **D22b**) Also on disc:
D17e, 16g.

1. AVE VERUM

D22d.   CA MX 3096. 1981.
Choeur d'enfants du comté de Flandre, Regis Decool, director.

D22e.   Solstice SOL FR 780 504. *Trois Siècles de Musique Vocale
Sacrée pour solistes.* Carey, baritone; Massart, boy soprano.

D23. PSAUME 111 "BEATUS UIR QUI TIMET DOMINUM" (1977)

Coronata COR 5001. 1985. *Jean Langlais Vokalwerk I.*
Marlies Schauerte, soprano; Helga Schauerte, organ; Kammerchor
Schmallenberg, Ulrich Schauerte, director; Ansgar Ballhorn,
producer. Also on disc: **D6, 9, 15d, 18b, 18d, 22a, 26b.**

D24. PSAUME SOLENNEL 3 "LAUDATE DOMINUM DE CAELIS" (1964)

Solstice SOL 14. 1980. *Jean Langlais à Notre-Dame de Paris.*
Recorded Dec. 10 and 11, 1979, under the supervision of the
composer; Jehan Revert, conductor. La Maîtrise de Notre-Dame de
Paris, Jehan Revert, director; Les Petits Chanteurs de
Sainte-Marie d'Antony, Patrick Giraud, director; La Maîtrise de la
Résurrection, Francis Bardot, director; L'Ensemble de Cuivres
Roger Delmotte; le Quatuor de Trombones de Paris; Pierre
Cochereau, great organ, Jacques Marichal, choir organ.
Also on disc: **D17f, 80h.**

SACERDOS ET PONTIFEX, "TU ES PETRUS" (1959) *See*: D128.

D25. SOLEMN MASS (1969)

Vantage SLBP-1015. *Christ in Majesty.* Recording of the world
première at the National Shrine of the Immaculate Conception,
Washington, D. C., Nov. 10, 1969 during the Pontifical Con-
celebrated Mass for Peace commemorating the tenth anniversary of
the dedication of the Upper Church and Veterans Day Observance.
Joseph Michaud, Music director; 350 singers including Catholic
University Chorus, National Shrine Chorale, and massed military
choirs: United States Air Force Academy Catholic Choir, United
States Naval Academy Catholic Chapel Choir, Holy Trinity Chapel
Choir of West Point; Brass choirs from Catholic University School
of Music; Jean Langlais, organ; Howard Solomon, recording
engineer; A. Alan Botto, producer. Also on disc: Preludial organ
recital by Jean Langlais, **D42e, 57k, 95, 106b, 112b, 113b.**

UBI CARITAS (1986) *See*: D128.

D26. UENITE ET AUDITE (1958)

D26a. CND 47. Contrepoint Vocal Ensemble; Gaussens.

D26b. Coronata COR 5001. 1985. *Jean Langlais Vokalwerk I.*
Marlies Schauerte, soprano; Helga Schauerte, organ; Kammerchor
Schmallenberg, Ulrich Schauerte, director; Ansgar Ballhorn,
producer. Also on disc: **D6, 9, 15d, 18b, 18d, 22a, 23.**

D27. UILLE D'IS, LA (1947)

D27a. Erato LDE 1012A. 25 cm. 1955. *Chansons de la Mer/
Folklore Français.* Claudette Gagnepain, soloist.

D27b. Spoken Arts 213. Contrepoint Vocal Ensemble; Gaussens, director.
(*See*: D131) M. P. Thiery, soprano soloist.

INSTRUMENTAL

ORGAN

D28. ADORATION (1968)

Wealden WS 109. Robert Husson; All Saints, Blackheath, Kent. Also on disc: **D60d, 69m.**

D29. ADORATION DES BERGERS (1929)

Musical Heritage Society MHS 7275. 1985.
Jean Langlais/Complete organ works, vol. 3.
Ann Labounsky; Calvary Episcopal Church, Pittsburgh; Frederick J. Bashour, producer. In 3-disc set 837273M, recorded September 1984. Also in set: **D58a, 63, 64, 65a, 76.**

D30. AMERICAN SUITE (1959-60)

6. SCHERZO CATS

D30a. Association de l'orgue Silbermann de Mulhouse. Unnumbered. 1974. *Marie-Louise Jaquet.* Temple de Saint Jean, Mulhouse, France. Recorded 1973. Also on disc: **D37f, 57v.**

D30b. Austin CM 7245, CS 7245 (stereo). circa 1964. *Praise Him with organs.* Frederick Swann, St. Martin's Church, New Canaan, Conn. Produced by Mirrosonic Records for Austin Organs, Inc.

D30c. Organ Historical Society. *Central Connecticut.* Rosalind Mohnsen; Derby United Methodist Church, Derby, Conn. Recorded in June 1975 during OHS Convention recital. Also on disc: **D57z.**

AVE MARIA, AVE MARIS STELLA, *see* **TROIS PARAPHRASES GREGORIENNES, D53.**

B.A.C.H. *See:* D130.

CHANT DE PAIX, *see* **NEUF PIECES, D57.**

D31. CHANTS DE BRETAGNE, HUIT (1974)

D31a. Arion ARN 36 331. 1976. *Jean Langlais/Huit chants de Bretagne et improvisation sur le thème Adoromp Holl.* Jean Langlais; Sainte-Clotilde; Claude Morel, recording engineer. Also on disc: **D85.**

D31b. Musical Heritage Society MHS 4129. 1980. *Jean Langlais/ Complete organ works [1].* Ann Labounsky; St. Peter's Cathedral, Erie, PA; Frederick J. Bashour, producer. In 3-disc set MHS 834127K, recorded August 1979. Also on disc: **D37a, 40y, 53c, 57a, 59c, 67c.**

D32. CHARACTERISTIC PIECES, THREE (1957)

Musical Heritage Society MHS 4712. 1983. *Jean Langlais/Complete organ works, vol. 2.* Ann Labounsky; St. Peter's Cathedral, Erie; Frederick J. Bashour, producer. In 3-disc set MHS 843712K, recorded June 1982. Also in set: **D51, 66a, 68a, 69f, 73a, 74.**

DEUHIEME CONCERTO POUR ORGUE *See:* **CONCERTO, DEUHIEME,** D77.

D33. DOMINICA IN PALMIS [IN DIE PALMARUM] (1954)

D33a.   Musical Heritage Society MHS 9320184. 1987.
Jean Langlais/Complete organ works, vol. 4.
Ann Labounsky; Calvary Episcopal Church, Pittsburgh; Frederick J.
Bashour, producer. In 3-disc set recorded September 1984. Also
in set: D44, 48, 49a, 50a, 52a, 54a, 55, 60c, 61, 62b, 70.

D33b.   Repertoire Recording Society RRS-3. 1971.
Jean Langlais et le chant grégorien.
Rollin Smith; Church of St. Paul the Apostle, New York City.
Recorded July 1 and 8, 1971. Also on disc: D40ff, 53d, 69i.

D34. ESQUISSES GOTHIQUES, TROIS (1975)

D34a.   Arion ARN 38 486. 1979. *Les orgues de Masevaux/*
Musiques pour deux orgues. Marie-Louise Jaquet, Kern organ;
Georges Delvalée, Schwenkedel organ; Saint Martin de Masevaux,
France; Claude Morel, recording engineer. Recorded in 1978.

D34b.   Mark MC 8651. 1978. *Music for two organs/Langlais:*
Romanesque & Gothic sketches. Ann Labounsky, gallery
organ, Robert Grogan, chancel organ; National Shrine of the
Immaculate Conception, Washington, DC. Recorded October 1976.
Also on disc: D35a.

D34c.   Motette Ursina M 1016-33, reissued M 10160. 1978.
Jean Langlais/Six esquisses pour deux orgues.
Jean Langlais, Marie-Louise Jaquet; Altstädter Nicolai-Kirche,
Bielefeld, Germany. Recorded 1978. Also on disc: D35b.

D35. ESQUISSES ROMANES, TROIS (1975)

D35a.   Mark MC 8651. 1978. *Music for two organs/Langlais:*
Romanesque & Gothic sketches. Ann Labounsky, gallery
organ, Robert Grogan, chancel organ; National Shrine of the
Immaculate Conception, Washington, DC. Recorded October 1976.
Also on disc: D34b.

D35b.   Motette Ursina M 1016-33, later numbered M 10160. 1978.
Jean Langlais/Six esquisses pour deux orgues.
Jean Langlais, Marie-Louise Jaquet; Altstädter Nicolai-Kirche,
Bielefeld, Germany. Recorded 1978. Also on disc: D34c.

D36. FETE (1946)

D36a.   Bridge Records 2241. 1972. *Organ masterpieces.*
Roger Nyquist.

D36b.   Priory PR 148. 1984. *French organ music from Salisbury*
Cathedral. Colin Walsh. Also on disc: D67f.

D36c.   St. Cecilia STC 1001. *Roger Sayer organ recital.* Blackburn
Cathedral, England.

D36d.   Unicorn-Kanchana DKP 9007.   1979. *Jennifer Bate plays showpieces for organ.* Royal Albert Hall, London; John Taylor, producer.

D36e.   Vista VPS 1032. 1976. *The organ of Norwich Cathedral.* Graham Barber; Michael Smythe, producer and recorder.

D36f.   Wealden WS 151. R. Humphrey, Winchester Coll. Chapel.

D37. FOLKLORIC SUITE (1952)

complete work

D37a.   Musical Heritage Society MHS 4127. 1980.
Jean Langlais/Complete organ works [1.]
Ann Labounsky; St. Peter's Cathedral, Erie, PA; Frederick J. Bashour, producer. In 3-disc set MHS 834127K, recorded August 1979. Also in set: D31b, 40y, 53c, 57a, 59c, 67c.

1. FUGUE SUR O FILII

D37b.   Lumen LD 1.110. 45 rpm. *Musique d'orgue pour le temps de Pâques.* Noëlie Pierront; Saint-Merry, Paris.
Also on disc: D38d, 40q.

2. LEGENDE DE SAINT-NICOLAS (1937)

D37c.   Solstice SOL 1. 1978. *Langlais joue Langlais.*
Jean Langlais; Sainte-Clotilde. Recorded March 1976. Also on disc: D41b, 42d, 53h, qq, 57h, s, u, 57aa, 59k, 67h.

3. CANTIQUE

D37d.   FMA 211 276. 1976. *Francine Carrez-Olivier.* Amis de l'orgue Cathedrale de St. Quentin. André Thiébault, engineer.
Also on disc: D40m.

3. CANTIQUE   4. CANZONA

D37e.   Alpha ACA 548. The Abbey Recording Co. 1985. *Organ works of Jean Langlais.* Marjorie Bruce; Paisley Abbey, Scotland. Also on disc: D37h, 39b, 47, 53n, 57b, 59e, 65b.

4. CANZONA

D37f.   Association de l'orgue Silbermann de Mulhouse. Unnumbered. 1974. *Marie-Louise Jaquet.* Temple de Saint Jean, Mulhouse, France.   Recorded 1973.   Also on disc: D30a, 57v.

D37g.   Erato LDE 3024. 1955. *Œuvres modernes pour orgue.* Jean Langlais; Sainte-Clotilde, Paris. Also on disc: D53t, 69c.

5. RHAPSODIE SUR DEUX NOELS

D37h.   Alpha ACA 548. The Abbey Recording Co. 1985. *Organ works of Jean Langlais.* Marjorie Bruce; Paisley Abbey, Scotland.
Also on disc: D37e, 39b, 47, 53n, 57b, 59e, 65b.

D37i.   Motette Ursina M 1044. 1983. *Weihnachtliche orgelmusik aus dem Altenberger Dom.* Paul Wisskirchen; Altenberg Cathedral, Altenberg, Germany.

D38. HOMMAGE A FRESCOBALDI (1951)

complete work

D38a.   Psallite Psal 158/060 674 PET. 1975. *Das Orgelportrait/ Französische orgelmusik aus der Benediktinerabtei Gerleve/W.* Edgar Krapp; Benedictine Abbey, Gerleve.

1. PRÉLUDE AU KYRIE 2. OFFERTOIRE 3. ELÉVATION 4. COMMUNION 5. FANTASIE

D38b.   CBS 51236. CBS Grammofoonplaten B.V., Holland. 1981. *Albert De Klerk speelt Vierne-Langlais.* No. 10 in the series *Orgelwerken/Albert De Klerk speelt.* Augustinuskerk, Amsterdam; Joop L. U. Reiziger, producer.

4. COMMUNION

D38c.   Vista VPS 1004. 1973. *The organ of St. Martin-in-the-Fields.* Robert Vincent; Michael Smythe, producer and recording engineer. Recorded May 1973.   Also on disc: **D56c.**

5. FANTAISIE

D38d.   Lumen LD 1.110. 45 rpm. *Musique d'orgue pour le temps de Pâques.* Noëlie Pierront; Saint-Merry, Paris. Also on disc: **D37b, 40q.**

7. THEME ET VARIATIONS

D38e.   Proprius PROP 7707. 1975. *Vox Humana: Orgelmusik från Ryssland, Polen, Frankrike och Sverige.* Erik Lundkvist; Nätra Kyrka.

8. EPILOGUE

D38f.   Medias Music MEM 0008. *L'Orgue virtuose.* Michelle Leclerc, Belley, France. Recorded 1986.

D39. HOMAGE TO JEAN-PHILIPPE RAMEAU (1962-64, 1987)

D39a.   Motette M 11170. Complete 1987 version, Hommage à Rameau. Naji S. Hakim, organ; Basilique du Sacré-Cœur de Montmartre, Paris.   Recorded April 17, 1987. (*See*: **D129**)

4. EVOCATION (1964)

D39b.   Alpha ACA 548. The Abbey Recording Co. 1985. *Organ works of Jean Langlais.* Marjorie Bruce; Paisley Abbey, Scotland. Also on disc: **D37e, h, 47, 53n, 57b, 59e, 65b.**

D39c.   Turnabout TV-S 34319. *Modern French organ music.* Single record release from the Vox Box set of 3 discs, SVBX 5315. (*See*: **D39d**) Jean-Claude Raynaud; Basilica of St. Sernin, Toulouse, France.

D39d.   Vox SVBX 5315. 1973. Side 2 of 6 sides.
A Survey of the world's greatest organ music/France/
Volume VI/The 20th century French composer.
Jean-Claude Raynaud; Basilica of St. Sernin, Toulouse, France.

D40. INCANTATION POUR UN JOUR SAINT (1949)

D40a.   Abbey Records LPB 797. 1979. *St. David's Cathedral*
Organ. Nicholas Jackson; St. David's Cathedral, Wales.

D40b.   Academica, München (Munich).   K 22177 Stereo LC 5145.
Orgelmusik im olympischen Dorf.   Winfried Englhardt;
Katholische Kirche Frieden Christi im olympischen Dorf München.

D40c.   Aeolian-Skinner AS 321. 1966. *Music at St. Luke's.*
Bob Whitley; St. Luke's Episcopal Church, San Francisco;   Ed
Karlow, engineer.

  Amadeó AVRS 6457. *See:* MHS 3776, **D40v.**

D40d.   Bourdon FK-1. *French music for the organ.*
Edward Eigenschenk; St. Ita's Church, Chicago; Fred   Kruse,
recording engineer; Peter Bartok, disk mastering; Norman
Pellegrini, production director. Recorded in 1956.

D40e.   Calig-Verlag CAL 30 473. (Munich) *Österliche orgelmusik*
Süddeutscher und Französischer meister. Hans Maier; Basilika
Ottobeuren.

D40f.   Cambridge CRS 407 (mono) 1407X (stereo). *Choral and organ*
music by Jean Langlais.   Theodore Marier; Church of the
Advent, Boston. Also on disc: **D11, 15c.**

D40g.   Chalfont C77.002.   Issued as Polydor 2460 262.   *The*
Magnificent Liverpool Cathedral Organ. Noel Rawsthorne.

D40h.   Citadel 116.001. 1970/71. *Orgelwerken van Jean Langlais.*
Jean Langlais; St. Bavokerk, Haarlem, Holland.
Also on disc: **D42b, g, 52c, e, 53q, 56b, 57n, t, w, 68g, 69p.**

D40i.   Connaisseur Musik [Epsilon] EPS 4514/ESR 4514.   Edward Fry;
All Saints, Clifton, Bristol. Also on disc: **D52f, 56a, 69q.**

D40j.   Deutsche Grammophon Gesellschaft DGM 19091.
Also issued as LPEM 19091 and 25 35 748, also Heliodor 89816.
Issued Polydor International, 1969; reissued 1980.
Orgelmusik im Kölner Dom.   Josef Zimmermann, Cologne
Cathedral, Germany. Also on disc: **D53s, 69r.**

D40k.   EMI Electrola 053-28 948. *Orgelkonzert in der Zisterzienser*
Abtei Himmerod. Peter Raimund van Husen; Cistercian Abbey,
Himmerod.

D40l.   Erato LDE 3049. 1960. *Œuvres pour orgue d'inspiration*
grégorienne. Jean Langlais; Sainte-Clotilde; Gregorian chants
sung by male choir directed by René Malherbe.
Also on disc: **D49b, 53e, 53k, 58c, 124.**

D40m.   FMA 211 276. 1976. *Francine Carrez-Olivier.* Amis de   l'orgue

Cathedrale de St. Quentin. André Thiébault, engineer.
Also on disc: **D37d.**

D40n.　FSM 43 504 AUL. *Alte und neue orgeln.* Fritz Soddemann.

D40o.　GEMA 2892 071. 1980. *Papst Johannes Paul II. bei Künstlern und Publizisten.* Hans Maier (Minister of Culture, Bavaria); Herkulessaal der Münchener Residenz. Recorded during the visit of Pope John Paul II to Munich on November 19, 1980.

D40p.　KO/LEC. Le Kiosque d'Orphée (Paris). *Récital Michelle Leclerc.* Sens Cathedral.

D40q.　Lumen LD 1.110. 45 rpm. *Musique d'orgue pour le temps de Pâques.* Noëlie Pierront; Saint-Merry, Paris.
Also on disc: **D37b, 38d.**

D40r.　Lyrichord LLST 7353. 1981. *The Aeolian-Skinner organ.* John Obetz; RLDS Auditorium, Independence, MO; William Winholtz, producer. Recorded in 1980. Also on disc: **D53a.**

D40s.　Mark Records MC 8711. *Music at St. John's II.* Albert Russell; St. John's Episcopal Church, Lafayette Square, Washington, DC; Roger Allen, recording engineer.

D40t.　Mirrosonic Records CS 7015. Produced for M. P. Moller Organ Company. *Music for the organ.* Frederick Swann; The Interchurch Center, New York City.

D40u.　Mirrosonic Records DRE 1012. 1958. *The first international congress of organists.* John Huston; St. John's College, Cambridge, England. Recorded July 30, 1957 during ICO recital.

D40v.　Motette Ursina M 1006. *Ludger Mai spielt virtuose orgelmusik.* Ludger Mai; St. Matthias-Kirche, Berlin-Schöneberg.

D40w.　Motette Ursina M 1023. 1979. *Jean Langlais spielt Französische orgelmusik in der Abteikirche Marienstatt.* Recording of concert played at Marienstatt Abbey, Germany, on Nov. 5, 1978. Also on disc: **D53ff, 91, 97c, 125.**

　　　Motette M 11170. Naji S. Hakim, recorded April 17, 1987, Basilique du Sacré-Cœur de Montmartre, Paris. (*See*: **D129**)

D40x.　Musical Heritage Society MHS 3776. *Organ music in the Vienna Hofburgkapelle.* Alois Forer. Original issue: Amadeó AVRS 6457.

D40y.　Musical Heritage Society MHS 4127. 1980. *Jean Langlais/Complete organ works [1].* Ann Labounsky; St. Peter's Cathedral, Erie, PA; Frederick J. Bashour, producer. In 3-disc set MHS 834127K, recorded August 1979. Also in set: **D31b, 37a, 53c, 57a, 59c, 67c.**

D40z.　Odeon CSD 3565 (stereo) CLP 3565 (mono). 1966. [HMV 154609-1] *Great Cathedral Organ Series #10/Hereford Cathedral.* Melville Cook.

D40aa. Organo Org 90 008 F.   *Die Oberlinger-Orgel in St. Jakobus Friedberg-Ockstadt.*   Gert Augst.

Polydor, *see* Chalfont, **D40g.**

D40bb. Priory PR 128. *The organ of St. George's Chapel Windsor Castle.* John Porter; John Porter, producer.

D40cc. Psallite PSAL 176/060 875PET. *Die orgel der Pfarrkirche Saint-Paul-Saint-Louis, Paris.* Mireille Tissot.

D40dd. RCA LSC 10272. circa 1970. *Feike Asma at the Grote Kerk, Maassluis.*

D40ee. REM 10847. 1978. *Flute et orgue.*   Bruno Mathieu; St. Louis, Lyon.

D40ff. Repertoire Recording Society RRS-3. 1971. *Jean Langlais et le chant grégorien.* Rollin Smith; Church of St. Paul the Apostle, New York   City. Recorded July 1 and 8, 1971. Also on disc: **D33b, 53d, 69i.**

D40gg. Special Edition Records. 1974.   *Kay Holford plays organ music from the last four centuries.* Kay Holford; Univ. of Houston and First Presbyterian   Church, Houston, TX. Recorded November 17, 1973.

D40hh. Studio RM NDC 336311.   Notre-Dame-du-Cap, Québec.   *Claude Lavoie.*   Claude Lavoie; Church des Saints-Martyrs   Canadiens, Québec.   Available through Casavant Organ Company circa 1963.

D40ii. TMC 002. 1980. *Trio Récital.* Pierre Cortellezzi, organ. Three pro- fessors of the Conservatoire National de Region de Nancy in recital; other works with Jacques Mule, flute, and Dino Tomba, trumpet.

D40jj. Tempo FR 760310.   1976.   *Jean Langlais/Œuvres d'orgue inspirées du chant grégorien.* Pierre Cogen; Basilica of Sainte-Clotilde. Recorded in March 1976.   Also on disc: **D50b, 53l, 69k.**

D40kk. Vista VPS 1063. *The organ of Beverley Minster.* Alan Spedding. Also on disc: **D56e.**

D40ll. Vista VRS 1927. J. Lemckert; Laurenskerk, Rotterdam.

D40mm. Wealden Studios WS 192. Cathedral Organ Series.   1980. *Organ music from Peterborough Cathedral played by Andrew Newberry.* Recorded 30 November/1 December 1979 by Alan Brandon, Julian Sturdy.

D41. IMPLORATIONS, TROIS

1. POUR LA JOIE

D41a. Cantilena MC 1821. 1985. *Henk Klop aux grandes orgues Cavaillé-Coll Ste. Clotilde-Paris.*

3. POUR LA CROYANCE

D41b. Solstice SOL 1. 1978. *Langlais joue Langlais.* Jean Langlais;

Sainte-Clotilde, Paris. Recorded March 1976. Also on disc: **D37c, 42d, 53h, qq, 57h, s, u, aa, 59k, 67h.**

D42. LIURE ŒCUMENIQUE (1968)

4. NOTRE DIEU EST UNE PUISSANTE FORTERESSE

D42a. Motette M 1003. 1980. later M10480. *Die historische Didier-orgel in der Kathedrale Notre Dame in Laon/ Grandes orgues de la Cathédrale de Laon.* Marie Ducrot; Notre Dame Cathedral, Laon, France. Also on disc: **D42c, f, 57y.**

D42b. Citadel 116.001. 1970-71. *Orgelwerken van Jean Langlais.* Jean Langlais; St. Bavokerk, Haarlem, Holland. Also on disc: **D40h, 42g, 52c, e, 53q, 56b, 57n, 57t, w, 68g, 69p.**

9. KYRIE "ORBIS FACTOR"

D42c. Motette M 1003. 1980. later M10480. *Die historische Didier-orgel in der Kathedrale Notre Dame in Laon/ Grandes orgues de la Cathédrale de Laon.* Marie Ducrot; Notre Dame Cathedral, Laon, France. Also on disc: **D42a, f, 57y.**

D42d. Solstice SOL 1. 1976. *Langlais joue Langlais.* Jean Langlais; Sainte-Clotilde, Paris. Also on disc: **D37c, 41b, 53h, qq, 57h, s, u, aa, 59k, 67h.**

D42e. Vantage SLBP-1015. *Christ in majesty.* Jean Langlais. Prelude for the premiere of *Solemn Mass* Nov. 10, 1969 at the National Shrine of the Immaculate Conception in Washington, D. C. Also on disc: **D25, 57k, 95, 106b, 112b, 113b.**

10. KYRIE, DIEU, PERE ETERNEL

D42f. Motette M 1003. 1980. later M10480. *Die historische Didier-orgel in der Kathedrale Notre Dame in Laon/ Grandes orgues de la Cathédrale de Laon.* Marie Ducrot; Notre Dame Cathedral, Laon, France. Also on disc: **D42a, c, 57y.**

12. GLOIRE A DIEU, AU PLUS HAUT DES CIEUH

D42g. Citadel 116.001. 1970-71. *Orgelwerken van Jean Langlais.* Jean Langlais; St. Bavokerk, Haarlem, Holland. Also on disc: **D40h, 42b, 52c, e, 53q, 56b, 57n, 57t, w, 68g, 69p.**

D43. MEDITATIONS SUR L'APOCALYPSE, CINQ (1972-73)

D43a. Arion ARN 38 312. 1976. *Jean Langlais/Cinq méditations sur l'Apocalypse.* Marie-Louise Jaquet; Sainte-Clotilde, Paris; Claude Morel, recording engineer.

5. LA CINQUIEME TROMPETTE

D43b. Guild Records GRSP 7022. *John Scott plays Liszt at St. Paul's Cathedral.* London, England.

D44. MEDITATIONS SUR LA SAINTE TRINITE, TROIS (1962)

Musical Heritage Society MHS 9320184. 1987.

Jean Langlais/Complete organ works, vol. 4.
Ann Labounsky; Calvary Episcopal Church, Pittsburgh, PA; Frederick
J. Bashour, producer. In 3-disc set recorded September 1984. Also
in set: D33a, 48, 49a, 50a, 52a, 54a, 55, 60c, 61, 62b, 70.

D45. MINIATURE (1958)

Mirrosonic Records Ltd. CS 7145.   circa 1965.   *A sound
adventure.*   Marilyn Mason; University of Michigan, Ann Arbor.

D46. MOSAIQUE, VOLUME I (1959, 1975-76)

2. DOUBLE FANTAISIE (1975)

D46a.   Disques Syrinx LX 301. Marseille, France. Lyrinx 0976-003. 1976.
Musique   pour   deux   organistes.   Marie-Louise   Jaquet,
Anne-Catherine Plasse; Abbey of Saint Victor, Marseille.

D46b.   FSM 68 203 EB. 1982. *Virtuose orgelmusik zu vier händen.*
Elisabeth Sperer, Winfried Englhardt; St. Bonifaz Abtei, Munich.

D46c.   Paula 6. 1980. *Final* section only.   Peter Langberg and Kirsten
Kolling Langberg; Løgumkloster Church, Denmark; Leif R. Svendsen,
producer.

D47. MOSAIQUE, VOLUME II (1976)

5. SALVE REGINA

Alpha ACA 548. The Abbey Recording Co. 1985. *Organ works
of Jean Langlais.* Marjorie Bruce; Paisley Abbey, Scotland.
Also on disc: D37e, 37h, 39b, 53n, 57b, 59e, 65b.

D48. NOELS AVEC VARIATIONS (1979)

Musical Heritage Society MHS 9320184. 1987.
Jean Langlais/Complete organ works, vol. 4.
Ann Labounsky; Calvary Episcopal Church, Pittsburgh, PA; Frederick
J. Bashour, producer. In 3-disc set recorded September 1984. Also
in set: D33a, 44, 49a, 50a, 52a, 54a, 55, 60c, 61, 62b, 70.

D49. OFFERTOIRES POUR TOUS LES TEMPS, DEUX (1943)

complete work

D49a.   Musical Heritage Society MHS 9320184. 1987.
Jean Langlais/Complete organ works, vol. 4.
Ann Labounsky; Calvary Episcopal Church, Pittsburgh, PA; Frederick
J. Bashour, producer. In 3-disc set recorded September 1984. Also
in set: D33a, 44, 48, 50a, 52a, 54a, 55, 60c, 61, 62b, 70.

I. PARAPHRASE DE LA MESSE "Stelliferi conditor orbis"

D49b.   Erato LDE 3049. 1960. *Œuvres pour orgue d'inspiration
gégorienne.*   Jean Langlais; Sainte-Clotilde, Paris; Gregorian
chants sung by male choir directed by René Malherbe. Also on disc:
D401, 53e, 53k, 58c, 124.

D50. OFFRANDE A MARIE (1971)

D50a.   Musical Heritage Society MHS 9320184. 1987.
Jean Langlais/Complete organ works, vol. 4.
Ann Labounsky; Calvary Episcopal Church, Pittsburgh, PA; Frederick
J. Bashour, producer. In 3-disc set recorded September 1984. Also
in set: **D33a, 44, 48, 49a, 52a, 54a, 55, 60c, 61, 62b, 70.**

D50b.   Tempo FR 760310.   1976. *Jean Langlais/Œuvres d'orgue
inspirées du chant grégorien.* Pierre Cogen; Sainte-Clotilde,
Paris. Recorded March 1976. Also on disc: **D40jj, 531, 69k.**

D51. OFFRANDE A UNE AME, DIPTYQUE (1979)

Musical Heritage Society MHS 4713. 1983.
Jean Langlais/Complete organ works, vol. 2. Ann Labounsky;
St. Peter's Cathedral, Erie, PA; Frederick J. Bashour, producer. In
3-disc set MHS 843712K, recorded June 1982. Also in set: **D32,
66a, 68a, 69f, 73a, 74.**

D52. ORGAN BOOK (1956)

complete work

D52a.   Musical Heritage Society MHS 9320184. 1987.
Jean Langlais/Complete organ works, vol. 4.
Ann Labounsky; Calvary Episcopal Church, Pittsburgh, PA; Frederick
J. Bashour, producer. In 3-disc set recorded September 1984. Also
in set: **D33a, 44, 48, 49a, 50a, 54a, 55, 60c, 61, 62b, 70.**

1. PRELUDE

D52b.   Carthagène DS 35. 1982. (originally issued as Carthagène 730 529)
Marie Ducrot à l'orgue St. Martin de Pau.
Musique française pour orgue/vol. 4. Marie Ducrot; L'Eglise
Saint Martin, Pau. Also on disc: **D68b.**

D52c.   Citadel 116.001. 1970/71. *Orgelwerken van Jean Langlais.*
Jean Langlais; St. Bavokerk, Haarlem, Holland. Also on disc: **D40h,
42b, g, 52e, 53q, 56b, 57n, t, w, 68g, 69p.**

10. PASTICCIO

D52d.   Carthagène 730 517. *Musique française pour orgue/vol. 2.*
Marie Ducrot; Laon Cathedral, Jean Philippe Mousnier, producer.
Also on disc: **D59f.**

D52e.   Citadel 116.001. 1970/71. *Orgelwerken van Jean Langlais.*
Jean Langlais; St. Bavokerk, Haarlem, Holland. Also on disc: **D40h,
42b, g, 52c, 53q, 56b, 57n, t, w, 68g, 69p.**

D52f.   Connaisseur Musik [Epsilon] EPS 4514/ESR 4514. Edward Fry.
Also on disc: **D40i, 56a, 69q.**

D52g.   Delos DEL 25443.   1978.   *Masterworks for organ by
Grunenwald & Langlais.* David Britton; First Presbyterian
Church, Trenton, New Jersey. Also on disc: **D59a.**

D52h. Lyrichord LL 187/LLST 7187. 1969. *Twentieth-century French organ music.* Robert Noehren; St. John's Cathedral, Milwaukee. Also on disc: **D53z, 57g, q, 59g.**

D52i. Vista VPS 1024. 1975. *Organ music from the Church of the Holy Rude, Stirling.* Richard Galloway; Scotland; Michael Smythe, producer and recording engineer. Recorded in June 1975.

D53. PARAPHRASES GREGORIENNES, TROIS (1933–34)

complete work

D53a. Lyrichord LLST 7353. 1981. *The Aeolian Skinner organ.* John Obetz; RLDS Auditorium, Independence, MO; William Winholtz, producer. Recorded in 1980. Also on disc: **D40r.**

D53b. Mixtur MXT 2005. 1978. *Jean Langlais, Petr Eben, Susan Landale.* Susan Landale; Martin Luther Gedächtniskirche, Berlin-Mariendorf. Recorded in April 1977. Also on disc: **59b.**

D53c. Musical Heritage Society MHS 4128. 1980. *Jean Langlais/ Complete organ works [1].* Ann Labounsky; St. Peter Cathedral, Erie, PA; Paul Engle, Frederick J. Bashour, recording engineers. In 3-disc set MHS 834127K recorded August 1979. Also in set: **D31b, 37a, 40y, 57a, 59c, 67c.**

D53d. Repertoire Recording Society RRS-3. 1971. *Jean Langlais et le chant grégorien.* Rollin Smith; Church of St. Paul the Apostle, New York City. Recorded July 1 and 8, 1971. Also on disc: **D33b, 40ff, 69i.**

1. MORS ET RESURRECTIO

D53e. Erato LDE 3049. 1960. *Œuvres pour orgue d'inspiration grégorienne.* Jean Langlais; Sainte-Clotilde, Paris; Gregorian chants sung by male choir directed by René Malherbe. Also on disc: **D40l, 49b, 53k, 58c, 124.**

D53f. F.T.L. 1369. 1985. *Raphaël Tambyeff à l'orgue de Saint Vincent de Paul à Paris.* Raphaël Tambyeff; St. Vincent de Paul, Paris; Philippe Guillaumie, engineer. Recorded July 1984.

D53g. RPCo. unnumbered. Pressed by Recorded Publications Co. *Organ music at Wheaton College.* Edmund B. Wright; Gerald G. LeCompte, recording engineer.

D53h. Solstice SOL 1. 1976. *Langlais joue Langlais.* Jean Langlais; Sainte-Clotilde, Paris. Also on disc: **D37c, 41b, 42d, 53qq, 57h, s, u, aa, 59k, 67h.**

2. AVE MARIA, AVE MARIS STELLA

D53i. Aeolian-Skinner AS 318. *Two great organs.* Albert Russell; Philharmonic Hall, Lincoln Center, New York City.

D53j. Coronata COR 001. 1980. Pierre Cortelezzi. Also on disc: **D53r.**

D53k. Erato LDE 3049. 1960. *Œuvres pour orgue d'inspiration grégorienne.* Jean Langlais; Sainte-Clotilde, Paris; Gregorian chants sung by male choir directed by René Malherbe. Also on disc: **D40l, 49b, 53e, 58c, 124.**

D53l. Tempo FR 760.310. Paris, France. 1976. *Jean Langlais/ Œuvres d'orgue inspirées du chant grégorien.* Pierre Cogen; Sainte-Clotilde, Paris. Recorded in March 1976. Also on disc: **D40jj, 50b, 69k.**

3. HYMNE D'ACTIONS DE GRACES "TE DEUM"

D53m. Aeolian-Skinner XTV 20628. *The king of instruments/volume II - organ literature: Bach to Langlais.* Unnamed staff organist; First Presbyterian Church, Kilgore, Texas. Reissued as WAS II (Washington Records).

D53n. Alpha ACA 548. The Abbey Recording Co. 1985. *Organ works of Jean Langlais.* Marjorie Bruce; Paisley Abbey, Scotland. Also on disc: **D37e, h, 39b, 47, 57b, 59e, 65b.**

D53o. Argo ZRG 807. 1975. *Peter Hurford at St. Albans.* Chris Hazell, producer; Michael Mailes, Ronald Cohen, engineers.

Arsica 1624. P. Heuser; Kevelaar Basilica. (*See*: D126)

D53p. Calliope CAL 1931. *Le Livre d'or de l'orgue français - 31/ Marcel Dupré - Jean Langlais - André Fleury.* André Fleury; Cathédrale Saint-Bénigne de Dijon; André Garnier, recording engineer. Also on disc: **D67k.**

D53q. Citadel 116.001. 1970-71. *Orgelwerken van Jean Langlais.* Jean Langlais; St. Bavokerk, Haarlem, Holland. Also on disc: **D40h, 42b, g, 52c, e, 56b, 57n, t, w, 68g, 69p.**

D53r. Coronata COR 001. 1980. Pierre Cortelezzi. Also on disc: **D53j.**

D53s. Deutsche Grammophon Gesellschaft DGG 19091. LPEM 19091, also 25 35 748. Issued Polydor International 1969, reissued 1980. *Orgelmusik im Kölner Dom.* Josef Zimmermann; Cologne Cathedral, Germany. Also on disc: **D40j, 69r.**

D53t. Erato LDE 3024. 1955. *Œuvres modernes pour orgue.* Jean Langlais; Sainte-Clotilde, Paris. Also on disc: **D37g, 69c.**

D53u. Exon Audio EAS 16. Barry Ferguson; Wimborne Minster, Dorset.

D53v. Exon Audio EAS 21. David Ponsford; Wells Cathedral.

D53w. Fontana 894.151 ZKY. circa 1970. *French organ music.* Feike Asma; Grote Kerk, Dordrecht, Holland.

D53x. Gothic Records 27979802. 1979. *Easter.* Frederick Swann; The Riverside Church, New York City; Fred Miller and Harry Munz, recording engineers.

D53y. Kendall 2553. 1952. *French organ music.* Catharine Crozier; Kilbourn Hall, Eastman School of Music, Univ. of Rochester, Rochester, N.Y. Red vinylite.

D53z.   Lyrichord LL 187/LLST 7187. 1969. *Twentieth-century French organ music.* Robert Noehren; St. John's Cathedral, Milwaukee. Also on disc: **D52h, 57g, q, 59g.**

D53aa. Meridian E 77034. *Popular organ music.* Christopher Herrick; Westminster Abbey, London.

D53bb. Meridian E 77105. *Organ favourites from Norwich.* Michael Nichols; Norwich Cathedral; John Shuttleworth, producer.

D53cc. Mitra   MIT 16 163. F. Leinhäuser; Liebfrauenkirche, Obermesel.

D53dd. Mixtur MXT CVO 102 (Canto di Vangelo 0102). *Orgel Nieuwe Zuiderkerk, Rotterdam.* Jef Dubbeldam.

D53ee. Motette Ursina M 1006-33. *Ludger Mai spielt virtuose orgel-musik.* St. Matthias-Kirche, Berlin-Schöneberg.

D53ff. Motette Ursina M 1023. 1979. *Jean Langlais spielt französische orgelmusik in der Abteikirche Marienstatt.* Jean Langlais. Recording of concert played at Marienstatt Abbey on Nov. 5, 1978. Also on disc: **D40w, 91, 97c, 125.**

D53gg. Motette M 11170. Naji S. Hakim, Basilique du Sacré-Cœur de Montmartre, Paris. Recorded April 17, 1987. (*See*: **D129**)

D53hh. Move MS 3048. *Peter Nicholson plays the organ of Melbourne Cathedral.*

D53ii. Odeon CSD 1609 (stereo) CLD 1879 (mono) [HMV]. *Great cathedral organ series/Coventry Cathedral.* David Lepine.

D53jj. Proprius PROP 7784. 1977. *Langlais/Te Deum & Deuxième Concerto/Honegger/Fugue et Choral.* Kjell Johnsen; Engelbrekt Church, Stockholm. Recorded 1977. Also on disc: **D77.**

D53kk. Psallite Psal 44/290 667 PET. *Rieger-Orgel des Münsters, Mönchengladbach.* Viktor Scholz.

D53ll. Rittenhouse RS 1003. *A two-organ recital.* Earl Ness and William Whitehead; First Baptist Church, Philadelphia. Also on disc: **D67n.**

D53mm. RSCM 112/5. *Tri Centennial Festival Service.* S. Campbell.

D53nn. Ryemuse SALR 1204 (stereo) ALR 1204 (mono). *20th-century organ music.* Noel Rawsthorne; Liverpool Cathedral.

D53oo. Schudi Organ Co. Schudi 001. Garland, Texas. 1979. *George C. Baker at St. Thomas Aquinas, Dallas.* Recorded January 2-3, 1979.

D53pp. SC GLX 73 806 Christophorus. *Orgelkonzert im Stift Haug.* Klaus Linsenmeyer.

D53qq. Solstice SOL 1. 1976. *Langlais joue Langlais.* Jean Langlais; Sainte-Clotilde, Paris. Also on disc: **D37c, 41b, 42d, 53h, 57h, s, u, aa, 59k, 67h.**

D53rr.   Unidisc UD 30 135A. *André Fleury aux grandes orgues de la Cathédrale de Dijon.* Also on disc: **D67m.**

D53ss.   Vista VPS 1107. 1982. Nicholas Jackson. Also on disc: **D83d.**

D53tt.   Wealden WS 140. E. Park; Enfield Parish Church.

D53uu.   Wealden WS 142. Jack Hindmarsh; Haileybury College Chapel, Herts. Also on disc: **D68d.**

D53vv.   Woodward MW 912. St. Nicholas Church, Great Yarmouth.

D53ww. [Label and recording number unknown.] *We praise thee.*
Jerome Meachen; Church of the Redeemer, Sarasota, Florida; Don Smith, engineer. Recorded May 13, 1971.

D54. PETITES PIECES, DOUZE (1960, 1962)

complete work

D54a.   Musical Heritage Society MHS 9320184. 1987.
Jean Langlais/Complete organ works, vol. 4.
Ann Labounsky; Calvary Episcopal Church, Pittsburgh, PA; Frederick J. Bashour, producer. In 3-disc set recorded September 1984. Also in set: D33a, 44, 48, 49a, 50a, 52a, 55, 60c, 61, 62b, 70.

DIH UERSETS DANS LES MODES GREGORIENS (1962)

D54b.   Pilgrim Recordings JLPS155. Lionel Dakers; Exeter Cathedral. Four of the *Ten Versets* recorded as *Four Versets in Gregorian modes.*

D55. PIECES BREUES, DEUH (1983)

Musical Heritage Society MHS 9320184. 1987.
Jean Langlais/Complete organ works, vol. 4.
Ann Labounsky; Calvary Episcopal Church, Pittsburgh, PA; Frederick J. Bashour, producer. In 3-disc set recorded September 1984. Also in set: D33a, 44, 48, 49a, 50a, 52a, 54a, 60c, 61, 62b, 70.

D56. PIECES MODALES, HUIT (1956)

1. MODE DE RE

D56a.   Connaisseur Musik [Epsilon] EPS 4514/ESR 4514. Edward Fry; All Saints, Clifton, Bristol.
Also on disc: **D40i, 52f.**

1. MODE DE RE   2. MODE DE LA

D56b.   Citadel 116.001. 1970/71. *Orgelwerken van Jean Langlais.*
Jean Langlais; St. Bavokerk, Haarlem, Holland. Also on disc: **D40h, 42b, g, 52c, e, 53q, 57n, t, w, 68g, 69p.**

4. MODE DE SI   8. MODE DE SOL

D56c.   Vista VPS 1004. 1973. *The organ of St. Martin-in-the-Fields.* Robert Vincent; Michael Smythe, recording engineer and producer. Recorded in May 1973. Also on disc: **D38c.**

5. MODE DE FA

D56d. Festivo Stereo 086. *Daniel Roth aux grandes orgues van den Heuvel de Strijen.* (Holland)   Also on disc: **D57p.**

7. MODE DE SOL

D56e. Vista VPS 1063. *The Organ of Beverley Minster.*
Alan Spedding.   Also on disc: **D40kk.**

D57. PIECES, NEUF (1942-43)

complete work

D57a. Musical Heritage Society MHS 4128. 1980.
Jean Langlais/complete organ works [1].
Ann Labounsky; St. Peter's Cathedral, Erie, PA; Frederick J. Bashour, producer. In 3-disc set MHS 834127K, recorded August 1979. Also on disc: **D31b, 37a, 40y, 53c, 59c, 67c.**

2. CHANT DE JOIE

D57b. Alpha ACA 548. The Abbey Recording Co. 1985. *Organ works of Jean Langlais.* Marjorie Bruce; Paisley Abbey, Scotland.
Also on disc: **D37e, h, 39b, 47, 53n, 59e, 65b.**

3. CHANT DE PAIX

D57c. Aeolian-Skinner AS 326. *The king of instruments.*
Alexander Boggs Ryan; Cathedral Church of Christ the King, Kalamazoo, Michigan.

D57d. Alpha ACA 536, CACA 536 (Cassette). The Abbey Recording Co. 1984. *Organ music from Wells Cathedral.*
Christopher Brayne; Wells Cathedral, England. Also on disc: **D57l.**

D57e. Decca Ace of Diamonds SDD-R404. *Romantic organ music.*
Edward Fry; St. Monica's Chapel, Westbury-on-Trym, Bristol.

D57f. Gallo 3087. 1978.   René Oberson.

D57g. Lyrichord LL 187/LLST 7187. 1969. *Twentieth-century French organ music.*   Robert Noehren; St. John's Cathedral, Milwaukee.
Also on disc: **D52h, 53z, 57q, 59g.**

D57h. Solstice SOL 1. 1976. *Langlais joue Langlais.*
Jean Langlais; Sainte-Clotilde, Paris.
Also on disc: **D37c, 41b, 42d, 53h, qq, 57s, u, aa, 59k, 67h.**

D57i. Towerhill T-1002. 1979. *John Rose plays the Beckerath organ at Pomona College.* John Rose.

D57j. United Sound USR 5002. *The organ on Mormon Temple Hill.*
Norberto Guinaldo; The Church of Jesus Christ of Latter Day Saints, Interstake Center, Oakland, California. Also on disc: **D59l.**

D57k. Vantage SLBP-1015. *Christ in majesty.* Jean Langlais;
The National Shrine of the Immaculate Conception, Washington, D. C.

Recorded November 10, 1969 in concert.
Also on disc: **D25, 42e, 95, 106b, 112b, 113b.**

4. CHANT HEROIQUE

D57l. Alpha ACA 536, CACA 536 (Cassette). The Abbey Recording Co. 1984. *Organ music from Wells Cathedral.* Christopher Brayne; Wells Cathedral, England. Also on disc: **D57d.**

D57m. Avant Quart AQ 3001 AT. 1969. *Hommage à Jean Langlais.* Susan Ingrid Ferré; Sainte-Clotilde, Paris. Also on disc: **D60a, 62a, 93a, 97a, 100.**

D57n. Citadel 116.001. 1970/71. *Orgelwerken van Jean Langlais.* Jean Langlais; St. Bavokerk, Haarlem, Holland. Also on disc: **D40h, 42b, g, 52c, e, 53q, 56b, 57t, w, 68g, 69p.**

D57o. Eclipse ECS 626. Decca Ltd. 1972. *Organ music from Corpus Christi College, Cambridge.* Edward Higginbottom; Gavin Barrett, producer.

D57p. Festivo Stereo 086. 1977. *Daniel Roth aux grandes orgues van den Heuvel de Strijen.* (Holland). Also on disc: **D56d.**

D57q. Lyrichord LL 187/LLST 7187. 1969. *Twentieth-century French organ music.* Robert Noehren; St. John's Cathedral, Milwaukee. Also on disc: **D52h, 53z, 57g, 59g.**

D57r. McIntosh Music 106. *An adventure in high fidelity organ sound.* William Watkins; Calvary Methodist Church, Washington, DC.

D57s. Solstice SOL 1. 1976. *Langlais joue Langlais.* Jean Langlais; Sainte-Clotilde, Paris. Also on disc: **D37c, 41b, 42d, 53h, qq, 57h, u, aa, 59k, 67h.**

6. DE PROFUNDIS

D57t. Citadel 116.001. 1970-71. *Orgelwerken van Jean Langlais.* Jean Langlais; St. Bavokerk, Haarlem, Holland. Also on disc: **D40h, 42b, g, 52c, e, 53q, 56b, 57n, w, 68g, 69p.**

D57u. Solstice SOL 1. 1976. *Langlais joue Langlais.* Jean Langlais; Sainte-Clotilde, Paris. Also on disc: **D37c, 41b, 42d, 53h, qq, 57h, s, aa, 59k, 67h.**

7. MON AME CHERCHE UNE FIN PAISIBLE

D57v. Association de l'orgue Silbermann de Mulhouse. Unnumbered. 1974. *Marie-Louise Jaquet.* Marie-Louise Jaquet; Temple de Saint Jean, Mulhouse, France. Recorded 1973. Also on disc: **D30a, 37f.**

D57w. Citadel 116.001. 1970-71. *Orgelwerken van Jean Langlais.* Jean Langlais; St. Bavokerk, Haarlem, Holland. Also on disc: **D40h, 42b, g, 52c, e, 53q, 56b, 57n, t, 68g, 69p.**

D57x. Jecklin 161. *Jean Langlais/Cesar Franck.* René Oberson; Fraumünster Zürcher, Switzerland. Also on disc: **D67a.**

D57y.   Motette M 1003. 1980. later M10480. *Die historische Didier-orgel in der Kathedrale Notre Dame in Laon.* Marie Ducrot; Notre Dame Cathedral, Laon, France.   Also on disc: **D42a, c, f.**

D57z.   Organ Historical Society.   *Central Connecticut.*   Rosalind Mohnsen; Derby United Methodist Church, Derby, Conn.   Recorded in June 1975 during OHS Convention recital. Also on disc: **D30c.**

D57aa. Solstice SOL 1. 1976. *Langlais joue Langlais.*
Jean Langlais; Sainte-Clotilde, Paris.
Also on disc: **D37c, 41b, 42d, 53h, qq, 57h, s, u, 59k, 67h.**

D58. PIECES, UINGT-QUATRE pour harmonium ou orgue (1933-39)

complete work

D58a.   Musical Heritage Society MHS 7273-74. 1985.
Jean Langlais/Complete organ works, vol. 3.
Ann Labounsky; Calvary Episcopal Church, Pittsburgh, PA;
Frederick J. Bashour, producer.   In 3-disc set MHS 837273M, recorded September 1984. Also in set: **D29, 63, 64, 65a, 76.**

Uolume I

12. HOMMAGE A FR. LANDINO

D58b.   Organ Historical Society RPC.   *1966 National convention.* John Skelton; Federated Church of Sandwich, Mass.   Recorded during the 11th national convention of the Organ Historical Society on Cape Cod, June 21-23, 1966.

Uolume II

13. HOMO QUIDAM

D58c.   Erato LDE 3049. 1960. *Chants grégoriens et œuvres d'orgue inspirées du chant grégorien.* Jean Langlais; Sainte-Clotilde, Paris; Gregorian chants sung by male choir directed by René Malherbe. Also on disc: **D40l, 49b, 53e, k, 124.**

15. PRIERE

D58d.   30977 SM 43. 1980. *Chant grégorien et orgue: St. Benoit.*
Dom Claude Gay; Solesmes Abbey, France.

D59. POEMES EUANGELIQUES (1932)

complete work

D59a.   Delos DEL 25443. 1978. *Masterworks for organ by Grunenwald & Langlais.*   David Britton; First Presbyterian Church, Trenton, New Jersey. Also on disc: **D52g.**

D59b.   Mixture MXT 2005. 1978. *Jean Langlais, Petr Eben, Susan Landale.*   Susan Landale; Martin Luther Gedächtniskirche, Berlin-Mariendorf. Recorded in April 1977. Also on disc: **D53b.**

D59c.   Musical Heritage Society MHS 4127.   1980.   *Jean Langlais/ Complete organ works [1].* Ann Labounsky; St. Peter's Cathedral, Erie, PA; Paul Engle, Frederick J. Bashour, recording engineers. In 3-disc set MHS 834127K recorded August 1979. Also in set: **D31b, 37a, 40y, 53c, 57a, 67c.**

1. L'ANNONCIATION

D59d.   ES 313-15.   Bernard Bartelink.

2. LA NATIVITE

D59e.   Alpha ACA 548.   The Abbey Recording Co., Oxford, England.   1985. *Organ works of Jean Langlais.* Marjorie Bruce; Paisley Abbey, Scotland.   Also on disc: **D37e, h, 39b, 47, 53n, 57b, 65b.**

D59f.   Carthagene 730 517. *Musique française pour orgue/vol. 2.* Marie Ducrot; Cathédrale de Laon. Jean Philippe Mousnier, producer. Also on disc: **D52d.**

D59g.   Lyrichord LL 187/LLST 7187. 1969. *Twentieth-century French organ music.*   Robert Noehren; St. John's Cathedral, Milwaukee. Also on disc: **D52h, 53z, 57g, q.**

D59h.   McIntosh Music 1005. *A program of organ music.* Harold Ash; New York Ave. Presbyterian Church, Washington, DC.

D59i.   Music From Central. 1979. *Music from Central, vol. 1.* John Ferguson; Central Lutheran Church, Minneapolis, Minn.

D59j.   Richardson RSS 6. G. Dale.

D59k.   Solstice SOL 1. 1976. *Langlais joue Langlais.* Jean Langlais; Sainte-Clotilde, Paris. Also on disc: **D37c, 41b, 42d, 53h, qq, 57h, s, u, aa, 67h.**

D59l.   United Sound USR 5002. *The organ on Mormon Temple Hill.* Norberto Guinaldo; The Church of Jesus Christ of Latter Day Saints, Interstake Center, Oakland, California.   Also on disc: **D57j.**

D59m.   W-806. *Music for Christmas.* James Welch; Memorial Church, Stanford University, CA.

D59n.   Wealden WS 112. M. Cobb. Church of St. Lawrence Jewry.

D59o.   Wealden WS 126. R. Manns.

D59p.   Wicks Concert Series SHC 42366. 1966.   *The dedication of the organ/Sacred Heart Cathedral/Rochester, New York.* Kent Hill; Frank A. Morris, recording engineer and producer. Recorded January 19, 1966.

D59q.   Wilson Audio W806. J. Webb.

D60. POEM OF HAPPINESS (1966)

D60a.   Avant Quart AQ 3001 AT. 1969. *Hommage à Jean Langlais.* Susan Ingrid Ferré; Sainte-Clotilde, Paris. Also on disc: **D57m, 62a, 73c, 93a, 97a, 100.**

D60b.   Festivo 097. 1984.
*Bruno   Mathieu/L'Orgue   Cavaillé-Coll   de   L'Eglise   St.
Antoine des Quinze-Vingts à Paris.* Also on disc: D72.

D60c.   Musical Heritage Society MHS 9320184. 1987.
Jean Langlais/Complete organ works, vol. 4.
Ann Labounsky; Calvary Episcopal Church, Pittsburgh, PA; Frederick
J. Bashour, producer. In 3-disc set recorded September 1984. Also
in set: D33a, 44, 48, 49a, 50a, 54a, 55, 61, 62b, 70.

D60d.   Wealden WS 109. Robert Husson; All Saints, Blackheath, Kent. Also
on disc: D28, 69m.

D61. POEM OF LIFE (1965)

Musical Heritage Society MHS 9320184. 1987.
Jean Langlais/Complete organ works, vol. 4.
Ann Labounsky; Calvary Episcopal Church, Pittsburgh, PA; Frederick
J. Bashour, producer. In 3-disc set recorded September 1984. Also
in set: D33a, 44, 48, 49a, 50a, 52a, 54a, 55, 60c, 62b, 70.

D62. POEM OF PEACE (1966)

D62a.   Avant Quart AQ 3001 AT. 1969. *Hommage à Jean Langlais.*
Susan Ingrid Ferre; Sainte-Clotilde.
Also on disc: D57m, 60a, 73c, 93a, 97a, 100.

D62b.   Musical Heritage Society MHS 9320184. 1987.
Jean Langlais/Complete organ works, vol. 4.
Ann Labounsky; Calvary Episcopal Church, Pittsburgh, PA; Frederick
J. Bashour, producer. In 3-disc set recorded September 1984. Also
in set: D33a, 44, 48, 49a, 50a, 52a, 54a, 55, 60c, 61, 70.

D63. PRELUDE A LA MESSE "ORBIS FACTOR" (1956)

Musical Heritage Society MHS 7275. 1985.
Jean Langlais/Complete organ works, vol. 3.
Ann Labounsky; Calvary Episcopal Church, Pittsburgh, PA;
Frederick J. Bashour, producer.In 3-disc set 837273M, recorded
September 1984. Also in set: D29, 58a, 64, 65a, 76.

D64. PRELUDES, HUIT (1983-84)

Musical Heritage Society MHS 7275. 1985.
Jean Langlais/Complete organ works, vol. 3.
Ann Labounsky; Calvary Episcopal Church, Pittsburgh, PA;
Frederick J. Bashour, producer. In 3-disc set MHS 837273M,
recorded September 1984. Also on set: D29, 58a, 63, 65a, 76.

D65. PROGRESSION

complete work

D65a.   Musical Heritage Society MHS 7274-75. 1985.
Jean Langlais/Complete organ works, vol. 3.
Ann Labounsky; Calvary Episcopal Church, Pittsburgh, PA;
Frederick J. Bashour, producer.In 3-disc set 837273M, recorded
September 1984. Also on disc: D29, 58a, 63, 64, 76.

4. OFFERING

D65b. Alpha ACA 548. The Abbey Recording Co. 1985.
Organ works of Jean Langlais. Marjorie Bruce; Paisley Abbey,
Scotland. Also on disc: D37e, h, 39b, 47, 53n, 57b, 59e.

D66. SUITE BAROQUE (1973)

complete work

D66a. Musical Heritage Society MHS 4713-14. 1983. *Jean Langlais/
Complete organ works, vol. 2.* Ann Labounsky; St. Peter
Cathedral, Erie; Frederick J. Bashour, producer. In 3-disc set MHS
843712K recorded June 1982.
Also in set: D32, 51, 68a, 69f, 73a, 74.

6. VOIX HUMAINE 7. GRAND JEU

D66b. Coronata COR 4001. 1983. *Orgeln im Elsass.* Jean Langlais;
Maseveau Congres GDD 1983. Recorded August 4, 1983 in concert,
Church of St. Martin, Masevaux. Also on disc: D89, 93c, 111, 112a.

7. GRAND JEU

D66c. Disques Christal SCA 019. 1985. *Saint Georges, Selestat.*
Remi Hoffbeck.

D67. SUITE BREVE

complete work

D67a. Jecklin 161. *Jean Langlais/César Franck.* René Oberson;
Fraumünster Zürcher, Switzerland. Also on disc: D57x.

D67b. Lismor LILP 5068. 1977. *Great Organ Music.*
George McPhee; Paisley Abbey, Scotland.

D67c. Musical Heritage Society MHS 4129. 1980. *Jean Langlais/
Complete organ works. [1].* Ann Labounsky; St. Peter Cathedral,
Erie, PA. In 3-disc set MHS 834127K, recorded August 1979.
Also in set: D31b, 37a, 40y, 53c, 57a, 59c.

D67d. Philips 65 28 001. *Jehan Alain/Jean Langlais.*
Recording by Cathedral Recordings Ltd.
Also released as Philips Fourfront 4F07012.
Nicolas Kynaston; Buckfast Abbey, Buckfastleigh, Devon.

D67e. Priory PR 116. 1982. *The organ at Guildford Cathedral.*
Philip Moore; Paul Crichton, Philip Moore, producers; Paul Crichton,
recording engineer. Recorded April 22 and 25, 1982.

D67f. Priory PR 148. 1984. *French organ music from Salisbury
Cathedral.* Colin Walsh; Paul Crichton, producer and recording
engineer. Recorded on April 10-11, 1984. Also on disc: D36b.

2. CANTILENE

D67g. Aeolian-Skinner AS 317. *The king of instruments/Phillip
Steinhaus.* All Saints Church, Pontiac, Michigan.

3. PLAINTE

D67h.   Solstice SOL 1. 1976. *Langlais joue Langlais.*
Jean Langlais; Sainte-Clotilde, Paris.
Also on disc: D37c, 41b, 42d, 53h, qq, 57h, s, u, aa, 59k.

4. DIALOGUE SUR LES MIXTURES

D67i.   Aeolian-Skinner AS 315. Reissued as Washington Records WAS XIV
(mono), SWAS XIV (stereo). *New dimensions in organ sound/
The king of instruments, vol. XIV.*   Catharine Crozier;
Auditorium, World Headquarters Reorganized Church of Jesus Christ
of Latter Day Saints, Independence, MO. Also on disc: D68h.

D67j.   Argo ZRG 864. 1977. *The organ at Hexham Abbey.* Gillian Weir;
Chris Hazell, producer; Stan Goodall, Simon Eadon, engineers.

D67k.   Calliope CAL 1931. *Le livre d'or de l'orgue français - 31
Marcel Dupré - Jean Langlais - André Fleury.*
André Fleury; Cathédrale Saint-Bénigne de Dijon; André Garnier,
Engineer. Grand Prix du Président de la République.
Also on disc: D53p.

D67l.   Mirrosonic DRE 1004. 1958. *The first international congress
of organists, vol. II.* Robert Baker; Temple Church, London,
England. Recorded July 28, 1957 during ICO Congress.

D67m.   Unidisc UD 30 135A. *André Fleury aux grandes orgues de
la Cathédrale de Dijon.* Also on disc: D53rr.

D67n.   Rittenhouse RS 1003. circa 1964. *A two-organ recital.*
Earl Ness and William Whitehead, organs; First Baptist Church,
Philadelphia. Also on disc: D53ll.

D68. SUITE FRANÇAISE (1948)

complete work

D68a.   Musical Heritage Society MHS 7712. 1983. *Jean Langlais/Com-
plete organ works, vol. 2.* Ann Labounsky; St. Peter's Cathedral,
Erie; Frederick J. Bashour, producer. In 3-disc set MHS 843712K,
recorded June 1982. Also in set: D32, 51, 66a, 69f, 73a, 74.

1. PRELUDE SUR LES GRANDS JEUX   2. NASARD

D68b.   Carthagene DS 35. 1982. (originally issued as Carthagène 730 529)
*Marie Ducrot à l'orgue St. Martin de Pau.
Musique française pour orgue/Vol.4.*
Marie Ducrot; L'Eglise Saint Martin, Pau. Also on disc: D52b.

2. NASARD

D68c.   Audiophile AP-42.   *Organ music of France.* Robert Noehren;
Collingwood Presbyterian Church, Toledo, Ohio. Red vinylite.

D68d.   Wealden WS 142.   Jack Hindmarsh; Haileybury College Chapel,
Hertfordshire. Also on disc: D53uu.

D68e.   Wealden WS 159. N. Jackson. Church of St. Lawrence Jewry.

D68f.   WRC 1-4478. *Music for Organ.* Ian Sadler; Yorkminster Park Baptist Church, Toronto, Canada.

4. FRANÇAISE

D68g.   Citadel 116.001. 1970/71. *Orgelwerken van Jean Langlais.* Jean Langlais; St. Bavokerk, Haarlem, Holland. Also on disc: **D40h, 42b, g, 52c, e, 53q, 56b, 57n, t, w, 69p.**

6. ARABESQUE SUR LES FLUTES

D68h.   Aeolian-Skinner AS 315. Reissued as Washington Records WAS XIV (mono), SWAS XIV (stereo).*New dimensions in organ sound/ The king of instruments series, vol. XIV/Aeolian-Skinner organs.* Catharine Crozier; Auditorium, World Headquarters, Reorganized Church of Jesus Christ of Latter Day Saints, Independence, Missouri. Also on disc: **D67i.**

D68i.   Klip KST 1002 (stereo tape). J. Eargle; First Presbyterian Church, Kilgore, Texas.

D69. SUITE MEDIEVALE (1947)

complete work

D69a.   Cameo C4020. *The organ of the Philadelphia Academy of Music--vol. 2.* William Whitehead.

D69b.   Disques RDG 30 10 76. *Maurice Clerc aux grandes orgues de la Cathédrale de Dijon.* Richesses des Orgues de Bourgogne, vol. 2. Raymond Garnier, recording engineer; Jean Dufour, technical assistant.

D69c.   Erato LDE 3024. 1955. *Œuvres modernes pour orgue.* Marie-Claire Alain; Sainte-Clotilde, Paris. Also on disc: **D37g, 53t.**

D69d.   Gregorian Institute of America M-107 (mono), S-207 (stereo). Toledo, Ohio. *Henry Hokans at the organ of All Saints Church, Worcester, Mass.*

D69e.   Motette 2002-33. *Musik aus der Abtei Marienstatt.* Marie Ducrot; Gregorian themes sung by choralschola der Abtei Marienstatt, Dr. Gabriel Hammer, director.

D69f.   Musical Heritage Society MHS 4713. 1983.*Jean Langlais/Complete organ works, vol. 2.* Ann Labounsky; St. Peter's Cathedral, Erie; Frederick J. Bashour, producer. In 3-disc set MHS 843712K, recorded June 1982. Also in set: **D32, 51, 66a, 68a, 73a, 74.**

D69g.   Priory PR 173. 1985. *French organ music from Salisbury Cathedral, volume 2.* Colin Walsh.

D69h.   Psallite PSC 17 250265 (17/250). *Das Orgelportrait [6]. Die Doppelorgel der Abteikirche Maria Laach.* Günter Berger; Benedictine Abbey Maria Laach.

D69i.   Repertoire Recording Society RRS-3. 1971. *Jean Langlais et le chant grégorien.* Rollin Smith; Church of St. Paul the Apostle, New York City. Also on disc: **D33b, 40ff, 53d.**

D69j.   SKE 30-683. 1980. *L'Orgue de Engelberg.*
Pére Norbert Hegner; Engelberg Monastery, Switzerland.

D69k.   Tempo FR 760.310. 1976. *Jean Langlais/Œuvres d'orgue
inspirées du chant grégorien.*   Pierre Cogen; Sainte-Clotilde,
Paris. Recorded in 1976. Also on disc: **D40jj, 50b, 53l.**

D69l.   Vista VPS 1057. 1977. *The organ in Worcester Cathedral.*
Donald Hunt.

D69m.   Wealden WS 109. Robert Husson; All Saints, Blackheath, Kent.
Also on disc: **D28, 60d.**

D69n.   Wealden Prestige WS 200. Allan Wicks; Canterbury Cathedral.

D69o.1. PRELUDE 3. IMPROVISATION 5. ACCLAMATIONS

Bourdon FK-1. *French music for the organ.*
Edward Eigenschenk; St. Ita's Church, Chicago; Fred Kruse, recording
engineer; Peter Bartok, disk mastering; Norman Pellegrini,
production director. Recorded in 1956.

D69p.1. PRELUDE (ENTREE)   2. TIENTO (OFFERTOIRE)

Citadel 116.001. 1970/71. *Orgelwerken van Jean Langlais.*
Jean Langlais; St. Bavokerk, Haarlem, Holland.
Also on disc: **D40h, 42b, g, 52c, e, 53q, 56b, 57n, t, w, 68g.**

2. TIENTO (OFFERTOIRE)

D69q.   Connaisseur Musik EPS 4514/Epsilon ESR 4514. Edward Fry.
Also on disc: **D40i, 52f, 56a.**

D69r.   Deutsche Grammophon Gesellschaft DGG 19091. LPEM 19091.
Also 25 35 748. Issued 1969 Polydor International; reissued 1980.
Orgelmusik im Kölner Dom. Josef Zimmermann; Cologne
Cathedral, Germany. Also on disc: **D40j, 53s.**

4. MEDITATION

D69s.   Eurosound ES 46402. L. Toebusch.

D69t.   Mirrosonic CS 7232-B. *The organs of Fifth Avenue
Presbyterian Church, New York.* Richard Bouchett.

D69u.4. MEDITATION   5. ACCLAMATIONS

Productions Charlevoix PC12. Cassette. *Jean-Marie Bussières.*

D70. SUPPLICATION (1972)

Musical Heritage Society MHS 9320184. 1987.
Jean Langlais/Complete organ works, vol. 4.
Ann Labounsky; Calvary Episcopal Church, Pittsburgh, PA; Frederick
J. Bashour, producer. In 3-disc set recorded September 1984. Also
in set: **D33a, 44, 48, 49a, 50a, 52a, 54a, 55, 60c, 61, 62b.**

D71. SYMPHONIE, PREMIERE (1941-42)

Alpha ACA 521. The Abbey Recording Co. 1984. *The Sainte Clotilde tradition.* Marjorie Bruce; Paisley Abbey, Scotland; George McPhee, producer. Recorded on 16,17,18 September 1983.

D72. SYMPHONIE, TROISIEME (1959, 1979)

Festivo 097. 1984. *Bruno Mathieu/L'Orgue Cavaillé-Coll de L'Eglise St. Antoine des Quinze-Vingts à Paris.* Also on disc: D60b.

TE DEUM *See:* **TROIS PARAPHRASES GREGORIENNES, D53.**

D73. TRIPTYQUE (1956)

D73a.   Musical Heritage Society MHS 4714. 1983. *Jean Langlais/Complete organ works, vol. 2.* Ann Labounsky; St. Peter's Cathedral, Erie; Frederick J. Bashour, producer. In 3-disc set MHS 843712K, recorded June 1982. Also in set: D32, 51, 66a, 68a, 69f, 74.

D73b.   Vista VPS 1029. 1976. *French organ music from Blackburn Cathedral.* Jane Parker-Smith; Michael Symthe, producer and recording engineer. Recorded October 1974.

2. Trio

D73c.   Avant Quart AQ 3001 AT. 1969. *Hommage à Jean Langlais.* Susan Ingrid Ferré; Sainte-Clotilde, Paris. Also on disc: D57m, 60a, 62a, 93a, 97a, 100.

D73d.   WRC1-2106. World Records. Robarts Recordings. [EMI] *The great organ sounds of David Palmer.* David Palmer; All Saints' Church, Windsor, Canada.

D74. TRIPTYQUE GREGORIEN (1978)

Musical Heritage Society MHS 4714. 1983. *Jean Langlais/Complete organ works, vol. 2.* Ann Labounsky; St. Peter's Cathedral, Erie; Frederick J. Bashour, producer. In 3-disc set MHS 843712K, recorded June 1982. Also on disc: D32, 51, 66a, 68a, 69f, 73a.

D75. TRUMPET TUNE (1987)

Classic Masters. Jonathan Dimmock, Cathedral of St. John the Divine, New York City. Christopher Greenleaf, producer. Recorded May, 1987.

D76. VOLUNTARIES, THREE (1969)

Musical Heritage Society MHS 7274. 1985. *Jean Langlais/Complete organ works, vol. 3.* Ann Labounsky; Calvary Episcopal Church, Pittsburgh; Frederick J. Bashour, producer. In 3-disc set MHS 837273M, recorded September 1984. Also in set: D29, 58a, 63, 64, 65a.

ORGAN AND INSTRUMENTS

D77. CONCERTO, DEUXIEME, FOR ORGAN AND STRING ORCHESTRA (1961)

Proprius PROP 7784. 1977. *Langlais/Te Deum & Deuxième concerto/Honegger/Fugue et choral.* Kjell Johnsen, organ; Kjell Ingebretsen, conductor; Engelbrekt Church, Stockholm. Recorded June 9-10, July 13, 1977. Also on disc: D53jj.

D78. CONCERTO, TROISIEME: RÉACTION, FOR ORGAN, STRING ORCHESTRA, AND TIMPANI (1971)

ABC Records ABCL 8103. 1981. *Poulenc concerto in g minor/ Langlais concerto no. 3 (Réaction).* Original version, uncut. Michael Dudman, organ; Sydney Symphony Orchestra; Patrick Thomas, conductor; David Hinder, producer; Rupert Mazlin, Allan Maclean, sound engineers; Sydney Town Hall, Australia.

BRASS

FRENCH HORN AND ORGAN

D79. AVE MARIS STELLA (1934)

Medias Music MEM 003. 1985. *Ave Maria.* Gilbert Esposito, French horn; Robert Martin, organ, Notre-Dame de la Garde, Marseille.

TRUMPET AND ORGAN

D80. CHORALS, SEPT, POUR TROMPETTE (1972)

    I. DE PROFUNDIS/AUS TIEFER NOT (DU FOND DE LA MISERE)
    II. EIN FESTE BURG (DIEU EST LE REMPART DE NOTRE VIE)
    III. VATER UNSER (NOTRE PERE AU ROYAUME DES CIEUX)
    IV. COMMANDMENTS/O DASS DOCH BALD DEIN FEUER BRENNTE
        (LORSQUE NOUS SOMMES DANS LES PLUS GRANDES DETRESSES)
    V. IN DULCI JUBILO
    VI. JESU, MEINE FREUDE
    VII. LOBE DEN HERREN

D80a.   Concerto Bayreuth FSM CB 16003. *Trumpet und orgel.* Ludwig Güttler, trumpet; Christoph Kircheis, organ. IV. VI. VII.

D80b.   Crystal Records S365. 1980. *The Voice of trumpet & organ.* Byron Pearson, trumpet; Arthur Vidrich, organ; First Baptist Church, Detroit; David Lau, recording engineer. I. II. Recorded in 1977.

D80c.   Disques Corelia CC 684463. 1984. *Orgue et cuivres à Saint Louis des Invalides.* Jean-Bernard Beauchamp, trumpet; Louis Kalck, organ; Paris. II. III. IV.

D80d.   Erato STU 71272, MCE 71272 (cassette). 1980. *Trompette et orgue/Vol. 10.* Maurice André, trumpet; André Luy, organ; Lausanne Cathedral, Switzerland. Recorded in February1979. II. III. V. VI. Also on disc: D83b.

D80e. International Pelgrims Group I.P.G. Aristocrate; S.F.S. 7.315. Decca QS 7.315. 1975. Original recording by Société Française du Son. 1975. *Trompette & orgue/Quatre compositeurs français contemporains.* André Bernard, trumpet; Jean Louis Gil, organ. Recorded June 1975 at Saint-Salomon-Saint-Grégoire, Pithiviers (Loiret). **II. IU. UII.** Also on disc: **D82a.**

D80f. Motette M 2004. *Works for trumpet and organ.* Freddy Grin, trumpet; Dick Klomp, organ; Marienstatt Abbey. Recorded July 1979. **I. U. UI. UII.** Also on disc: **D82b, 83c.**

D80g. Motette M 5012. 1984. Freddy Grin, trumpet; H. B. Orlinski, organ. **U. UII.** Also on disc: **D82c.**

D80h. Solstice SOL 14. 1980. *Jean Langlais à Notre-Dame de Paris.* Roger Delmotte, trumpet; Pierre Cochereau, organ. trumpet works recorded Feb. 3, 1980. **I. III. IU.** Also on disc: **D17f, 24.**

D81. PASTORALE ET RONDO (1982)

Motette Ursina M 2011. 1983. *Trompete und orgel Köln/Festive music from Altenberg Cathedral.* Edward H. Tarr, trumpet; Wolfgang G. Haas, trumpet; Paul Wisskirchen, organ.

D82. PIECE POUR TROMPETTE (1971)

D82a. International Pelgrims Group I.P.G. Aristocrate; S.F.S. 7.315. Decca QS 7.315. 1975. Original recording by Société Française du Son. 1975. *Trompette & orgue/Quatre compositeurs français contemporains.* André Bernard, trumpet; Jean Louis Gil, organ. Recorded June 1975 at Saint-Salomon-Saint-Grégoire, Pithiviers (Loiret). Also on disc: **D80e.**

D82b. Motette M 2004. *Works for trumpet and organ.* Freddy Grin, trumpet; Dick Klomp, organ. Recorded at Marienstatt Abbey, Germany, July 1979. Also on disc: **D80f, 83c.**

D82c. Motette M 5012. 1984. Freddy Grin, trumpet; H. B. Orlinski, organ. Also on disc: **D80g.**

D83. SONATINE (1976)

D83a. Crystal Records S661. 1982. *Voices of trumpets and organ.* Don Tison, trumpet; Arthur Vidrich, organ; First Baptist Church, Ann Arbor, Michigan; David Lau, recording engineer. Recorded in August 1979.

D83b. Erato STU 71272, MCE 71272 (cassette). 1980. *Trompette et orgue/Vol. 10.* Maurice André, trumpet; André Luy, organ; Lausanne Cathedral, Switzerland. Recorded in February 1979. Also on disc: **D80d.**

D83c. Motette M 2004. *Works for trumpet and organ.* Freddy Grin, trumpet; Dick Klomp, organ; Marienstatt Abbey, Germany. Recorded in July 1979. Also on disc: **D80f, 82b.**

D83d. Vista VPS 1107. 1982. Maurice Murphy, trumpet; Nicholas Jackson, organ; St. David's Cathedral, Wales. Also on disc: **D53ss.**

WOODWINDS

FLUTE AND ORGAN

D84. CINQ PIECES (1974)

D84a.   REM 10847.   1978. *Flute et orgue.* J. P. Prades, flute; Bruno Mathieu, organ, St. Louis, Lyon. Also on disc: **D40ee.**

D84b.   RLP 5011. 1979/80. *Flute and organ.*
Bent Larsen, flute; Peter Langberg, organ.

IMPROVISATION RECORDINGS MADE BY JEAN LANGLAIS

IMPROVISATION ON

D85. ADOROMP HOLL

Arion ARN 36 331. 1976. *Jean Langlais/Huit chants de Bretagne et improvisation sur le thème Adoromp Holl.* Sainte-Clotilde, Paris;   Claude Morel, recording engineer. Also on disc: **D31a.**

D86. ALLELUIA, MESSE DU TRES SAINT-SACREMENT &

CONFITEBOR TIBI, OFFERTOIRE DE LA MESSE DU SAINT NOM DE JESUS

Medias Music MEM 0009F, 009FC45. 1986. *Jean Langlais improvise à Sainte Clotilde.* Recorded November 11, 1986; released as part of Langlais' eightieth birthday celebration. Improvisation on two themes. Robert Martin, recording engineer. Also on disc: **D97b.**

D87. BRETON THEMES

GAIF 387 cassette. 1987. *Improvisation sur deux thèmes bretons.* Recorded January 31, 1987 at Sainte-Clotilde, Paris, for Groupe des Aphasiques d'Ile-de-France.

D88. CE QUE LE DIEU VEUT, CE SOIT FAITE TOUJOURS

Cantilena MC 1820. 1985. *Improvisations par Jean Langlais/ Ste. Clotilde-Paris.* Leo Dijns, recording engineer. Also on disc: **D93b, 94, 98, 99.**

D89. THE CHORALE "HERR GOTT, DICH LOBEN ALLE WIR"

Coronata 4001. *Orgeln im Elsass.* Recorded on August 4, 1983 in concert played on Kern organ of "der katholischen Kirche St. Martin im Masevaux-Mitschnitt." Also on disc: **D66b, 93c, 111, 112a.**

D90. CHORALFANTASIE ÜBER "AUS TIEFER NOT"

Motette Ursina M 1037. 1981. *An der Cavaillé-Coll-Orgel von Ste. Clotilde-Paris: Jean Langlais.* Also on disc: **D92.**

D91. CONDITOR ALME SIDERUM

Motette Ursina M 1023. 1979. *Jean Langlais spielt französische orgelmusik in der Abteikirche Marienstatt.* Concert of November 5, 1978. Also on disc: **D40w, 53ff, 97c, 125.**

D92. FANTASIE ÜBER B.A.C.H.

Motette Ursina M 1037. 1981. *An der Cavaillé-Coll-Orgel von Ste. Clotilde-Paris: Jean Langlais.* Also on disc: **D90.**

D93. KYRIE "ORBIS FACTOR"

D93a.　Avant Quart AQ-3001-AT. 1969. *Hommage à Jean Langlais.* Sainte-Clotilde. Also on disc: **D57m, 60a, 62a, 73c, 97a, 100.**

D93b.　Cantilena MC 1820. 1985. *Improvisations par Jean Langlais/Ste. Clotilde-Paris.* Leo Dijns, recording engineer. Also on disc: **D88, 94, 98, 99.**

D93c.　Coronata 4001. *Orgeln im Elsass.* Recorded on August 4, 1983 in concert played on the Kern organ of "der katholischen Kirche St. Martin im Masevaux-Mitschnitt." Also on disc: **D66b, 89, 111, 112a.** The five other organists on this record are Hans Martin Balz, Jean-Claude Zehnder, Hermann J. Busch, Guy Bovet, and Daniel Roth.

D94. LOUANGE A DIEU

Cantilena MC 1820. 1985. *Improvisations par Jean Langlais/ Ste. Clotilde - Paris.* Also on disc: **D88, 93b, 98, 99.**

D95. THE LOURDES HYMN

Vantage SLBP-1015. *Christ in Majesty.* Played November 10, 1969 at the conclusion of the recessional (after *Solemn Mass* premiere), National Shrine of the Immaculate Conception, Washington, D.C. Also on disc: **D25, 42e, 57k, 106b, 112b, 113b.**

D96. PUER NATUS EST

Motette Ursina M 5004. 1983. *Weihnachten in der Abtei Marienstatt.*

D97. SALVE REGINA

D97a.　Avant Quart AQ-3001-AT. 1969. *Hommage à Jean Langlais.* Sainte-Clotilde. Also on disc: **D57m, 60a, 62a, 73c, 93a, 100.**

D97b.　Medias Music MEM 0009F, 009FC45. 1986. *Jean Langlais improvise à Sainte Clotilde.* Recorded on November 11, 1986; released as part of Langlais' eightieth birthday celebration. Improvisation on two themes, the solemn and simple tone melodies of the *Salve Regina.* Robert Martin, recording engineer. Also on disc: **D86.**

D97c.　Motette Ursina M 1023. 1979. *Jean Langlais spielt französische orgelmusik in der Abteikirche Marienstatt.* Concert of November 5, 1978. Also on disc: **D40w, 53ff, 91, 125.**

D98. SEIGNEUR JESUS, NE PAS REBUTE

Cantilena MC 1820. 1985.
Improvisations par Jean Langlais/Ste. Clotilde - Paris.
Also on disc: D88, 93b, 94, 99.

D99. VENI CREATOR

Cantilena MC 1820. 1985.
Improvisations par Jean Langlais/Ste. Clotilde - Paris.
Also on disc: D88, 93b, 94, 98.

D100. VENI CREATOR & EIN' FESTE BURG

Avant Quart AQ-3001-AT. 1969. *Hommage à Jean Langlais.*
Sainte-Clotilde. Also on disc: D57m, 60a, 62a, 73c, 93a, 97a.

WORKS OF OTHER COMPOSERS RECORDED BY JEAN LANGLAIS

Recorded at the Basilica of Sainte-Clotilde, Paris unless otherwise
stated.

BACH, JOHANN SEBASTIAN

[Entries by BWV number]

D101. BWV 533 PRELUDE AND FUGUE IN E MINOR

Motette Ursina M 1072. 1981. *Langlais Spielt - Plays - Joue
BACH.* Marienstatt Abbey organ, Germany.
Also released as Motette M 1066. *Orgelwerke von Joh. Seb.
Bach/Jean Langlais an der orgel der Abtei Marienstatt.*
Also on disc: D102b, 103, 104b, 105, 106a, 107.

D102. BWV 565 TOCCATA AND FUGUE IN D MINOR

D102a. Match Records MR 17.517; Trianon A17.017. 25 cm. 1957.
Récital Jean Langlais à l'orgue de César Franck.
Also on disc: D104a, 108.

D102b. Motette Ursina M 1072. 1981. Not on Motette M 1066.
Langlais Spielt - Plays - Joue BACH. Marienstatt Abbey organ,
Germany. Also on disc: D101, 103, 104b, 105, 106a, 107.

D103. SIX ORGELBÜCHLEIN CHORALES

BWV 610 JESU, MEINE FREUDE
BWV 621 DA JESUS AN DEM KREUZE STUND
BWV 622 O MENSCH, BEWEIN DEIN SÜNDE GROSS
BWV 625 CHRIST LAG IN TODESBANDEN
BWV 637 DURCH ADAMS FALL IST GANZ VERDERBT
BWV 638 ES IST DAS HEIL UNS KOMMEN HER

Motette Ursina M 1072. 1981. Motette M 1066.
Langlais Spielt - Plays - Joue BACH. Marienstatt Abbey
organ, Germany. Also on disc: D101, 102b, 104b, 105, 106a, 107.

**D104. BWV 645 WACHET AUF, RUFT UNS DIE STIMME
(EVEILLEZ-VOUS, LA VOIX DU VEILLEUR VOUS APPELLE)**

D104a. Match Records M.R. 17.516, Trianon A17.016. 25 cm. 1957.
Récital Jean Langlais. Also on disc: **D108, 113a.**

D104b. Motette Ursina M 1072. 1981. Motette M 1066.
Langlais Spielt - Plays - Joue BACH. Marienstatt Abbey
organ, Germany. Also on disc: **D101, 102b, 103, 105, 106a, 107.**

**D105. BWV 653 AN WASSERFLÜSSEN BABYLON
BWV 659 NUN KOMM DER HEIDEN HEILAND**

Motette Ursina M 1072. 1981. Motette M 1066.
Langlais Spielt - Plays - Joue BACH. Marienstatt Abbey
organ, Germany. Also on disc: **D101, 102b, 103, 104b, 106a, 107.**

D106. BWV 680 WIR GLAUBEN ALL AN EINEN GOTT

D106a. Motette Ursina M 1072. 1981. Motette M 1066.
Langlais Spielt - Plays - Joue BACH. Marienstatt Abbey
organ, Germany. Also on disc: **D101, 102b, 103, 104b, 105, 107.**

D106b. Vantage SLBP-1015. *Christ in majesty.*
Recorded in concert, November 10, 1969, National Shrine of the
Immaculate Conception, Washington, D. C.
Also on disc: **D25, 42e, 57k, 95, 112b, 113b.**

D107. BWV 727 HERZLICH TUT MICH VERLANGEN

Motette Ursina M 1072. 1981. Motette M 1066.
Langlais Spielt - Plays - Joue BACH. Marienstatt Abbey
organ, Germany. Also on disc: **D101, 102b, 103, 104b, 105, 106a.**

D108. JESUS QUE MA JOIE DEMEURE, transcription Maurice Duruflé.

Match Records M.R. 17.516, Trianon A17.016. 25 cm. 1957.
Récital Jean Langlais. Also on disc: **D104a, 113a.**

BACH, K. PH. EMM.

D109. SONATA IN D MAJOR

Erato EFM 42.035. 25 cm. 1957. Series Fiori Musicali.
Recital Jean Langlais/Musique ancienne.
Also on disc: **D114, 122, 123.**

BOYVIN, JACQUES

D110. DIALOGUE SUR LA VOIX HUMAINE

Match MR 17.517; Trianon A17.017. 25 cm. 1957.
Récital Jean Langlais à l'orgue de César Franck.
Also on disc: **D102a, 115.**

D111. GRAND DIALOGUE, SECOND LIVRE D'ORGUE

Coronata 4001. 1983. *Orgeln im Elsass.* Church of St. Martin in
Masevaux. Also on disc: **D66b, 89, 93c, 112a.**

CALVIERE, ANTOINE

D112. PIECE D'ORGUE

D112a. Coronata 4001. 1983. *Orgeln im Elsass.* Church of St. Martin in Masevaux. Also on disc: **D66b, 89, 93c, 111.**

D112b. Vantage SLBP-1015. *Christ in Majesty.*
Recorded Nov. 10, 1969, in recital at the National Shrine of the Immaculate Conception in Washington, D.C.
Also on disc: **D25, 42e, 57k, 95, 106b, 113b.**

COUPERIN, FRANÇOIS

D113. OFFERTOIRE SUR LES GRANDS JEUX (Mass for the Convents)

D113a. Match Records M.R. 17.516, Trianon A17.016. 25 cm. 1957.
Récital Jean Langlais. Also on disc: **D104a, 108.**

D113b. Vantage SLBP-1015. *Christ in Majesty.*
Recorded November 10, 1969, in recital.
Also on disc: **D25, 42e, 57k, 95, 106b, 112b.**

COUPERIN, LOUIS

D114. CHACONNE EN SOL MINEUR

Erato EFM 42.035. 25 cm. 1957. Series Fiori Musicali.
Recital Jean Langlais/Musique ancienne.
Also on disc: **D109, 122, 123.**

DU MAGE, PIERRE

D115. GRAND JEU

Match MR 17.517; Trianon A17.017. 25 cm. 1957.
Récital Jean Langlais à l'orgue de César Franck.
Also on disc: **D102a, 110.**

FAURE, GABRIEL

D116. MARIA MATER GRATIAE (Motet, Op. 47, no. 2)

Erato EFM 18012. 1958-1961. Musical Heritage Society MHS 4349. 1981. *Wedding Music.* Stéphane Caillat Vocal Ensemble, Stéphane Caillat, director; Jean Langlais, organ, Guy Laporte, engineer. Also on disc: **D117.**

D117. MESSE BASSE

Erato EFM 18012. 1958-1961. Musical Heritage Society MHS 4349. 1981. *Wedding Music.* Stéphane Caillat Vocal Ensemble, Stéphane Caillat, director; Jocelyne Chamonin, soprano soloist; Jean Langlais, organ, Guy Laporte, engineer. Also on disc: **D116.**

FRANCK, CESAR

D118. Twelve works. D118a and 118b are 3-disc sets.

CANTABILE	**PRELUDE, FUGUE ET VARIATION**
FANTAISIE EN LA MAJEUR	**PRIERE**
FANTAISIE EN UT MAJEUR	**TROIS CHORALS**
FINALE	**1. MI MAJEUR**
GRANDE PIECE SYMPHONIQUE	**2. SI MINEUR**
PASTORALE	**3. LA MINEUR**
PIECE HEROIQUE	

D118a. Arion ARN 336 008. 1975. *César Franck à Sainte-Clotilde.*
Claude Morel, engineer.

D118b. Gregorian Institute of America. M-108-10. S-208-10. 1964.
The Complete organ works of César Franck.

D119. GRANDE PIECE SYMPHONIQUE

D119a. Ducretet-Thomson LAG-1017. 1953. (London DTL 93071)
César Franck: pièces d'orgue. Also on disc: D120.

D119b. Opal 811. 1983. originally ADU-142-1.
Charles Tournemire/Jean Langlais/ Cesar Franck: Pupil and successors at Sainte-Clotilde.
Historical reissue, transfer effected by Denis Hall.

D120. FINALE and PRIERE

Ducretet-Thomson LAG-1017. 1953. (London DTL 93071)
César Franck: pièces d'orgue. Also on disc: D119a.

MESSIAEN, OLIVIER

D121. APPARITION DE L'EGLISE ÉTERNELLE
LES BERGERS (La Nativité du Seigneur)   O SACRUM CONVIVIUM

Ducretet-Thomson 270 C 003. 1954. *Messiaen/Langlais*
Janine Collard, Mezzo-soprano on *O Sacrum Convivium.*
Also on disc: D16b.
The first recording made by Langlais, and the first French LP recording of Messiaen. (*See:* B370)

PACHELBEL, JOHANN

D122. NEUF VERSETS DE MAGNIFICAT DU 6e TON

Erato EFM 42.035. 25 cm. 1957. Series Fiori Musicali.
Recital Jean Langlais/Musique ancienne.
Also on disc: D109, 114, 123.

PURCELL, HENRY

D123. TROMPETTE ET AIR

Erato EFM 42.035. 25 cm. 1957. Series Fiori Musicali.
Recital Jean Langlais/Musique ancienne.
Also on disc: D109, 114, 122.

TOURNEMIRE, CHARLES

D124. **PIECES FROM** *L'ORGUE MYSTIQUE*

COMMUNION from **NATIVITE DE LA SAINTE-VIERGE (17th Office, 3rd Cycle, opus 57)**   and complete office, 5 pieces:
EPIPHANIE (7th Office, 1st Cycle, opus 55)

Erato LDE 3049. 1960. *Œuvres pour orgue d'inspiration grégorienne.* Gregorian chants sung by male choir diected by René Malherbe.   Also on disc: **D401, 49b, 53e, 53k, 58c.**

VIERNE, LOUIS

D125. **SUR LE RHIN** and **CARILLON DE WESTMINSTER**

Motette Ursina M 1023. *Jean Langlais spielt Französische orgelmusik in der Abteikirche Marienstatt.* Recording of concert played on Nov. 5, 1978. Also on disc: **D40w, 53ff, 91, 97c.**

ADDENDA

Information on the following discs was received after the discography was compiled:

D126.   Arsica 1624. P. Heuser, organ; Kevelaar Basilica.
Composition: **Te Deum** (*See*: W162, D53)

D127.   Guilde Internationale du Disques CHS 2348. Olivier Alain; St. Merry, Paris. Composition: **Neuf Pièces pour orgue** [partial?] (*See*: W165, D57)

D128.   *Jean Langlais Vokalwerk II.*   Scheduled for release in Spring,1988, by Coronata.
Marlies Schauerte, soprano; Helga Schauerte, organ; Kammerchor Schmallenberg, Ulrich Schauerte, director; Ansgar Ballhorn, producer. Basilica of Sainte-Clotilde, Paris. Recorded June 19, 21, 1987. Compositions include **Hymn of Praise "Te Deum Laudamus," Lauda Jerusalem Dominum, Mass in Ancient Style, Missa Misericordia Domini, Sacerdos et Pontifex "Tu es Petrus," Ubi Caritas** (*See*: W35, W36, D11, W43, W117, W73)

D129.   Motette M 11170. Naji S. Hakim, organ; Basilique du Sacré-Cœur de Montmartre, Paris.   Recorded April 17, 1987.   Compositions: **Hommage à Rameau, Te Deum, Incantation pour un jour Saint** (*See*: W138, W162, W141, D39a, D53gg)

D130.   Priory PR 214. 1987. *Widor and Langlais.* Christopher Brayne, organ; Wells Cathedral, England.
Composition: **B.A.C.H.** (*See*: W125)

D131.   Spoken Arts 213. Contrepoint Vocal Ensemble/Gaussens.
Compositions: **La Ville d'Is, Le Lin** (#3 of Trois Chansons Populaires Bretonnes, 1954), and **Guillaume, Antoine, et Pierre** (#2 of Trois Noëls, 1959). (*See*: D27b, W26, W50)

Bibliography

"*See*" citations refer to individual works and particular performances of those works as described in the "Works and Performances" section (*e.g.*, *See*: W12). "D" citations refer to the "Discography" section. *Diapason* is a French record review, while *The Diapason* is an American organ journal. References to individual compositions follow the general reference section.

GENERAL REFERENCES

B1. Abel, Jean. "Cinq minutes avec le compositeur Jean Langlais. « Grâce à la musique, oublier ses soucis »." *Le Provençal* (Marseille), July 4, 1976. Interview with Langlais in Marseille.
"-- quand vous considérez l'ensemble de vos œuvres, quel jugement portez-vous?
-- Sans doute y a-t-il des pages que je n'écrirais pas aujourd'hui. Mais enfin, j'ai été constamment de bonne volonté. Je n'ai jamais fait une concession et jamais je n'en ferai. J'ai cherché toute ma vie la poésie." (JA: When you consider the whole body of your works, what is your opinion? JL: There are certainly some pages that I would not write today. Nevertheless, I have always been sincere. I never made any concession, and I never will. All my life I've looked for poetry.)

B2. Alain, Olivier. "Chants grégoriens et œuvres d'orgue inspirées du chant grégorien." Album notes for Erato LDE 3049 disc, 1960.
Excellent discussion of influences in the styles of French composers from Franck to Langlais.

B3. Alston, Vernon. "Organ recital reveals power of musicianship." *State-Times* (Baton Rouge), March 13, 1962.
Langlais' compositions expressed "the poetry and grandeur France rightfully claims for her artists."

B4. Arnold, A. N. "Royal Festival Hall organ recitals." *Musical Opinion* 102 (December 1978): 104.
Langlais, "always a welcome visitor to these shores," in London, October 11, 1978. André Marchal, in the audience, gave the theme for the concluding improvisation. *Te Deum* was the encore after a prolonged ovation. (*See*: B27, another review of the same recital.)

B5. Assistant, Un. "Solennité artistique du 19 Janvier." *Chronique du Patronage St. Pierre*, February 1936.

January 19, 1936 recital included four pieces of 16th to 18th
century masters, Bach, Franck, Tournemire, Dupré, his own
Nativité, and an improvisation.   He was described as "the young
and already famous Jean Langlais,...with eyes closed to the light of
day, but whose interior vision is luminous and profound."

B6. "Auditions des ouvrages des élèves des classes de Composition et des
lauréats du Prix de Rome." *Le Courrier Musical,* December 15,
1934.
Deux pièces for organ by Langlais, student of Paul Dukas, were
played by the composer and Gaston Litaize in a two-piano version.
(Probably two sections of *Trois Paraphrases grégoriennes,
Ave Maria* and *Te Deum.*)

B7. Barber, Clarence H.   "Jean Langlais and Ste. Clotilde organ visited by
American." *The Diapason* 37, no. 9 (August, 1946): 8.
Account of Langlais playing high and low masses during his first
year as organist of Ste. Clotilde, with interview.

B8. Barnard, L. S. "Philip Dore's French music lectures." *Musical Opinion*
76 (February 1953): 299–301.
Sixth lecture, given November 5, 1952, University of London at the
London College of Music, in a course "The Renaissance of French
Organ Music." Reports begin in December 1952 issue. Langlais is
one who uses plainchant "rigged up in a very up-to-date manner."

B9. Barrett, Gavin. "London organ recitals." *Musical Opinion* 94 (December
1970): 156.
Langlais' blindness frees him from being tied to the printed score,
consequently his performances "breathe." *Incantation pour un
jour saint* and *Chant de paix* are cited as his most popular
organ works with British audiences.

B10. Barrillon, Raymond. "La poétesse américaine Ellen Keller est à Paris."
Parisien Libere, November 16, 1946.
Helen Keller visited classes at the National Institute for the Young
Blind, staying the longest time in the room where the students,
directed by Langlais at the organ, sang for her.

B11. "Basilique Sainte-Clotilde/concert spirituel." *Chronique du Congrès,*
part 2 of *Actes du Troisième Congrès International de
Musique Sacrée.* Paris: Edition du Congrès, 1959.
Page 69 lists the works played by Langlais on July 3, 1957 for the
Third International Congress of Sacred Music in Paris.   Concert
photos of Langlais and the Ensemble Vocal de Beauvais.

B12. Beckley, Paul V. "Blind Paris organist explores keys for debut here
Tuesday." *New York Herald Tribune,* April 19, 1952.
Interview the day before Langlais' first New York recital, with
photo of husband and wife at the organ of Central Presbyterian
Church, Park Avenue. Remarks about his methods of composition and
his fondness for bicycling. "He explained that he makes his way by
following the sound of the wheels of a bicycle ridden ahead of him
by his wife. He admitted   he would not like to attempt this on
Fifth Ave., but he indicated   the measure of his self-confidence
when he confided that he had often taken his children along on such
jaunts, riding on the handlebars."

B13. Beechey, Gwilym. "The organ music of Jean Langlais." *Musical
Opinion* 101 (July 1978): 405–413, 438.

Published organ music 1936-1977, with frank evaluations. His early works brought him popularity, but two of his most significant works (*Premiére Symphonie* and *Essai*) are not widely played.

B14. Berens, Fritz. "Langlais: notes on a French organist." *The Fort Worth Press*, February 23, 1975, 31A.
Recital February 21 in Ed Landreth Auditorium, TCU, played prior to his first honorary doctorate. Improvisation is the prevailing tendency found in Langlais's compositions. "It often seemed as if the composer were playing with sound, exploring proviously (sic) unheard sound combinations. The result was always interesting, often fascinating, pointing to possibilities of sound the contemporary composer may some day fully utilize."

B15. Berry, Ray. "Recitals and concerts." *The American Organist* 39, no. 4 (April 1956): 127.
Langlais' concert at Central Presbyterian Church on March 5, 1956, during his third American tour.

B16. Bertault, Julien. "Jean Langlais. Organiste et compositeur aveugle." **(Blind Organist and Composer.)** *Le Nouveau Messager de la Vendee* (La Roche sur Tyon, France), August 23, 1971.
Brief biography; the author's friendship with Langlais started in 1923 in Paris.

B17. Bertho, Hervé. "Le « cas » Jean Langlais compositeur et aphasique." *Ouest-France* (Rennes), April 29, 1986. [Reprinted, *Le Valentin Haüy*, 1986, no. 3: 5.]
Aftermath of Langlais' 1984 stroke. "Le cas du compositeur et organiste Jean Langlais, atteint de paralysie et surtout d'aphasie, demeure énigmatique: il a perdu l'usage de la parole et de la lecture mais joue à nouveau de l'orgue." **(The case of the organist composer Jean Langlais, struck by paralysis and especially by aphasia, remains enigmatic: he has lost some speech and reading functions, but plays the organ again.)**

B18. Biba, Otto. "Berichte/Internationale Orgeltagung der GdO in Paris." *Ars Organi* 54 (October 1977): 207-08.
Members of the group *Gesellschaft der Orgelfreunde* visited Langlais at Sainte-Clotilde on August 5, 1977.

B19. Billings, David A. "An interview with Jean Langlais." Typescript, 1981, 8 pages.
Transcription of interview led by Jim Cunningham at Pittsburgh's public-broadcasting station WQED-FM on September 21, 1981, with Langlais, his wife Marie-Louise, and Ann Labounsky Steele.

B20. -----. "Langlais in Pittsburgh." *The American Organist* 16, no. 2 (February 1982): 35-36.
Report on radio interview, PBS WQED-FM, September 21, 1981, Langlais' recital that evening at Calvary Episcopal Church, and six masterclasses at Duquesne University's School of Music.

B21. Bingham, Seth. "Come, let us worship on wings of music; be lifted on high." *The Diapason* 45, no. 12 (November 1, 1954): 21.
Report on the week-long celebration in France, June 1952, of the 100th anniversary of the death of Louis Braille. Langlais conducted the choir at the memorial service in the Cathedral of Notre-Dame de Paris.

B22. -----. "The choral masses of Jean Langlais." *Caecilia* (Omaha) 86, no. 2 (Summer1959): 73-82.
Analysis of four choral masses which have been published and recorded: *Mass in Ancient Style, Messe Solennelle, Missa "in simplicitate," Missa Salve Regina.*

B23. -----. "Jean Langlais, French organ composer." *Organ Institute Quarterly* 3, no. 3 (Summer 1953): 13-24.
Brief description and comments on organ works published 1945-52. English translation of Dufourcq's notes on organ works published 1931-34 in *La Musique d'Orgue Française de Jehan Titelouze à Jehan Alain.*

B24. -----. "Langlais thrills New York audience at his debut recital." *The Diapason* 43, no. 7 (June 1, 1952): 8.
Langlais' first recital in New York City was at Central Presbyterian Church on April 22 before a large audience which included many famous New York and New England organists.   As performer, composer, and improvisor he made a superb impression.

B25. -----. "The organist's liturgical role." *Caecilia* (Omaha) 88, no. 1 (Spring 1961): 15-28.
Excellent background on the controversy of the role of organ music in the Catholic churches of France, particularly Paris, following the Instruction issued in Rome in 1958 by the Sacred Congregation of Rites. Translation of eleven questions posed by Norbert Dufourcq to Canon Martinot, professor in the Faculty of Theology at Toulouse, with summary of answers. [From "Le rôle liturgique de l'orgue à la lumière des dernières *Instructions romaines,*" in *L'Orgue* 90.] The Parisian practice of low mass seeming to be an organ recital with silent liturgy is no longer tolerated. Includes comments by 12 organists or clergy. Langlais' works are mentioned twice by clergy as being unsuitable for service playing, as are most works by Vierne, Widor, Franck, Alain, Tournemire, Dupré, and the Handel organ concertos. These should be reserved for organ recitals.

B26. Birkby, Arthur.   "Jean Langlais/an interview with the organist-composer." *Clavier* 11, no. 3 (March 1972): 29-31.
Conversation on Langlais' life, other French organists, and the status of the church organist in France. "A salary of forty dollars per month is considered quite good for a French organist; thus, it is always necessary to supplement one's income by teaching, or by having some business enterprise in spare time. Langlais, himself, teaches many students at the Schola Cantorum; and his world travels as a recitalist are well known."

B27. Birley, Margaret. "Organ and choral recitals." *The Musical Times* 119 (December 1978): 1077.
Review of Langlais at Royal Festival Hall, London, October 11, 1978. "His *Visions prophétiques* was predominantly rhetorical, with vehement discords and sudden changes of colour and texture; equally persuasive was the *Complainte de Pontkalleg,* simple modal variations on a Breton folksong."

B28. Bloch, Catherine.   "Maître Jean Langlais donnera un récital à Saint-Félix-Lauragais."   *La Depeche Du Midi* (Toulouse), September 5, 1969.
Interview in Escalquens, native area of his wife Jeannette.

B29. Boeglin, Paul. "Une interview de Jean Langlais. « J'aime tout ce qui est beau... »." *L'Alsace* (Mulhouse), June 9, 1972.
Langlais speaks of the creativity of the French organ composers Franck and Tournemire. Influences on his own career and works were his teachers Dupré, Marchal, Dukas; his fellow student Messiaen; and the organ at Sainte-Clotilde.

B30. Boros, Ethel. "Organist's recital bliss at museum." *Cleveland Plain Dealer*, November 19, 1964.
Review of Langlais at the Cleveland Museum of Art. "...he showed once again his complete control of his imposing instrument."

B31. *Boys Town Times*, unsigned. October 13, 1961, 1.
Photo of Langlais receiving award from Archbishop Gerald T. Bergin with caption "The Medal of St. Caecilia, an exclusive Boys Town award, is given in recognition of outstanding contributions to the field of liturgical music." (*See*: B36)

B32. Brierre, Anne. "En vacances à Escalquens/Le Maître d'orgues Jean Langlais prépare sa prochaine tournée, aux États-Unis." *Sud-Ouest*, August 31, 1964.
An interview with Langlais, vacationing at the home of his wife's family in Escalquens before starting his ninth recital tour in America, forty concerts in three months. His photo caption is: "La vie d'artiste? Une existence d'abnégation, mais aussi de joies profondes et irremplaçables."(An artist's life? A self-sacrificial existence,but also with deep and irreplaceable joys.)

B33. Brousse, J.-J. "Vivre sans voir." (Life without sight.) *Detective* (France), November 8, 1963.
Langlais spoke of his childhood, marriage, children, and career; photo of him teaching an American at his Parisian apartment.

B34. Burns, Richard C., and Wayne Leupold. "The use of recordings in establishing performance practices for 19th/20th century organ music." *Association for Recorded Sound Collections, Journal* 8, no. 3 (1976): 32-46.
Dr. Robert S. Lord, on a panel at the AGO Regional Convention of 1973 in Syracuse, N.Y., discussed the Franck recordings made by Tournemire, Langlais' comments on these recordings, and his performance style of Franck.

B35. Butcher, Harold. "Jean Langlais, blind organist, scores success at concert." *The New Mexican* (Santa Fe), March 22, 1962.
Langlais showed his immense power as a musician and the "poetic" quality of the new Moller organ. "The large audience became intensely aware of the depth and meaning of organ music."

B36. "Caecilian medal is presented to Jean Langlais." *Boys Town Times* (Nebraska), September 8, 1961, 1.
Citation for tenth Caecilian Medal: "Mr. Langlais, as organist of the Basilica of Saint Clotilde in Paris, carries on eminently the tradition of his great predecessors Cesar Franck and Charles Tournemire. All the world is his debtor, not only for the exquisite artistry of his performances, but for his first rank contribution to contemporary organ literature and his many compositions destined to enhance Christian worship." (*See*: B31)

B37. Cantrell, Scott. "Langlais, Jean." *High Fidelity* 30, no. 7 (July 1980): 70. Reprinted in *Records in Review, 1981 Edition*, 177–178. Great Barrington, MA: Wyeth Press, 1981.
Review of Labounsky recording. (*See:* B125) Improvisatory, richly colored works with a large stylistic range from "gentle modality to uncompromising dissonance."

B38. Carbou, François. "Langlais joue Langlais." Translated by Susan Landale. Liner notes for disc Solstice 1.
Langlais spoke about 11 works on January 21, 1978.

[B321a] Case, Del Williams. "A study and performance of three organ works by Langlais, Dupré and Messiaen." D.M.A. diss., University of Southern California, 1973. (*See:* B321a, Poèmes Evangéliques)

B39. Chasse, Charles. "Jean Langlais, organiste breton et aveugle, a succédé à César Franck dans l'église de Ste-Clotilde." *Le Telegramme* (Brest), 24 and 25 December 1947.
Two-part article: biography, Langlais playing the Vesper service, and interview. Compositional influences are Breton themes, architecture of Beethoven, classicism of Dukas and Dupré, Bartok's use of folk melodies, and Albert Roussel's *Festin de l'Araignée*.

B40. Chatellard, Abbé Francis. "Plain chant sur les orgues savoyardes." *Messager Patriotique Thonon*, August 26, 1960.
Celebrations of the centenary of the return of Savoy to France (**"le Centenaire de la Savoie française"**) included Langlais at Megève.

B41. Ciccone, Louis. "Gaston Litaize et l'Institut National des Jeunes Aveugles." In *Gaston Litaize*, **Cahiers et mémoires de l'Orgue,** special number of the revue *L'Orgue*, 34 (1985): 24–25.
Litaize speaks of Langlais several times, calling him his best comrade (**"meilleur camarade"**) at the INJA. In 1964 Litaize succeeded Langlais as choir director of the school chorale. Page 37 has a photo of the Paris Conservatory 1930 *Classe d'orgue de Marcel Dupré* of ten students including Litaize and Langlais.

B42. Cogen, Pierre. Untitled insert with recording Tempo FR 760310, "Jean Langlais/Œuvres d'orgue inspirées du chant grégorien." 1976.
Analysis of the four recorded works, with chant themes: *Incantation pour un jour saint; Offrande à Marie; Ave Maria, Ave Maris Stella;* and *Suite médiévale.*

B43. Cohn, Arthur. *Recorded classical music (A critical guide).* New York: Schirmer Books, Macmillan Co., 1981.
Langlais has four listings (*see* : B278c, B303); his music is classified as chromatic but disciplined. "All the designs are clear and the textures avoid overload."

B44. Cooksey, Steven Lee. "Impressionistic aspects of twentieth-century French organ literature." Ph.D. diss., Washington University, St. Louis, 1972, iii–181.
Langlais is grouped with composers whose style is derived from the Romantic Era but who occasionally use impressionistic devices. *Chant de Paix*, *Hommage à Frescobaldi*, *Incantation, Poems Evangéliques, Suite médiévale*, and *Trois Paraphrases grégoriennes* are discussed and analysed.

B45. "Au Conservatoire de Paris." *Ouest-France* (Rennes), June 25, 1934.
Announcement of Langlais' second prize in musical composition at
the Paris Conservatory for two pieces for organ and orchestra (W4,
W5), with list of his other diplomas, prizes, and awards.

B46. Coqueux-Le Boel, Pierre. "Jean Langlais, compositeur et organiste
breton Docteur Honoris Causa aux U.S.A." *Ouest-France* (Rennes),
March 1975.
Langlais' reactions at being awarded an honorary doctorate at TCU
in Fort Worth, his musical life and compositions.

B47. Craig, Dale. "Master organist Langlais excels in Stanford show." *Palo
Alto Times*, February 15, 1967, 25.
Langlais' recital before a large audience at Stanford University.

B48. Cressard, Pierre. "L'Artiste doit être un apôtre." n.d., n.p.
Interview before Rennes recital, May 15,1941, with photo.

B49. Cunkle, Frank. "Jean Langlais falls on ice, breaks upper right arm." *The
Diapason* 57, no. 4 (March 1966): 21.
Accident in Paris, Christmas Day, 1965.

B50. -----. "Langlais in the Chicago area." *The Diapason* 58, no. 4 (March
1967): 35.
Recital of January 23 was "the most satisfactory one he has given
here." All seats sold out weeks ahead.

B51. -----. "We visit Jean Langlais." *The Diapason* 55, no. 8 (July 1964):
35.
Langlais at home and church in Paris, with five photos.

B52. Dalton, Sydney. "Performance by Langlais is rewarding." *The Nashville Banner*, February 16, 1962, 7.
" He has a biting harmonic sense that is almost acrid at times, but
it is always meaningful, as well as effective."

B53. Darasse, Xavier. "Langlais, Jean." *The New Grove Dictionary of
Music and Musicians*, edited by Stanley Sadie, 10: 452. London:
Macmillan Publishers Ltd., 1980.
Langlais, following Tournemire's tradition of using Gregorian
themes, shows great inventiveness while employing rich polymodal
harmonies.

B54. Denis, Pierre. "L'activité des «Amis de l'Orgue» saison 1966-1967."
L'Orgue 124 (October-December 1967): 1-2.
On October 20, 1966 the "Friends of the Organ" honored the
eightieth birthday of Marcel Dupré; Langlais was among his former
students who spoke and played.

B55. -----. "Les aveugles et l'école d'orgue française." *L'Orgue* 83 (April-
September 1957): 13-20.

B56. -----. "L'œuvre d'orgue de Jean Langlais." *L'Orgue* 100 (October-
December 1961): 180-194.
Excellent article: brief biography, discussion of influences on
Langlais' compositional style, characteristics of his musical
language, forms employed, and organ works composed 1930-1961.

B57. -----. "Les organistes français d'aujourd'hui. IV. Jean Langlais."
L'Orgue 52 (July-September 1949): 66-72.

Brief biography with good interview and photo of Langlais at Sainte-Clôtilde in 1949.

B58. -----. "Jean Langlais." *De Praestant* (Tongerlo, Belgium) October 1956, 77-80.

B59. Doar, Harriet. "Blind organist says practice ... practice." *The Charlotte Observer* (North Carolina), March 18, 1962, 5D.
Langlais' master class taught at Winthrop College the night before his 140th concert in the United States, on fifth U.S. concert tour.

B60. Dodane, Charles. "Chronique musicale/Jean Langlais aux grandes orgues de St-Jean." *La Depeche du Midi* (Toulouse), April 11, 1961.
Besançon recital of 9 April 1961, with discussion of sacred and secular influences in Langlais' works.

B61. -----. "Jean Langlais qui était l'invité des Amis de l'Orgue reste le musicien français le plus demandé en Amérique." *Le Journal de Nancy, L'Est Republicain*, Nov. 11, 1961.
Interview with Langlais at Cathedral Saint-Jean in Besançon, shortly before his three-month tour of the U.S.A. Photo of him playing the cathedral organ, with American student Lucie Howells, his guide and concert assistant, in the background.

B62. Duckworth, Manly. "27th Bach Festival one of finest ever." *Winter Park Herald* (Florida), March 3, 1962.
Langlais' second appearance at the Bach Festival, Rollins College. "His beautifully balanced program was devoted to Bach and his French precursors. His playing genuinely illuminates the music. There are the French virtues of clarity and sobriety."

B63. Dufourcq, Norbert. *La musique d'orgue française de Jehan Titelouze à Jehan Alain.* 2d ed. Paris: Librairie Fleury, 1949.
Langlais' works are discussed on pages 227-231.

B64. -----. "La musique religieuse en Europe jusqu'a 1940, II. Musique instrumentale." In *La musique, des origines à nos jours.* Paris: Librairie Larousse, 1946.
Page 429, the concept of the organ as a substutite for an orchestra, and the school of symphonic organ composers. Langlais is listed as one of the disciples of Tournemire.

B65. -----. "Panorama de la musique d'orgue française au XXe siècle. III: La génération de l'après guerre." *La Revue Musicale* 20 (March 1939): 103-117.
Discussion of Langlais' compositions is on page 108.

B66. -----. "Réflexions sur la musique d'orgue en France." *L'Orgue* 154 (April-June 1975): 33-39.
Comparison of Jehan Alain and Langlais is on page 37.

B67. -----. "Le rôle liturgique de l'orgue." *L'Orgue* 90 (April-June 1959): 52-55.
Canon Martinot interviewed, February 1959, on the organ's place in the Catholic liturgy in view of recent instructions from Rome. (For English translation, summary, and discussion, *see*: B25.)

B68. Einhardt, Eileen. "Organist enchants audience." *Illinois State Journal* (Springfield), October 25, 1969.
A standing-room-only audience heard Langlais play on the Casavant

organ of the First Methodist Church. "At the first note the atmosphere was charged with that peculiar excitement which attends the sure touch of a great artist."

B69. Erville, René. "En parlant avec Jean Langlais." *France-Amérique* (New York), April 18, 1954.
Interview about Langlais' 1952 and 1954 American tours.

B70. Eureka, Leonard. "Langlais surveys organ music." *Fort Worth Star-Telegram,* February 22, 1975.
Recital at TCU before Langlais received an honorary doctorate.

B71. Feder, Edgard. "Jean Langlais, un organiste célebre." *France-Amérique* (New York), April 27-May 3, 1978.
Review of the premieres given in New York by organist William Maul of *Concerto No. 3* and *Thème et Variations;* performance by the Bronx Choral Society, William Maul, conductor, of *Messe Solennelle.* The composer was in the audience.

B72. Ferré, Susan Ingrid. "A Survey of bibliographic materials on Langlais' organ compositions." *The Diapason* 66, no. 4 (March 1975): 6, 18.
Evaluation of 18 sources includes 3 D.M.A. dissertations (B124, B196, B258) with West's judged the most comprehensive, well-organized, and scholarly.

B73. "Festival Langlais." *Le Courrier Picard* (Amiens), September 23, 1969.
Announcement of a three-concert series of Langlais' sacred music to be held September 24, 25, 26 in the Cathedral of Amiens, organized by its titular organist, his former student Germain Desbonnet. Includes a letter from Langlais.

B74. Gapper, S. Gordon. "French organist has angelic touch." *The Flint Journal* (Michigan), February 5, 1962.
Recital in Court Street Methodist Church showed that organ music need not be pompous, but could be "music of sylvan clarity."

B75. Gendre, C. "Un enregistrement qui fera date dans l'histoire de l'orgue." *Revue du Son* 127 (November 1963): 497-99.
Report on recording of Franck's organ works (D117b) by the Société Intersonor (Société internationale d'enregistrements sonores) with photos of Langlais, the organ, and recording engineers. A drawing of the church shows microphone and recording equipment placement.

B76. Giraud, Patrick. "Jean Langlais/En hommage pour ses 80 ans." *Pueri Cantores* (Paris) 23 (March 1987): 28-29.
Birthday tribute in a magazine for young choristers.

B77. -----. "Le thème grégorien dans les œuvres pour orgue de Jean Langlais." Thesis, Institut Grégorien, Paris, and the Conservatory of Fribourg, Switzerland, July 1, 1964. 76 pages, including 12 pages of musical examples. (*See:* B78)

B78. -----. "Le thème grégorien dans les œuvres pour orgue de Jean Langlais." *L'Orgue* 122-123 (April-September 1967): 220-37.
Well-organized article using the thesis material cited above. Excellent analysis of 15 works published 1932-1961, covering themes, the methods used for transcribing melody, rhythmic preservation of chant lines, modal and non-modal combinations, and

religious aspects of the musical settings. This article has been a major source for some dissertations.

B79. Greene, David Mason. *Greene's Biographical Encyclopedia of Composers.* Garden City, N. Y.: Doubleday, 1985.
Langlais' entry is #2104, pages 1201-02.

B80. -----. "Long awaited." *Musical Heritage Society Review* 9, no. 15 (November 1985): 66.
Description of MHS 837273M, volume 3 in the organ works recorded by Ann Labounsky.

B81. Grondsma, Folkert. "Het orgeloeuvre van Jean Langlais." *Het Orgel* (Amersfoort, Holland) 83, no. 5 (May 1987): 163-169.
Survey of organ works by themes, harmonic structure, writing style, modal treatment, and rhythms/meters, with 25 musical examples. (Supplement to the article "Jean Langlais 80 jaar," B82.)

B82. -----. "Jean Langlais 80 jaar." *Het Orgel* 83, no. 2 (February 1987): 49-56.
Biography, organ works, and improvisations are covered in this Dutch article issued the month of Langlais' 80th birthday.

B83. -----. "Muziekwijzer." *Organist en Eredienst* (Holland), February 1975: 17-18.
Reviews of *Suite baroque, Cinq Méditations sur l'Apocalypse,* and the book *Jean Langlais - Un Indépendant.*

B84. Grunenwald, Jean-Jacques. "Le grand orgue de Saint-Pierre-de-Montrouge." *L'Orgue* 90 (April-June 1959): 44-46.
Discussion of the organ and organists of this Parisian church; Langlais was organist from 1934 to1945.

B85. Guenther, Eileen. "Jean Langlais honored in Washington on his 75th birthday." *The American Organist* 16, no. 2 (February 1982): 34-35.
Report of the concerts, lectures, and events of September 18-20 in Washington, D. C., where Langlais received the degree Doctor of Music, *honoris causa,* from the Catholic University of America.

B86. Guillemaud, B.-M. "De Paris à La Richardais/Le devoir de vacances de Jean Langlais sur les flots de la musique." *Ouest-France* (Saint-Malo), August 19, 1987.
Interview during summer vacation. Langlais mentions finishing the *Pièce pour clarinette et piano* the previous day.

B87. Gustafson, Bruce. "Hommage à Dufourcq." *The Diapason* 70, no. 11 (October 1979): 1, 8.
The famous French musicologist is saluted on his 75th birthday; his interview includes discussion of Langlais and Messiaen.

B88. Hadley, Benjamin. "Langlais in Oak Park." *The Diapason* 47, no. 4 (March 1, 1956): 33.
Sponsored by the Chicago Chapter, American Guild of Organists.

B89. Hameline, Daniel. "Jean Langlais ouvre la sixième saison des Soirées de Musique Sacrée de Guérande." *Ouest-France,* July 26, 1961.
Review of Langlais' recital of July 24 at the Collégiale St-Aubin, Guérande. Langlais does not like the word *interpréter.* He asks that performers just play his music, rather than interpret it.

B90. Hamrick, George Lee. "Organ music in 1965." *The American Organist* 49, no. 2 (February 1966): 16-18.
Survey of 2,741 works in 1,161 recital programs appearing in TAO. Langlais' *Song of Peace* had 35 performances. Seven other works are included on the chart ratings.

B91. Harkel, Paul. "L'Organiste virtuose Jean Langlais a donné un magnifique récital." *Voix Du Nord* (Lille), January 25, 1975.
Conservatory of Lille recital, part of the festivities marking the 150th anniversary of the invention of the Braille system of writing.

B92. Henderson, Charles H. "Editor's notes." *The American Organist* 16, no. 2 (February 1982): inside cover.
Editorial column tribute to Jean Langlais on his 75th birthday. "The remarkable fact is that he has not fallen into a set pattern of composing but has used each completed work as a stepping-stone for the next one, always with freshness and spontaneity."

B93. "Here & There." *The Diapason* 69, no. 8 (July 1978): 2.
Announcement of several premieres at concerts which Langlais attended in New York City and Pittsburgh: *Theme and Variations for Organ, Brass, and Strings; Mosaïque, Volume III;* and *Sonatine.*

B94. "Honorary member." *Music/The AGO-RCCO Magazine* 11, no. 3 (March 1977): 30.
The American Guild of Organists' citation of November 9, 1976 awarding honorary membership to Langlais "...a consummate musician whose devout faith, priceless Gallic sense of humor and staunch friendship for our country have earned for him the affection and admiration of countless members of our Guild."

B95. Houbart, François-Henri. "Entretien avec François-Henri Houbart." In *Gaston Litaize,* **Cahiers et mémoires de l'Orgue,** special number of the revue *L'Orgue,* 34 (1985): 1-7.
Litaize mentions Langlais' improvisations and studies with Tournemire. (Another interview: B41)

B96. Hume, Paul. "Blind French organist gives brilliant recital at Cathedral." *The Washington Post,* May 29, 1952, 35.
Influences of Franck, Pierne, and Tournemire are heard, combined with modern French dissonances and pre-Renaissance harmonies.

B97. "Informations Musicales/Récital d'orgue Jean Langlais." *Journal de l'ORTF* (Paris), 1972.
Review of the public concert broadcast from Studio 104 on November 10, 1972, "Les organistes de Sainte-Clotilde de Paris." Langlais played works by Franck, Tournemire, and his *Imploration pour la Croyance, Arabesques pour flûtes, Trois Pièces Liturgiques sur des thèmes grégoriens, Poem of Happiness, Chant héroïque,* and *Te Deum.* The strongest impression was made by the overwhelming *Imploration* with its contrast of vehement chords and suave melody, image of a tormented soul searching for peace.

Jaquet, see also Jaquet-Langlais.

B98. Jaquet, Marie-Louise. "Dialogue avec Jean Langlais." *Jeunesse et Orgue* (Bordeaux) 21 (1974): 6-11.
Interview, using twenty-five questions put by JEO.

B99. -----. "L'Ecole française des organistes aveugles, depuis la fin du XVIIIme siècle." *Jeunesse et Orgue* 26 (1976): 5-9; 27: 10-13.
Article written in connection with the 150th anniversary celebrations of the invention of the Braille system of writing for the blind. European blind organists and blind graduates of the organ classes at the Conservatoire de Paris are discussed.

B100. -----. "De Franse orgelmuziek na Jehan Alain." *Organist en Eredienst* (Holland), January 1980.
Dutch translation by Jenne Meyster of "La musique d'orgue après Jehan Alain."

B101. -----. "Hommage des Etats-Unis au compositeur Jean Langlais 21 Février 1975." *Le Louis Braille* 165 (May-June 1975): 1-2.
Concerts and honorary doctorate at Texas Christian University, with photo.

B102. -----. "Jean Langlais. Un indépendant. Essai sur son œuvre d'orgue." **(Jean Langlais. An independent. Essay on his organ works.) Cahiers et mémoires de l'Orgue,** special number of the revue *L'Orgue,* 144 bis (1972): 1-78.
Printed version of Jaquet's musicology thesis, B105. Studies the writing style, forms, Gregorian and folk themes, notation, rhythm, and registration of Langlais' organ compositions. Includes biographical details and photos.

B103. -----. "Die leichten Orgelwerke von Jean Langlais." **(The easy organ works of Jean Langlais.)** *Musica Sacra* 96/1 (1976): 30-40.
About 40 percent of Langlais' organ works are classified as easy, including parts of *Livre Œcumènique, Offrande à Marie, Hommage à Frescobaldi, Suite médiévale,* and *Neuf pièces.*

B104. -----. "La musique d'orgue après Jehan Alain." In "La Face Cachée de la Musique Française Contemporaine," *La Revue Musicale* (Paris) Double numero 316-317 (1979): 135-43.
Modern French organ composition after the Second World War.

B105. -----. "L'œuvre d'orgue de Jean Langlais." MA diss., Musicology: Faculté des lettres et sciences humaines, Paris, 1969. 1-177.
168 organ works are discussed; their roots are in medieval music, but 20th-century dissonance and impressionistic language are employed. Chapters deal with form, thematic aspect, style of writing, rhythm, and registration.

B106. -----. "Les œuvres récentes pour orgue de Jean Langlais (1973-1977)." *Jeunesse et Orgue* 35; 36 (spring; summer 1978) 4-8; 6-9.
Organ works published 1973 to 1977, with composition dates, editions, first performances, and a six-disc discography.

B107. -----. "Présence de la musique d'orgue française post-romantique et contemporaine aux Etats-Unis." **(Performances of post-Romantic and contemporary French organ music in the United States.)** *L'Orgue* 138 (April-June 1971): 54-58.
Analysis of 1,200 organ recital programs from *The Diapason* in 1970. Works of 33 French composers were played; top 4 were Messiaen 414 times, Langlais 375, Franck 325, and Dupré 272.

[B397.] Jaquet-Langlais, Marie-Louise. "Anniversaire." *Bretagne et Orgue*

1, 1986. (*See*: B397, Addenda)

[B398.] -----. "Jean Langlais/L'Histoire d'un nomination mouvementée." *La Tribune de l'Orgue* (Switzerland) 3, September 1987. (*See*: B398, Addenda)

[B382.] -----. "La vie et l'œuvre de Jean Langlais." Doctoral dissertation in progress, University of Paris. (*See*: B382, In Preparation)

B108. "Jean Langlais, catalogue general de ses œuvres 1929-1983." *Editions M. Combre*, Paris, 1983.
Six-page catalog with photo and short biography.

B109. "Jean Langlais, who arrives in U.S. Jan. 2." *The Diapason* 47, no. 2 (January 1, 1956): 5.
Announcement of the third American tour, with photo.

B110. "Jean Langlais recital." *The American Organist* 37, no. 4 (April 1954): 115-16.
Unsigned review of all-French recital at Central Presbyterian Church, New York City, March 22, 1954, praised Langlais' registrations. "...full organ tingled the spine without splitting the ears. And with it all, Mr. Langlais was so delighful to watch; never once did he act silly or emotional."

B111. "Jean Langlais to arrive April 17 for six weeks' tour." *The Diapason* 43, no. 5 (April 1, 1952): 1.
Announcement of cities on Langlais' first recital tour of the United States and Canada, April 20 through June 2.

B112. Joel. "La vie musicale/Inauguration des orgues de la chapelle Saint-Vincent." *Ouest-France* (Rennes), February 12, 1932.
Langlais' inaugural recital, chapel of the College of Saint Vincent.

[B336d.] Jones, Celia Grasty. "The French organ symphony from Franck to Langlais." D.M.A. diss., University of Rochester, Eastman School of Music, 1979, ix-151. (*See*: B336d, Première Symphonie)

B113. Kagl, Stefan. "Jean Langlais--leben und werk." *Ars Organi* 35, no. 1 (March 1987): 3-16.
Eightieth-birthday tribute article covers organ pieces 1927-1986, with brief biography and catalog of published works.

B114. Kimball, George H. "French organist impresses." *The Times-Union* (Rochester, N. Y.), October 18, 1969, 9C.
Reviews *Heroic Song*, *At Buffalo Bill's Grave*, two parts of *Ecumenical Book*, *Trio*, and *Poem of Happiness*.

B115. Kincaid, Dorothy. *Milwaukee Sentinel*, August 28, 1967, Part 1, 6.
Interview with Langlais during a party in his honor given by Mr. and Mrs. Armand Basile. Langlais was en route from Boys Town to Paris. Mrs. Basile was his former student and guide. Two photos.

B116. Kingston, Joseph T. "Great pipe organ brought to life by blind master." *Lancaster Intelligencer Journal*, April 3, 1962.
"Monday night, an awed audience of more than 800 persons, filling First Presbyterian Church auditorium to overflowing, heard one of the world's greatest living organists and composers-for-the-organ demonstrate that fact again and again."

B117. Knorr, Don. "Organist reunited with former pupil." *The Observer Dispatch* (Utica, N.Y.), Oct. 1, 1981.
"Jean Langlais today described the rigors and rewards of being one of the foremost organists and composers for that instrument in the world." Interview conducted with Langlais, Marie-Louise Jaquet-Langlais, and Douglas Himes in Utica; rehearsal photo.

B118. Kotek, Raymond Anthony. "The French organ mass in the twentieth century." D.M.A. diss., University of Illinois, 1974, vi-248.
Excellent study on the literature written especially to be played at Low Mass, and its disappearance during the 1960's due to liturgical changes. The Langlais works included are *Homage à Frescobaldi, Suite médiévale, Office pour la Sainte Famille*, and *Office de la Sainte Trinité.*

B119. Kountz, Frederick J. "Special wisdom apparent in Peristyle organ recital." *Toledo Times,* February 12, 1962.
Review opens with quote from Bertrand Russell on our age's tendency to increase technical skills while decreasing wisdom. "Undoubtedly Lord Russell would find greater comfort in association with the likes of Mr. Langlais than he finds out of his estimation of the present state of civilization....the imagery in such a piece as the "Boys Town" section from his American Suite, the reduction of the elemental disorder of the day into a pattern of order, stems from something more than the sharpening of several senses resultant upon the loss of one. It stems basically out of the French love of order and of the justice that exists only in order."

B120. Kratzenstein, Marilou. "A survey of organ literature and editions: France, since 1800." *The Diapason* 64, no. 12 (November 1973): 3-6, 8.
Langlais' "melodically attractive and colorful" works have become some of the most frequently performed organ pieces of this century. A list of works is included.

B121. -----. *Survey of organ literature and editions.* Ames: Iowa State University Press, 1980.
Book version, in expanded form, of *The Diapason* article series.

B122. Krellwitz, Janet Berggren. "The use of Gregorian chant in the organ works of Jean Langlais: Analysis and recital." Ed. D. diss., Columbia University Teachers College, 1981, vii-100.
Rhythmic, modal, and compositional techniques in sixteen works, including *Poèmes Evangéliques, Suite médiévale* , and *Trois Paraphrases Grégoriennes.*

B123. Kunz, Stefan. "Die orgelmusik von Jean Langlais." Thesis, Musikhochschule in Saarbrücken, Germany, 1980.

B124. Kurr, Doreen Barbara. "The organ works of Jean Langlais." D.M.A. diss., University of Washington, 1971, ix-235.
Organ works through *Trois Implorations.* Chapters: evolution of organ compositional style (3 works), symphony and trio sonata (2), suites (7), collections (12), and independent works (11).

B125. Labounsky, Ann. "Jean Langlais, complete organ works." November, 1979, 6 pages. Album insert for Musical Heritage Society MHS 834127, three-disc set in box, January 1980.
Biography, program notes on *Incantation, Folkloric Suite, Trois Paraphrases grégoriennes, Neuf Pièces, Suite brève,*

and *Huit Chants de Bretagne*, the first part of projected seven volume series of the complete organ works on twenty-one discs.

B126. -----. "Jean Langlais, complete organ works, vol. 2." January 1983, 4 pages. Album insert for Musical Heritage Society MHS 834712K, three-disc set in box, April 1983. Program notes with musical analysis for *Suite française, Offrande à une âme, Suite médiévale, Suite baroque, Triptyque Grégorien*.

B127. -----. "Jean Langlais, complete organ works, vol. 3." January 1985, 8 pages.
Album insert for Musical Heritage Society MHS 83727M, three-disc set in box, released November 1985. Program notes for *Vingt-quatre Pièces, Three Voluntaries, Progression, Eight Preludes, Prélude à la messe "Orbis factor," Adoration des Bergers*.

B128. -----. "Jean Langlais, complete organ works, vol. 4." January 1985.
Album insert for Musical Heritage Society MHS 932018A, three-disc set in box, July 1987. Program notes for *Poem of Life, Poem of Peace, Poem of Happiness, Offrande à Marie, Dominica in Palmis, Trois méditations sur la Sainte Trinite, Deux Offertoires, Supplication, Noëls avec variations, Organ Book, Deux Pièces brèves, Douze petites Pièces*.

B129. -----. "Organ works of Jean Langlais." *Sacred Music Handbook*. 4th ed. Pittsburgh: Duquesne University School of Music, 1987: 40-47.
Chronological list of organ compositions 1929-1987, rated for difficulty and keyed to recordings by Miss Labounsky for Musical Heritage Society. Distributed by Duquesne University Bookstore.

B130. -----. "The organ works of Jean Langlais/A practical sampling." *The American Organist* 21, no. 7 (July 1987): 48-49.
Pieces suitable for church services, grouped by season and topic.

B131. -----. "Progression/Triptyque Grégorien/Offrande à une âme." *The American Organist* 16, no. 2 (February 1982): 37-38.
Three works composed in 1978-79, years of change for Langlais. Program notes have information on dedicatees, first performances, and musical motifs.

B132. -----. "You the reader/Langlais tour." *The American Organist* 48, no. 2 (February 1965): 3.
Langlais' guide for his sixth American tour shares her impressions, including observations on his adaption to different organs.

[B383.] -----. *See also* : dissertation in preparation, B383, non-print, B387.

B133. Labounsky, Ann, and Robert Sutherland Lord. "Langlais honored at Duquesne Convocation." *Music/The AGO-RCCO Magazine* 11, no. 3 (March 1977): 35-36.
Account of week-long Convocation on Sacred Music, Duquesne University, Pittsburg; a festival of Langlais' music. He received his second honorary Doctor of Music degree, played a concert, and taught. Includes Langlais interview and letter.

B134. Lacas, Pierre-Paul. "Langlais Jean." *Diapason* (Boulogne), January 1977.

A review of Arion ARN 36 331 (*see*: D31a, D85). *Huit Chants de Bretagne,* where the folk melody reigns, follows in the path of Langlais' *Rhapsodie sur deux Noëls (Folkloric Suite)* and *Suite Française. The Cinq méditations sur l'Apocalypse* were of a more complex and even violent style.

B135. Lamotte, Gérard. "En la collégiale de Saint-Félix-Lauragais un récital d'orgue par Jean Langlais: l'étrange pouvoir de la musique sacrée." *La Depeche du Midi*(Toulouse), September 18, 1969.
September 7 recital, recently renovated 18th century Babiny organ.

B136. Langlais, Jean. "A la memoire d'André Marchal." *Le Louis Braille* (Association Valentin Haüy, Paris)191 (4ème trimestre 1980): 2-3.
Memorial tribute to André Marchal, his teacher and colleague.

B137. -----. "A propos du concours Jean-Sébastien Bach de Wiesbaden." *L'Orgue* (January-March 1978): 31-3
Langlais, member of the jury for the Bach competition in Wies-baden, Germany on November 4-7, 1977, comments on the performance style and registration of the eleven final-round candidates.

B138. -----. "Bouquets for Dr. Bingham." *Music/The AGO-RCCO Magazine* 6, no. 4 (April 1972): 34.
90th birthday tribute, with congratulations from Europeans Flor Peeters, André Marchal, Langlais, and Norbert Dufourcq. Langlais remarks that he often plays the compositions of Seth Bingham.

B139. -----. "Cesar Franck." Typescript of lecture given at Masevaux on August 7, 1982.

B140. -----. "Charles Tournemire." *Bulletin de Sainte-Clotilde* (Paris), 1949.
Short article on tenth anniversary of Tournemire's death.

B141. -----. "The composer between man and music." *Interface, Journal of New Music Research*9, no. 3-4 (December 1980) 175-76.
Five questions (127-28) to contemporary composers. Langlais' reply dealt with the abandonment of classical traditions.

B142. ----. "En bref." *Le Louis Braille* (Association Valentin Haüy, Paris) 205 (2ème trimestre 1984): 22.
Short review of recital played in AVH auditorium by Italian organist Ruggero Livieri on February 29, 1984.

B143. ----. "Hommage à Marcel Dupré." *Le Courrier Musical de France* 35 (1971): 117.
Dupré died on May 30, 1971. Former students express admiration and appreciation for his teaching and influence on their musical lives; pages 112-19.

B144. -----. "Jean Langlais, organiste et compositeur revient des Etats-Unis et du Canada." *Le Louis Braille* (Association Valentin Haüy, Paris) 133 (January-February 1970), 1, 3.
An account written Dec. 30, 1969 about the eighth concert tour of America, which lasted fifty days, January 28 to April 9.

B145. -----. "Letters to the Editor." *The Diapason* 62, no. 10 (September 1971): 17.
Response to Clarence Watters (*see*: B219, B255) concerning styles of playing Franck. Langlais studied with three students of

Franck: Adolphe Marty, Albert Mahaut, and Joséphine Boulay. Comments on their performances of Franck organ works, as well as on his own playing of the *Fantasy in C* in Dupré's class of 1929.

B146.-----. "Letters to the Editor/Langlais expresses gratitude." *The Diapason* 58, no. 6 (May 1967): 25.
Seventh US tour, cut short because of pain in his right arm.

B147. -----. "Mon quatrième voyage artistique aux Etats-Unis." *Musique et Liturgie* 70-71 (July-October 1959): 15-17.`
The 41-concert tour of 1958-59, the fourth US tour, included the Boston premiere of Psalm 150. Influences on his *American Suite* are noted. The country of the skyscraper and air conditioner also has regional beauties: Colorado mountains, California "douceur," Texas sun, Georgia perfumes, and Florida lakes and seas.

B148. -----. "Mon second voyage artistique aux Etats-Unis." *Musique et Liturgie* 41 (September-October 1954): 72-74.
Anecdotes of his second American tour, from New York on February 3 to Toronto on March 30. Travel was by train and car, Louisiana to Minnesota, California to North Carolina. Sometimes the improvisation themes amazed him; in Birmingham, for a four-movement symphony: Allegro--first theme from the symphony of Franck, Andante--Pilgrims Chorus of Wagner, Scherzo--theme from a Mozart concerto, Final--Marguerite's theme from Faust by Gounod. He refused, requesting four other themes.

B149. -----. "Mon septième voyage aux Etats-Unis." *Le Louis Braille* 119 (September-October 1967): 1-4.
Reflections on the two-month tour of 1967; humorous comments on life and musical events in America.

B150. -----. "Mon septième voyage artistique aux Etats-Unis." *Musique et Liturgie* 91 (January-February 1963): 11-12. [Reprinted, *Le Louis Braille* 94, July 1963, 1, 3.]
Actually 5th American concert tour, January 28-April 9, 1962. A commentary on American musical life and incidents on his tour.

B151.-----. "Mon troisième voyage en Amérique." *Musique et Liturgie* 53 (September-October 1956) 7 (71) and 9 (73).
Comments on Boston *Missa Salve Regina*, 28 recitals, a recording, 285 hours of train travel, and the fast pace of American life.

B152. -----. "Mon voyage en Amérique." *Musique et Liturgie* 30 (November-December 1952): 10-11.
Impressions of his first trip to America; differences between American and French organs. Modern French music was welcomed by his audiences.

B153. -----. "Un organiste français aux Etats-Unis." *Musique et Liturgie* 103, (July-September 1965): 12-14. [Reprinted, *Le Louis Braille* 109, January-February 1966, 1, 3.]
Sixth American concert tour in 1964, 44 concerts in 61 days. The Mayor of New Orleans said Langlais' concert, and another important one coming soon (the Beatles!) proved they were an important cultural center. He was then given a key to the city.

B154. -----. "Paul Dukas n'est plus." 1935. 3 page typescript, hommage to Dukas.

B155. -----. "Propos sur le style de César Franck dans son œuvre pour orgue." *Jeunesse et Orgue* 37 (Autumn 1978): one page.
Langlais has heard four students of Franck say the same thing: that the composer played his own works with extreme freedom. Langlais considers Franck an innovator. He does not approve of radical changes in Franck's indicated registrations, such as the frequent addition of mixtures.

B156. -----. "Quelques réflexions sur l'orgue moderne." *Musique et Radio* (Paris) 432 (May 1947): 133-135.
The modern French organ school and organ registrations.

B157. -----. "Quelques souvenirs d'un organiste d'église." *L'Orgue* 137 (January-March 1971): 4-6.
A memoir of almost fifty years as a church organist.

B158. -----. "Qu'en pense notre organiste?" *Bulletin de Sainte-Clotilde*, February 1963: 4.
On a "Letters to the editor" page, [Nos lecteurs nous écrivent...] Langlais comments on the role of the liturgical organist, in response to the article "Comment prier sur de la beauté" in the November 1962 issue.

B159. -----. "Réponses." *L'Orgue* 100 (October-December 1961): 124-125.
Langlais answers 26 questions sent to notable French organists concerning the contemporary organ in church. Questions are on pages 91-92, "Questionnaire posé aux organistes français." Responses from 21 organists are printed, with extracts from responses of 14 additional organists and clergy.

B160. -----. *Tour Journals.* Unpublished.
The source for articles on his American travels, dictated to guides, they shared impressions and adventures with his children and friends on his return. Possibly other journals exist.

1. April 11-May 18, 1952. First American tour, diary of Jean and Jeannette Langlais, handwritten by Jeannette in 5" x 8" notebook, 19 pages, typed after return to France.

2. 1954. "Mon second voyage aux Etats Unis." 2 typed pages.

3. December 29, 1955-March 8, 1956. Third USA tour, dictated to his guide Monique LeGerdre, handwritten in 4" x 6" spiral notebook, 93 pages.

4. January 1, 1959. "4ème Voyage aus Etats-Unis." Dictated to Christianne Chivot. 57 typed pages in 5" x 8 1/2" stapled notebook.

5. January 26-April 2, 1962. "Sur le United States." Fifth USA tour, dictated to Marie Villey. 33 typed pages in 5" x 8 1/2" stapled notebook.

6. 1972. "Mon 14ème Voyage aux U.S.A." 3 typed pages.

7. 1975. "Mon XVème voyage aux U.S.A." 2 typed pages.

B161. Langley, Robin. "Recitals/Festival Hall." *The Musical Times* 111 (December 1970): 1259.
Langlais' recital of November 1 was impressive. His compositions showed influences of Tournemire, Messiaen, and Vierne.

B162. Le Comte, J.-B. "Jean Langlais." *Les Artistes d'aujourdui.* May 1, 1926.
Debut recital at the Association Valentin Haüy, Paris, with photo of the nineteen-year-old student of M. Marchal who will enter the organ class of the Conservatory. "C'est assurément un début intéressant et plein de promesses pour une carrière qui ne fait que s'ouvrir." (**It is surely an interesting debut and full of promises for a career which is only just beginning.**)

B163. Lord, Robert Sutherland. "Jean Langlais--on the occasion of his seventieth birthday." *The Diapason* 68 (Feb 1977): 2, 14-15.
Langlais seen as teacher, improviser, performer, and composer by a former student. "The art of Langlais, then, is one of an economy of notes with a preference for concise forms, resulting often in rather short pieces. The climax is often achieved through the polyphonic combination of several themes which have been introduced earlier in the piece." The accompanying table of works has misaligned attributions, which are corrected on page 2, *The Diapason*, March 1977.

B164. -----. "Organ music of Jean Langlais/comments on performance style." *The American Organist* 51, no. 1 (January 1968): 27-32.
Articulation, registration, and interpretation problems analyzed by one who is an authority on organ works of Tournemire and Langlais.

B165. -----. "The Sainte-Clotilde tradition." *The American Organist* 16, no. 2 (February 1982): 38-40.
Impact of the organists of Sainte-Clotilde, with their "depth and diversity of poetic evocation," on modern French organ music.

B166. -----. "The Sainte-Clothilde traditions--Franck, Tournemire, and Langlais: conversation and commentary with Jean Langlais." *The Diapason* 66, no. 4 (March 1975): 3.
Langlais answers questions about Tournemire's playing the works of Franck; Langlais' own study with pupils of Franck; and differences between the practice at St. Clothilde and the Widor-Dupré organ tradition.

B167. -----. "Sources of past serve Langlais in organ works." *The Diapason* 50, no. 2 (January 1959): 24; no. 3 (February 1959): 24.
Langlais' use of historical materials: chant, chorale melodies, the short forms of the classic period, modes, and programmatic dedications such as *Homage to Frescobaldi* show his search for new ideas and contemporary sounds starts with sounds of the past.

B168. MacCluskey, Thomas. "Jean Langlais proves virtuosity." *Rocky Mountain News* (Denver, Colorado), February 27, 1967, 67.
The texture of clear counterpoint possible with organ registration has been exploited extremely well by Langlais as master composer and performer.

B169. Machabey, Armand. "Audition de jeunes musiciens." *L'Information Musicale* (Paris), May 8, 1942.

Young French composers presented their unpublished works at the Parisian salon of Mme. Schildge-Bianchini on April 18,1942. Langlais' compositions were *Humilis, L'arbre* from *Mélodies,* and *(Deux) Chansons de Clément Marot.*

B170. -----. "Galerie de quelques jeunes musiciens parisiens/M. Langlais." *L'Information Musicale* 77, July 3, 1942.
The sixth in a series on young Parisian musicians notes that there is nothing aggressive or revolutionary in Langlais' style. The writer compliments his unique melodic lines and rich harmonic colors, particularly in *Vingt-quatre pièces* for organ.

B171. -----. *Portraits de trente musiciens français.* Paris: Richard-Masse Editeurs, 1949.
Profile article (pages 109-113) in a book on thirty French musicians. The *Vingt-quatre pièces* are examples of Langlais' gifts and his ability to create a complete work in thirty measures. Catalog of published works (eight organ, four vocal) and unpublished manuscripts (twenty-one works in various media).

B172. "Manifestation d'une solennelle grandeur et d'une haute qualité artistique." *La Republique Du Centre* (Orléans), May 8, 1963.
The Société du Conservatoire honored the 534th anniversary of Joan of Arc's liberation of Orleans by presenting a concert by Langlais and Jeannine (Janine) Collard. Four photographs: Langlais at the organ console, the singer J. Collard, the numerous audience, and a panoramic view of the nave with audience and organ facade.

B173. "Marbella makes musical history." *Club Marbella Magazine* (Spain), 2nd issue, n.d.
Three page article with photos about the 1975 mechanical-action organ built by Blancafort in Marbella. Langlais' concert at Easter 1977 was outstanding; he received standing ovations from a packed church. It was his first recital in Spain.

B174. Mardirosian, Haig. "Langlais: organ works, volume 3." *Fanfare* 9, no. 6 (July-August 1986): 161-62.
Review of Musical Heritage Society MHS 837273M. The second of *Three Voluntaries* (W205) is praised for its fluid counterpoint, "a particular treat to the ear."

B175. -----. "Orgue et trompette." *Fanfare* 4, no. 1 (September-October 1980): 271-72.
Three trumpet and organ works of Langlais recorded by Freddy Grin, solo trumpet of the Concertgebouw Orchestra, and organist Dick Klomp. (*See:* D80f, D82b, D83c)

B176. Mari, Pierrette. "Langlais Jean." *Diapason,* August 1967.
Review of Erato STU 70358, *Missa Salve Regina, Missa "in simplicitate," Trois Prières.* These works carry on the tradition of Franck, Widor, and Vierne. Like them, Langlais is not content to be one of the best French organists, but is also an eminent composer of religious music.

B177. McAlear, Robert. "A very special relationship." *Musical Heritage Review* 11, no. 9 (1987): 66-67.
The halfway point in Labounsky records of Langlais organ works.

B178. McLean, Eric. "Jean Langlais at Notre Dame." *The Montreal Star,* March 30, 1954.

Exotic colors, free rhythms, and an underlying French impressionism are the important features of Langlais' works.

B179. -----. "Organ recital by K. Gilbert." *The Montreal Star,* September 29, 1953.
"As played by Mr. Gilbert, both the Cantilene and the Dialogue sur les Mixtures were gems, and I left this recital more firmly convinced than ever that Langlais is probably the most imaginative composer for the organ today."

B180. Minne, André. "Musique française par l'organiste Jean Langlais." *Flandre Liberale* (Ghent, Belgium), July 9, 1962.
Langlais' recital of July 7 at the Cathedral St. Bavon was notable for his capability to utilize all the rich sounds of the cathedral organ, and as an expression of his exceptional gifts as organist, improviser, and composer.

B181. "Mitteilungen der GdO/veranstaltungen." *Ars Organi* 34, no. 4 (December 1986): 249.
Announcement of the concerts in Bonn honoring Langlais' 80th birthday, February 12-15, 1987, "Bonner Langlais-Tage," with seven organists and the Kammerchor Schmallenberg.

B182. Monahan, Matthew. "Blind musician-composer gets honorary degree." *The Duquesne Duke,* October 21, 1976, 6.
A Sacred Music Convocation featuring many Langlais works was held in honor of the Duquesne University School of Music's 50th anniversary. Interviewed the day before honorary doctorate award.

B183. Monceau-Barbaud, Yvonne. "La symphonie pour orgue en France." Thesis for doctorate, l'Institut de Musicologie, University of Strasbourg, 1985. 131 pages.
Analyzes Langlais' Organ Symphonies 1, 2, 3 plus the symphonies of other French composers such as Widor, Vierne.

B184. de Montremy, J.-M. "Jean Langlais selon ses modes." *La Croix,* September 1, 1981.   Excellent interview.

B185. Morrison, Deborah B. "His world of beauty--and Braille." *The Sun,* (Baltimore), March 1954.
Langlais' love of Brittany and his summer vacations there are discussed in this interview.

B186. Mougeolle, René. "Brève rencontre avec Jean Langlais." *Le Journal De Nancy, L'Est Republicain,* May 8, 1968.
Admiration for the USA and American students; displeasure with some young French clergy over the role of the organ in services.

B187. Muess, Pasteur Claude-Rémy. "Relevage du grand orgue de la Basilique Sainte-Clotilde à Paris." *Jeunesse et Orgue,* November 1983.
Renovation of the organ at Sainte-Clotilde in 1983 by Jacques Barbéris. Two November concerts celebrated the completion of this work. Madame Jacques Chirac, representing the Mayor of Paris, with other officials, attended the all-Langlais concert of November 22.

B188. Mulheron, Frank. "700 here cheer blind organist." *The Bridgeport Post* (Conn.), January 13, 1959.
Fourth American tour. The Langlais compositions were delightful,

easy to listen to, and of sensible length, unlike many "monstrocities" from the French organ school.

B189. Murray, Kathryn. "Messenger offers Arts Symposium to aid youth in choosing vocations in music, drama, art, journalism." *The Messenger* (Diocese of Covington, KY), March 21, 1954.
Langlais discusses a career in music. He mentions the need for good musicians in the Church. Langlais considers Ravel one of the greatest modern composers "for his pure inspiration."

B190. "La musique dominicale." *Notre-Dame de Paris,* June 5, 1985.
A list of the 20 most-played composers in the Sunday afternoon organ recital series at the Cathedral, January 7, 1968 through the end of 1984. The first six were: J. S. Bach (275 times), Louis Vierne (144), Marcel Dupré (108), César Franck (96), Jean Langlais (90), and Olivier Messiaen (69).

B191. Nalle, Billy. "Langlais in New York." *Music/The AGO-RCCO Magazine* 6, no. 11 (November 1972): 18-19, 43.
Recital at the Church of the Heavenly Rest, August 23, 1972 received a bad review, rare for Langlais. He was accorded "respect for a great musician," but the writer was disappointed.

B192. Nazzaro, William J. "Langlais, blind organist brilliant in ASU concert." *Arizona Republic* (Phoenix), February 20, 1967.
Langlais' organ compositions were in the French modern style, "conservative, romantic and just a bit heavy, but always listenable.... Jean Langlais is a splendid organist, one who plays music brilliantly and at the same time honestly, without calling attention to his own virtuosity rather than the music. It was a pleasure to hear him."

B193. Newall, R. H. "Newall talks with Jean Langlais." *Bangor Daily News,* January 15, 1971, 19.
Interview conducted in Langlais' Paris apartment.

B194. "Newsnotes." *The American Organist* 47, no. 9 (September 1964): 26.
Announcement, Langlais' tour September 30-December 9, photo.

B195. Norman, Margaret Victoria. "Historic techniques in selected organ works of Jean Langlais." MA diss., Musicology, University of Indiana, Bloomington, 1976, iv-125.
Excellent work, on the level of a doctoral dissertation. Studies compositions through *Offrande à Marie* (1971), with most examples taken from *Poèmes Evangéliques, Suite médiévale, Suite française, Neuf Pièces, Première Symphonie, Homage to Rameau,* and *Essai.* Very good explanation of the revival of interest in plainsong, and in the historic and modern techniques used by Langlais.

B196. Nyquist, Roger Thomas. "The use of Gregorian chant in the organ music of Jean Langlais." D.M.A. diss. [1 of 3 independent parts], University of Indiana, Bloomington, 1968, 1-55.
Langlais' general and rhythmic treatment of the Gregorian theme and formal treatment of the Gregorian phrase are analyzed in works through 1966.

B197. Perrigault, A. "A Dol-de-Bretagne, le prix François-Duine 1964 a été

remis au maître Jean Langlais, organiste pour l'ensemble de son œuvre." *Ouest-France*, July 30, 1964, 12.
Ceremony in the Town Hall. Langlais spoke of his Breton origins, and his devotion to his native region.

B198. Peterson, James B. "French organist Langlais magnificent at Boys Town." *Omaha World-Herald*, August 25, 1967.
Recital given in Dowd Memorial Chapel as part of the Fifteenth Annual Music Workshop at Boys Town. "His playing is distinguished by an imaginative use of tone color and nearly flawless technique."

B199. "Pipings/mixtures." *The American Organist* 21, no. 6 (June 1987): 34.
Announcement of the music sung and played at the "American Cathedral" in Paris on Feb. 8 in honor of Langlais' 80th birthday.

B200. "Propagande par l'exemple/L'activité d'un jeune." *Le Valentin Haüy* (March–April 1935): 38–39.
Short biography of the young professor of organ, National Institute for the Young Blind; reports his compositions being played in Paris. He recently directed his musical poem *La Voix du Vent* at Rennes, coordinating the orchestra, choir, and soprano soloist, a total of 80 persons.

B201. Proskowetz, Pat. "Blind organist gives BR recital." *Morning Advocate*, Baton Rouge, March 13, 1962, 6-A.
Langlais "said here Monday morning that family finances pre(v)ented him from having music lessons and that he did not have the opportunity to use a piano until he was 10."

B202. Putnam, Thomas. "Ovation for a Paris organist." *Chicago Sun-Times*, January 25, 1967, 35.
Interesting reactions to the Langlais works: the "anxious" *Chant héroïque*, the "happy and simple" *Rhapsodie on two noels*, and a *Trio* that "limned a childlike world of calliopes." *Storm in Florida* was filled with the "suspense of background music."

B203. Ragsdale, Nancy Laughbaum. "Langlais attracts 1400 to recital, 91 to master class." *The Diapason* 50, no. 5 (April, 1959): 11.
Report by the Dean of the Oklahoma City AGO Chapter, with photo.

B204. Ramsey, Basil. "Church and organ news/Royal Festival Hall." *The Musical Times* 100 (June 1959): 350.
Review of Langlais' April 1 recital in London. "...this brilliant player is at his best in early and modern French music."

B205. Raugel, Félix. "L'Ecole Française de l'orgue moderne." *Musique et Liturgie* 57/58 (May–August 1957): 23 (55).
This volume, *La Musique Religieuse dans le monde*, contains reports given at the IIIe Congrés International de Musique Sacrèe (3rd International Congress of Sacred Music) in Paris, July 1-8, 1957. Musicologist Raugel gives a succinct account of French organ composers and virtuosi of the 19th and 20th centuries.

B206. -----. "Jean Langlais." *Die Musik in Geschichte und Gegenwart*. Edited by Friedrich Blume. Basel: Bärenreiter, 1960, vol. 8: 191.

B207. "Recital offerings of 1950 are analyzed." *The Diapason* 42, no. 4 (March 1, 1951): 1-2.
Example of the annual compilation and ranking of favorite works,

Bach's *Toccata and Fugue in d minor* being the top. 84 Langlais performances were reported; he ranks 18th. Two years previously there were 58 performances of his works reported; he ranked 32nd in the March 1, 1950 issue.

B208. Redmond, Michael. "Music in Jersey. Langlais plays up 'tradition'." *The Star-Ledger* (Madison, New Jersey), October 28, 1976.
Interview before recital in Madison. "'A composer is really an unfortunate sort of fellow. He is obliged to compose; he does not know why. Very often I have said, 'This is my last work.' A week afterwards, I am struggling with a new one.'"

B209. Regan, Sue. "Sacred Music 'Week' honors Jean Langlais." *The Duquesne Duke*, October, 1976.
Interview at Duquesne University during Langlais's 16th trip to America. "He ardently refuses to categorize his compositions or describe the evolution of his style. 'They are all different. You must never do the same thing twice.'"

B210. Reno, Doris. "Blind organist's recital thrills Trinity audience." *The Miami Herald*, February 1, 1967.
"An artist who pays equal attention to the poetry and the intensity his instrument is capable of expressing, and never overbalances on the side of sheer power."

B211. Rostand, Claude. *French Music Today.* Translated by Henry Marx. New York: Merlin Press, 1957. Originally published as *La Musique française contemporaine.* Collection « *Que Sais-je* » No. 517 (Paris: Presses Universitaires de France, 1952, 1956).
Pages 93–94 note that Langlais' early organ works have "a distinctive poetic climate... Later his art became more gentle, more relaxed, spontaneous and on a higher intellectual plane. Examples are *Vingt-quatre Pièces, Deux Offertoires pour tous les Temps* and, above all, his First Symphony, which is remarkable for the vigor of style and structure."

B212. Roubinet, Michel. "Tetes et affiches/Jean Langlais." *Diapason*, February 1987.
Recognition of Langlais' 40 years at Sainte-Clotilde and 80th birthday on February 15.

B213. Russell, Thomas. *L'Art Musical* (Paris), 28 April 1939.
Felix Aprahamian, secretary of the Organ Music Society, gave a conference at the University of London on "Modern French Organ Music," using works of the young composers Jean Langlais, Olivier Messiaen, Maurice Durufle, and André Fleury.

B214. "Les Sables: M. Jean Langlais au grand orgue de St-Pierre-des-Sables." *Ouest Eclair*, July 21, 1937.
Langlais played two masses at the Church of Saint-Pierre at the invitation of the curate. Compliments on his compositions and improvisations.

B215. Sarnette, Eric. "Revue de l'édition musicale/orgue." *Musique et Radio* 552 (May 1957): 183–84.
Comments on the repertoire of most organists outside large cities, and their past reluctance to play contemporary music. Fortunately, this has now changed. "The works by Marcel Dupré, Tournemire, Messiaen, Langlais penetrate everywhere, in France as well as abroad."

B216. Schmidt, Heinrich. "Französische orgelmusik." *Musik und Kirche* 26 (September/October 1956): 252-53.
Review of Langlais' recitals in Essen, Düsseldorf, and Cologne. His *Messe Solennelle* was sung in Düsseldorf.

B217. Schmitt, Francis P. "Twice through the rubble." Chap. 11 in *Church Music Transgressed.* New York: The Seabury Press, 1977, 103-106.
Report on church services attended in America and Europe in 1949 (the rubble of war) and in 1975 (the rubble of liturgical reform), with special attention to the status of Latin and Gregorian Chant. The section on Paris includes quotes from Langlais and an account of his musical role in the Sunday masses at Sainte-Clotilde.

B218. -----. "Workshop report." *Caecilia* (Omaha) 86, no. 3 (Autumn 1959): 87-89.
The seventh annual Liturgical Music Workshop, Boys Town, ended with the second American performance of the *Missa Salve Regina.* The composer expressed displeasure with the brass players, both here and at the Boston premiere. Organ recital programs for Langlais and his students are given. Photos include Langlais' guide, his son Claude (p. 106) and Langlais teaching a blind student from California (p.103).

B219. Schuneman, Robert. "Clarence Watters." *The Diapason* 62, no. 5 (April 1971): 4.
Review of Watters' Chicago recital on February 16 in which the two French styles of playing Franck organ works are discussed: a regular tempo, "steady sweep" pace vs. a freer, more rubato performance. Langlais is mentioned with Dupré, Duruflé, and Marchal. See replies by Watters (D255) and Langlais (D145).

B220. Sears, Lawrence. "Jean Langlais recital fine." *The Evening Star* (Washington, D.C.), January 16, 1967.
Opening recital of the seventh American tour, at Union Methodist Church. "He ended his sixth tour there in 1964 and was promptly re-engaged. The capacity audience heard a concert of distinguished playing which included the first performance of his new Poem of Peace."

B221. Seneca, Gérard. "Les musiciens laics plaident pour le chant grégorien." *L'Intransigeant* (Paris), January 8, 1967.
A plea for retaining Gregorian chant is signed by Langlais and others on the Commission des Musiciens-Experts, including Jacques Chailley, Maurice Duruflé, Marie-Madeleine Duruflé, and Gaston Litaize.

B222. Sergent, Maurice. "Le concours des 'Amis de l'Orgue'." *Le Courrier Musical,* July 13, 1931, 436.
The second performance and improvisation competition, held June 21, 1931 with Vincent d'Indy presiding over the twelve-member jury. Langlais won, in large part due to his improvisation on the *Ave Maris Stella.* In the final round he also played works by Bach, Franck, and Vierne. Included in the improvisation requirements were a *Prélude* and *Fugue* on a subject by Noël Gallon and a sonata movement on two themes by d'Indy.

B223. Singer, Samuel. "Jean Langlais recital solid, engaging, but Bach's role is small." *Philadelphia Inquirer,* October 7, 1964, 35.

The "diversity, craftsmanship and creativity" of Langlais' compositions are praised, especially the *Trio* from *Triptyque*.

B224. Sisler, Hampson A. "The sightless organ virtuoso." *The American Organist* 17, no. 9 (September 1983): 48-49.
Explores the world and motivations of blind organists; Langlais, Marchal, and Walcha are examples.

B225. Slominsky, Nicolas, ed. *Baker's Biographical Dictionary of Musicians*, 7th ed. New York: Schirmer Books, 1984.
Short entry for Langlais on page 1303.

B226. Smith, Emmet G. "Langlais Week at Texas Christian University." *Music/The AGO-RCCO Magazine* 9, no. 6 (June 1975): 26-27.
Langlais' first honorary doctorate, with seminars and concerts. 1,300 persons attended the closing concert and ceremony.

B227. Smith, H. Katherine. "Blind French organist will play here." *Buffalo Courier Express*, May 31, 1952.
21st recital on the first American tour included a 35-minute improvised symphony on four themes given just before the recital. His aural impressions of New York City, Omaha, and Texas.

B228. Southgate, Harvey. "Lightness and majesty." *Rochester Democrat and Chronicle* (N. Y.), October 18, 1969.
Langlais' writing is termed "elegant music."

B229. Stack, Dennis. "Music and musicians." *The Kansas City Times*, February 20, 1962.
The "most interesting" of his own works was the *Arabesque sur les flûtes*, while *Boys Town, Place of Peace* was a "truly beautiful, choral-like composition." Less impressive was the *Storm in Florida* from the same suite. "Many organists in the audience said they would rather have heard some of Langlais's less commercial organ works, such as his 'Four Preludes'."

B230. St. George, Paul. "Music." *The Pilot* (Boston), October 17, 1964.
To hear "Homage to Frescobaldi with its crystalline tinkling of flutes ... the recent 'Essai' (Trial), the Trio from the 'Triptych' --and the thunderous Acclamations on 'Lumen Christi' of Easter Vigil (Incantation for a Holy Day)--and to revel in the quintessence of French improvisatory art: this was delight indeed."

B231. Strüder, Brigitte. "Cinéma et orgue." *L'Orgue* 190 (April-June 1984): 30.
French report on the February 15, 1984, premiere in Bonn, Germany, of the documentary film on Langlais. (*See* : B385) Translation by Ann Labounsky in "Here & There" column of *The Diapason* 75, no. 9 (September 1984): 3.

B232. Sumner, William Leslie. "The organ in Ste. Clotilde: Paris." *The Organ* 47 (January 1968): 125-30.
Discussion of the organ and organists of this church.

B233. "Susan Ferre aids organist in American concert tour." *The Skiff* (Texas Christian University, Fort Worth), February 7, 1967, 10.
Interview with Langlais and his American guide, seventh US tour.

B234. Terrière, Henri. "Le maître Jean Langlais nous parle de sa vie et de son art." *Ouest-France*, n.d. [1962?]

Interview before recital at Eglise Saint-Germain, Rennes; questions on his foreign recital tours, his placement of blind graduates of the Institution as parish organists, his roots in Brittany, and the success of his compositions in France and abroad.

B235. Thomerson, Kathleen. "Errata in published editions of Langlais organ works." *Music/The AGO-RCCO Magazine* 12, no. 5 (May 1978): 36-37.
Updates the compilation of 1965 published in the *A.G.O. Quarterly.* (*See*: B236)

B236. -----. "Errors in the published organ compositions of Jean Langlais." *A.G.O. Quarterly* 10, no. 2 (April 1965): 47-54.
Corrections and performance comments for works published 1935 to 1962, taken from scores marked in private study with the composer beginning in 1955.

B237. -----. "Jean Langlais--an eightieth birthday tribute." *The Diapason* 78, no. 2 (February 1987): 8-9.
Report on European concerts given in honor of Langlais' eightieth birthday, and his activities and compositions of 1977-1986.

B238. -----. "Langlais' newest compositions." *The American Organist* 16 no. 2 (February 1982): 36-37.
Review of the organ works *Noëls With Variations, Rosace, Third Concerto, Third Symphony.*

B239. -----. "The organ music of Jean Langlais/discography of solo organ works and improvisations." *The Diapason* 73, no. 2 (February 1982): 18-20.
Eighty-one recordings, indexed by composition and by disc.

B240. -----. "Organ works of Jean Langlais." *Music/The AGO-RCCO Magazine* 11, no. 3 (March 1977): 30.
List of organ works composed 1929-1976.

B241. -----. "Recent organ works of Jean Langlais." *Music/The AGO-RCCO Magazine* 12, no. 5 (May 1978): 34-36.
Comments on Langlais' diversity of compositional techniques as illustrated in eight works written 1971-1977.

B242. Tortolano, William. "The mass and the twentieth century composer. A study of musical techniques and style, together with the interpretive problems of the performer." Vol. I: xxv-164 Vol. II: 46 musical examples. D.S.M. diss., University of Montreal, 1964.
A survey of 65 significant choral masses written 1903-1963. Analysis of forms, rhythm, melody, harmony, and polyphony, with comparisons of stylistic and technical trends. Five masses of Langlais (*Mass in Ancient Style, Messe Solennelle, Missa "in simplicitate," Missa Misericordiae Domini*, and *Missa Salve Regina*) are reviewed. Their stylistic cohesion, ingenious harmonies, and contrapuntal techniques are praised.

B243. -----. "Rhythm in the twentieth century mass." *Sacred Music* (St. Paul, Minn.) 95, no. 2 (Summer 1968): 5-15.
Chapter IV from his doctoral dissertation. (*See*: B242).
Langlais' *Missa Salve Regina* is discussed as a mass of fluctuating meter with Gregorian chant as a thematic basis, while *Mass in Ancient Style* is in the "one basic meter with polyphony" category. Langlais' awareness of word accents and the

rhythmic vitality of melodic lines are characteristics.

B244. -----. "Melody in 20th-century masses." *The Diapason* 60, no. 5 (April 1969): 18-19.
Adapted from Chapter V, "Melody," of *The Mass and the Twentieth Century Composer*, 1964. (*See*: B242).

B245. Towe, Teri Noel. "A most significant project." *Musical Heritage Review* 3 (Jan. 7, 1980): 16-17.
Announcement of the release of the first volume of recordings of Langlais' organ works by Musical Heritage Society. (*See*: B125)

B246. Tucker, Marilyn. "Langlais' concert in Berkeley." *San Francisco Chronicle*, February 13, 1967.
Langlais' quick ability to master the individual organs which he plays on tour, each different, is impressive. "...he played an instrument that was undoubtedly new to him, as easily as if he had been playing Sunday services there for thirty years."

B247. Valmarin. "Après Franck, Pierné, Tournemire, un breton: Jean Langlais est organiste de la Basilique Ste. Clotilde." *Ouest-France*, December 20, 1948.
Student days at the Conservatory. Langlais is grateful for the kindness of his friends there, such as the one who for a year copied his fugues from braille.

B248. Van Wye, Benjamin David. "The influence of the plainsong restoration on the growth and development of the modern French liturgical organ school." D.M.A. diss., University of Illinois, 1970, iv-137.
Excellent work on the use of plainsong by French organist-composers, the Low Mass with organ, and the Schola Cantorum. Examples cover 16th century versets from the Attaignant books through works and improvisations of Charles Tournemire.

B249. Verhoef, Kees. "Prachtig orgelspel door Jean Langlais." *Leids Dagblad*, (Holland), July 15, 1970.
Review of Langlais' organ recital of July 13 in the Nieuwe Kerk of the Dutch town of Katwijk-am-Zee, with comments on *Livre Œcuménique* chorals and his closing improvisation.

B250. Vermeersch, Sabine. "Het Gregoriaans in het orgeloeuvre van Jean Langlais." Laureaat Orgel, Lemmensinstitut, Leuven, Belgium, 1987.
Gregorian themes in the organ works of Langlais. This Flemish thesis was completed in March 1987.

B251. Vica, Carl. "Les sillons de la semaine." *La Vigie Marocaine*, (Casablanca), June 12, 1955.
Review of the first record made by Jean Langlais, Ducretet-Thomson 270 C 003, in 1954. Evaluated a very beautiful disc, to be appreciated by all musicians. (*See*: D16b)

B252. Vinton, John, ed. *Dictionary of Contemporary Music*. New York: E. P. Dutton & Co., Inc., 1974.
The Langlais entry on page 416 was prepared with the help of Marie-Louise Jaquet. "He uses modal harmonies, often combined with Gregorian chant, and often borrows forms, genres, and technical procedures from the 17th and 18th centuries."

B253. Walker, Charles Dodsley. "New York hears Langlais again." *Choral & Organ Guide* 7, no. 5 (June, 1954): 27-28.

Central Presbyterian Church recital of March 22. "Jean Langlais sums up his work in this way: 'I seek clarity in my music.'"

B254. Waters, Charles F. "Present century trends in the organ music of Germany and France." *The American Organist* 41, no. 10 (October, 1958): 374, 376.
French organ compositions divided into "plainsong" or "portrayal." Langlais works are used to illustrate both styles.

B255. Watters, Clarence. "Letters to the Editor." *The Diapason* 62, no. 7 (June 1971): 15.
Response to reviewer's remarks about "authentic" Franck performance practice and "tempo rubato." The two French camps are "the Widor-Dupré group ...(and) the Tournemire-Langlais adherents. It might be said that the two are involved in the age-old feud between the romantic and the aristocratic players." Watters' Parisian study in 1926, and his evaluation of the discipline and classicism of that "Paris School" of organists, is presented. (*See*: B145, 219)

B256. Wells, Tilden. "Large audience hears blind French organist." *Delaware Gazette*, February 6, 1954.
"The Langlais idiom is respectably contemporary, and at the same time accessible to ears accustomed to organ literature of the past. His music is possessed of a good deal of dissonance that produces no greatly startling effects because it is the logical outcome of compositional procedures."

B257. Welsh, Wilmer H. "Organist termed brilliant." *The Johnsonian* 15, no. 16 (Winthrop College, Rock Hill, South Carolina): 4.
Review of recital March 6, 1962 at Byrnes Auditorium, Winthrop College. "Those who did attend the Langlais recital were privileged to hear one of the greatest musicians of our time."

B258. West, Melvin. "The organ works of Jean Langlais." D.M.A. diss., Boston University, 1959, viii-259.
First doctoral dissertation on Langlais, written after his third American tour, studies 1932-56 works in detail. Scholarship and analysis are excellent. Harmonic examples include altered dominants, juxtaposed-triads, tone-clusters, chords of addition, modality, tonal centers, and unrelated chordal series. West discusses organ works in the context of techniques of other contemporary French composers, with musical illustrations.

B259. Wintermute, Edwin E. "Blind Parisian organist plays compositions here." *The State Journal* (Lansing, Michigan). n. d. [1959 tour]
United States premieres were "Pasticcio" from *Organ Book*, "a star-showering short display of musical brilliance; 'Scherzando,' another animated piece, taking as its theme the typical plaintive notes of a military drum and bugle band, travestying them for a while, without quite losing their solemn implications, and the academic but lovely 'Piece Modale No. 1'."

B260. Wolff, Alfred. "La chorale mixte des jeunes aveugles." *Petit Parisien*, January 4, 1936.
An account of a concert by the 40-member choir of the National Institution for the Young Blind directed by Jean Langlais.

B261. Wright, Searle. "Langlais makes American debut." *Choral & Organ Guide* 5, no. 5 (June, 1952): 20-21.

Crescent Avenue Presbyterian Church in Plainfield, N.J., April 20. Discussion of the French traditions of organplaying, interpretation, and composition. Langlais' improvisation showed "a truly artistic *musical individuality* literally pouring forth its personal poetry."

B262. Yorel, Paul. "Le maître Jean Langlais aux grandes orgues de Saint-Germain." *Ouest-Eclair* (Rennes), May 17, 1941, 3.
Benefit "concert spirituel" for the Secours National during wartime, when Langlais was organist of Saint-Pierre de Montrouge in Paris. Special mention of *La Nativité*, improvisation on *Puer natus est*, and the choral *O bone Jesu*.

B263. Yvel, Yann. "La Bretagne des arts et des lettres. Jean Langlais: « La ligne de conduite d'un artiste c'est la sincérité »." *La Bretagne à Paris*, Nov. 16, 1973.
Interview covering Langlais's Breton heritage, early life, methods of composition, and the "decadence" of some contemporary music.
Cesar Franck composed according to his own standards, and Langlais believes that is the path to follow.

REFERENCES TO INDIVIDUAL WORKS

ORCHESTRA

B264. DANSES, TROIS (1944)

B264a. Aubert, Louis. "De Beethoven à Hindemith et à Villa-Lobos." *Opéra*, March 9, 1949.
Refers to the second dance, *Sarabande*, as a poem.

B264b. Dufresse, Henri. "Ce qu'ils pensent/Instruments à vent." *Images Musicales* (Paris), March 25, 1949.

B264c. Michel, Gérard. "La Musique/Enfin, de vraies premières auditions." *Paroles Françaises* (Paris), March 18, 1949.
An original and well-written work, its lasting success is predicted.

B265. DIABLE QUI N'EST A PERSONNE, LE (1946)

Lalou, Etienne. "La création du «Diable qui n'est à personne»." *Radio 46*, February 7, 1946.
Announcement of the mystery drama broadcast with music by Langlais. Photo of actress Berthe Bovy.

B266. ESSAI SUR L'EVANGILE DE NOEL and

B267. HYMN D'ACTIONS DE GRACE (1935)

B266-67a. "La vie musicale." *Nouvelliste*, February 11, 1936.
Works by Langlais, Mihaud, Boccherini, and Beethoven, in series Concerts Classiques de Lyon. Both Langlais pieces were very favorably reviewed.

B266-67b. Caylot, A. M. "Concerts du Conservatoire." *L'Art Musical* (Paris), December 9, 1938.
Langlais was heard in the double roles of composer and virtuoso. His *Essai* had beautiful poetic color, with graceful writing. The co-ordination between organ and orchestra was excellent.

B266–67c. H., P. "Concerts musique/deuxième concert du Conservatoire." *Nancy Spectacles*, December 10, 1938.
Langlais' performance was received with long applause.

See also: B45.

B268. REMINISCENCES (1980)

B268a. "Ensemble Instrumental de Basse Bretagne." Concert program, Eglise Saint Julien Le Pauvre, Brest, France, May 18, 1981.
The composer's reason for the title is that he used two fragments of earlier works. He comments on the piece's free, rhapsodic structure.

B268b. *Le Télégramme* (Brest), August, 1980.
Review of the premiere of August 6. The strong, beautiful music sometimes evoked Poulenc with the harpsichord, but above all, Bartok and impressionism with the strings. This work showed that the harpsichord can be an instrument of the future as well as the past.

B269. SOLEIL SE LEVE SUR ASSISE, LE (1950)

B269a. A. A. "Le Soleil se lève sur Assise d'Albert Vidalie." *Gazette du Périgord Perigueux*, January 12, 1951.
Langlais' musical score was suggestive, but sometimes invaded [the dramatic score]. **[une partition suggestive, mais parfois envahissante.]**

B269b. "Le Soleil se lève sur Assise." *Savoie* (Chambery), December 23, 1950. Announcement of the radio program of December 30.

B269c. Richard, Roger. "Le Soleil se lève sur Assise." *Radio-Cinéma* (Paris), November 18, 1951.
Announcement of second broadcast of the radio drama, November 24, 1951. An exceptional work with very beautiful music.

B269d. *Radio-Cinéma* (Paris) 52, January 14, 1951.
Review of premiere.

B270. THEME, VARIATIONS ET FINAL (1937)

"Les Amis de l'orgue." *Excelsior* (Paris), June 6, 1938.
Results of the organ and orchestra composition contest, Les Amis de l'orgue. The jury (Maurice Emmanuel, Gustave Samazeuilh, Louis Aubert, Claude Delvincourt, Joseph Bonnet, Achille Philip, Alexandre Cellier, and André Marchal) unanimously awarded a prize of 2,000 francs to Jean Langlais for *Thème, Variations et Final*.

See also: B71, B93.

CHORAL and VOCAL

B271. ANTIENNES (1955)

Schalk, Carl. "Singing the Psalms." Translated by Kevin Donovan, S.J. *Church Music* 69-1 (1969): 27–31.
Interview with Fr. Gelineau. No mention of Langlais directly, but an excellent analysis of liturgical renewal in France and the problems encountered in French musical settings of scriptural texts. Gelineau's

rhythmic system and the French version of the Psalms are discussed. "I had asked a number of friends to contribute antiphons to the project."

B272. CANTATE A SAINT VINCENT DE PAUL (1946)

"A l'Ecole Saint-Vincent sous la Présidence de S. Em. le Cardinal Roques le maître Jean Langlais a inauguré hier les orgues de la chapelle." *Les Nouvelles de Bretagne* (Rennes), Feb. 11, 1952.
Langlais' dedicatory recital on the new chapel organ included a performance of this nine minute cantata (now lost) by the choir of the College of St. Vincent, directed by M. l'abbé Royer. The cantata was composed for the school's centenary in 1946.

B273. CANTIQUE dans GLOIRE AU SEIGNEUR (1948)

Gelineau, Joseph. "Supplément musical." *Musique et Liturgie* 4-5 (July-October 1948): 24.
Seigneur Jésus has a distinguised modal melody.

CHANSONS DE CLEMENT MAROT, DEUX (1931)   *See*: B169.

B274. CHANSONS FOLKLORIQUES FRANÇAIS, NEUF (1960)

B274a. Mari, Pierrette. *Guide du Concert et du Disques* (Paris), Nov. 30, 1962.
Review comments that the usual setting of folk melodies is quite simple, tending toward mediocrity. Langlais' settings, on the other hand, are judged to be subtle and intelligent, and the singers Collard and Maurane of highest quality. (*See*: D5a)

B274b. Dufourcq, Norbert. "Les petits riens de Chopin à J. Langlais." *La Nation Française* (Paris), Feb. 13, 1963.
Neuf Chansons populaires, Erato STE 60011, is described as a breath of fresh air (**"une bouffée d'air frais"**). (*See*: D5a)

B274c. Vendée, Gilles. "Disques de musique française in 1962." *Le Courrier Musical de France* 3 (1963): 113.
Review of Erato 42081 which notes that these ancient songs take on a youthful atmosphere in Langlais' settings. Particularly pleasing is "Quand le marin revient de la guerre." (*See*: D5a)

B275. CHANTS POUR LA MESSE (1953) [MESSE BREVE]

B275a. Bruyr, José. "Chants français pour la messe." *Disques* 120 (1961).
Review of Studio SM 33-74. (*See*: D13)

B275b. Hiégel, Pierre. "Disques classique." *Discographie Française* (Paris) 87.
Review of Studio SM 33-74, a very beautiful disc.

B276. DIEU, NOUS AVONS VU TA GLOIRE (1956)

Routley, Eric. *The Music of Christian Hymns*. Chicago: G.I.A. Publications, 1981.
Music printed as example 587, evaluated on page 181 as a masterpiece.

HUMILIS (1935) *See*: B169.

MELODIES (1936-38) *See*: B169.

B277. MASS IN ANCIENT STYLE (1952)

Marier, Theodore. "Mass in ancient style." *Caecilia* 84, no. 1 (February 1957): 56-57.
First Langlais mass published in the USA; inspired by a "challenge from the publisher McLaughlin and Reilly to write a simple mass for the average choir."

See also: B22, B242, B243.

B278. MESSE SOLENNELLE (1949)

B278a. Anderson, Roy. "Reviews: evening of music." *Choir Guide* 4, no. 3 (April 1951): 43-45.
First American performance, directed by Hugh Giles at Central Presbyterian Church, New York City, March 19, 1951. Not an unbiased review: "Now I am no sophisticate, so it will go hard for me to not give a sophisticated director a sophisticated review of sophisticated music.... Langlais uses a meaningless weaving of musical patterns that are so utterly confusing that the mind rejects an acceptance of them as having any goal.... Whenever he wants to build a climax he begins superimposing dissonances one right on top of the other and a few bars previous to his climax he opens up a blaring fifth so that by the time he gets to the climax, which is usually less dissonant than the preceding passages, the ears are so relieved that one feel(s) a sense of pleasure."

B278b. Arnold, Denis. "Instrumental." *Gramophone* 48, no. 573 (February 1971): 1338.
An extremely impressive work, strongly dependent on color, exploiting drama and rhetoric. (Review of Argo ZRG 662, *see*: D15a)

B278c. Cohn, Arthur. *Recorded Classical Music (A Critical Guide)*. New York: Schirmer Books, Macmillan Co., 1981.
Review of Argo recording on page 1033, mentioning its athleticism, passionate urgency, special aural impact, and exhilaration. (*See:* D15a)

B278d. Dufresse, Henri. "Messe de Jean Langlais." *Images Musicales* (Paris), February 23, 1951.
Performance given at the Association Valentin Haüy. Genius reigns in this music, the anguished and fervent cry of a twentieth-century man.

B278e. Hughes, Allen. "Three modern masses sung in Connecticut." *Musical America* 71, no. 10 (August 1951): 18.
On July 8 Hugh Giles presented Satie's *Messe des Pauvres*; Thomson's *Mass*; and Langlais' *Messe Solennelle* at Scott's Cove, near Darien. The Virgil Thomson work was deemed the most striking of the three.

B278f. Hume, Paul. "Jean Langlais." *The Washington Post*, September 21, 1981.
Langlais and Marie-Louise Jaquet-Langlais played on September 20 in the Shrine of the Immaculate Conception; *Messe Solennelle* and *Mass "Grant Us Thy Peace"* were sung. The former work had such "power and vital beauty" that it overshadowed the latter, written 30 years later. "No more glorious musical tradition exists today than that of the French organist and composer whose genius finds expression both in creating music for the church as well as in the art of improvisation. Jean Langlais is probably the outstanding exemplar of this tradition today."

B278g. Mardirosian, Haig. "Langlais: Messe Solennelle. O Salutaris Hostias. Ave Mundi Gloria. Libera Me. Corpus Christi. Trois

Prières. Venite et Audite. Psalm 111." *Fanfare* 9, no. 6 (July/August 1986): 161.
Review of Coronata COR 5001. Langlais' settings are "the music of faithful innocence." (*See*: D15d)

B278h. Mona, Joseph. "Jean Langlais aux claviers du Temple St-Etienne au 1er concert du Chant sacré." *L'Alsace*, October 9, 1973.
The choir "Chant sacré" featured the *Messe Solennelle*, with Langlais as organist, Madeleine Will as conductor. The reviewer comments that this major work, written in 1952, just prior to liturgical reforms in the Catholic Church in France, is being sung by a Protestant choir, while the Catholic choirs often seem to have turned their backs on it.

B278i. Pisciotta, Louis. "Messe Solennelle." *Caecilia* 84, no. 1 (February 1957): 57-59.
Praises "a highly imaginative use of motivic ideas, and a skillful handling of dissonance." Evaluated as "a splendid piece of musical craftsmanship" for a highly skilled choir.

See also: B22, B71, B216, B242.

B279. MISSA "IN SIMPLICITATE" (1952)

B279a. Blanchard, Roger. "Les disques." *Semaine Radio-phonique*, Paris, November 28, 1954.
The title "In simplicitate" shows Langlais' willingness to use a simple musical language, thus conforming to the *Motu proprio* of Pope Pius X.

B279b. Chailley, Jacques. "La musique religieuse." *Almanach des Disques*, 1955.
Held to be a "chef-d'œuvre," this record (Ducretet-Thomson 270 C 003) is recommended for all collections. (*See*: D16b)

B279c. "Commentaire des pièces musicales." *Musique et Liturgie* 32 (March-April 1953): 32. [first musical supplement]
Complete vocal score printed, no accompaniment. It was written the previous summer, particularly for a soloist who sings low masses.

B279d. Goléa, Antoine. "Jean Langlais." *Harmonie*, July 1967.
Review of Erato STU 70358. The music of this Mass is both simple and complex, the latter due to chant-like rhythms, a very free melodic line, and a harmonic texture both modal and chromatic. (*See*: D16d)

B279e. Mona, Joseph. "Musique française ancienne et contemporaine au «Concert du Dimanche» au Temple St-Jean." *L'Alsace*, December 5, 1972.
Marie-Louise Jaquet, with Claude Dubois-Guyot, soprano (soloist of Radio ORTF and the Parisian ensemble "Laetitia Musica", professor of voice at the music schools of Saint-Malo and Fougères). The *Missa "in simplicitate"* is described as full of ardent faith, austere and rich.

See also: B22, B176, B242.

B280. MISSA MISERICORDIAE DOMINI (1958)

Peloquin, C. Alexander. "Missa Misericordiae Domini." *Caecilia* 86, no. 3 (Autumn 1959): 115-16.
Review based on a study of the score and a performance at the 1959 Liturgical Music Workshop at Boys Town, sung by the Boys Town Choir at High Mass, with Langlais in the audience.

B281. MISSA SALVE REGINA (1954)

B281a. "L'Académie du Disque publie son palmarès." *Cunard Line*, January 1955, 3.
Short interview with Langlais about the first Christmas Eve mass televised by the R.T.F.; the first time the authorities at Notre-Dame had allowed commercial recording equipment to be used during mass.

B281b. Allan, Gilbert. "Confidences d'un choriste de la messe « Salve Regina »." *Figaro* (Paris), February 21, 1955.
An account of the difficulties and hardships when this mass was recorded February 18, 1955. (*See*: D17b)

B281c. Berry, Ray. "Third annual concert of the music commission of the Archdiocese of Boston." *The American Organist* 40, no. 4 (April 1957): 112-16.
American premiere on Jan. 7, 1956, in Sacred Heart Church, Roslindale, a suburb of Boston. The audience included clergy, musicians, and laity of many faiths, an aspect pointed out by Paul St. George, parish music director. Photos and program notes from the concert pamphlet, as well as parts of the review from the diocesan paper *The Pilot*. (*See*: B281r)

B281d. "Brillante Sainte-Cécile de la « Lyre Havraise » dont plusieurs membres ont été fêtés." *Le Havre-Presse*, December 9, 1968.
First performance in Le Havre, grand-messe in the church Saint-Vincent-de-Paul by the choir "Lyre Havraise," founded in 1868. The choir director was Bernard Dearing; organists were Claude Anacréon, titular, and Jean Lefebvre, choir organ. Town councillors and other dignitaries attended. Unsigned review, with photo.

B281e. Bruyr, José. "Messe de minuit télévisée." *Guide de Concert* (Paris), January 7, 1955.
Comments on the television program of the Christmas Eve midnight mass.

B281f. "Chronicle and Comment." *The Catholic Choirmaster* 42, no. 1 (Spring 1956): 83.
Three announcements concerning the *Salve Regina*, including the first New York performance.

B281g. Dumesnil, René. "Les disques/Henri Sauget--Jean Langlais." *Le Monde*, Dernière Edition, August 18/19, 1963.
This ingenious music aims to recreate the exceptional atmosphere of the Middle Ages in this Cathedral; nobly realized in the disc Erato 3023. (*See*: D17b)

B281h. -----. "Les disques/Ravel, par Robert Casadesus « Missa Salve Regina» de J. Langlais." *Le Monde*, 1ère Edition, August 7, 1955.
The mass is of singular beauty; a masterpiece, and magnificiently French. (*See*: D17b)

B281i. Hamon, Jean. "La Messe « Salve Regina »." *Combat*, Edition A (Paris), May 28, 1955.
Erato 3023 highly recommended, with special mention of the recording engineer Charlin, who surmounted the technical problems of the perilous acountics of Notre-Dame de Paris. (*See*: D17b)

B281j. -----. *Combat*, December 27, 1954.
The huge number of television viewers who heard the premiere of Langlais' mass should set a record for a first audition audience.

B281k. Mardirosian, Haig. "Langlais: Salve Regina Mass, Solemn Psalm No. 3." *Fanfare* 6, no. 1 (September/October 1982): 259.
Review of Solstice SOL 14. "The particular genius of the *Salve Regina Mass* lies in its discovery of how to deal with the heroic spaces of Notre Dame, Paris." (*See*: D17f)

B281l. Mona, Joseph. "Un somptueux concert inaugural." *L'Alsace.* n.d.
The *Mass Salve Regina* at the Neuvième festival de Masevaux, with organist Georges Bessonnet, les petits chanteurs de Ste-Marie d'Antony, le quatuor de cuivres du conservatoire Marcel Dupré de Mendon, Jean-Philippe Fetzer at the tribune organ with le quatuor liturgique de cuivres de Paris. Congregation directed by le Père Patrick Giraud, who was perfectly at home (**"qui se meut comme un poisson dans l'eau dans cette partition monumentale"**), like a fish in water, in this monumental score.

B281m. P., F. "Une messe de J. Langlais." *Disques*, April, 1955. [Reprinted in *Bulletin Sainte-Clotilde*, October 1955, 2-4.]
A work composed in December 1954, first performed on Christmas, recorded in February 1955, with the record released in April 1955! Numerous difficulties had to be surmounted, including the glacial cold in the Cathedral, but the recording was completed in one evening. The Erato disc is highly recommended. (*See*: D17b)

B281n. Petit, Pierre. "Les disques/Jean Langlais/Missa Salve Regina." *Conservatoire* (Paris), May 1955.
Langlais' style does not lose itself in byzantine complications; he writes for the faithful congregation in a language which they understand, but does not make the coarse concessions which weaken the music of some who write "for the public." (*See*: D17b)

B281o. R., A. "Une messe de Jean Langlais." *Reforme* (Paris), April 9, 1955.
A modern composer who brings back the breath of the Middle Ages.

B281p. Revert, Jehan. "La Messe "Salve Regina" de Jean Langlais." Insert with disc Solstice SOL 14. 1980.
The medieval atmosphere, the actual history of the Cathedral of Notre-Dame, is expressed in the music. The musical part of the congregation is included in the notes. (*See*: D17f)

B281q. Rostand, Claude. "La musique." *Carrefour* (Paris), June 15, 1955.
An immense ensemble has been perfectly captured on the Erato recording. The music is very beautiful in its simplicity. (*See*: D17b)

B281r. St. George, Paul. "Sing to God." *The Pilot* (Boston), January 14, 1956, 8.
Extensive review of the American premiere at Sacred Heart Church, Roslindale. Photos of Auxiliary Bishop Eric F. MacKenzie speaking, Jean Langlais at the organ, and Paul St. George conducting the congregational singing, with members of St. John's Seminary Choir. "In spite of the difficulty of making arrangements so near to Christmas, the church, which seats a thousand people, was full with standees in the rear.... the entire audience (most of whom had never seen the music before) after a brief rehearsal sang with incredible verve and fervor, demonstrating the feasibility and desirability of congregational participation at Mass."

B281s. Toulat, Jean. "Dans cinq ans toute la France télévisera."

Le Rouergat(Rhodesia), July 17, 1955.
An account of the role of television in liturgy and concert, showing that persons in England can attend Christmas Eve mass at Notre-Dame de Paris. Eight countries in Europe were linked in this Christmas service.

See also: B22, B151, B176, B218, B242, B243, B244.

B282. MOTETS, CINQ (1932-42)

B282a. P., F. "Discographie." *Musique et Liturgie* 90 (November-December 1962): 95.
Review of SM 45-87. The two-voice writing is expressive in its simplicity and purity of inspiration. (*See*: D18a)

B282b. Pierhal, Armand. "La royauté des concerts et leurs sujets." *Climats* (Paris), November 30, 1950.
The reviewer notes the series of five discs recently recorded by Les Petits Chanteurs de Fourvière at the Basilica of Fourvière. The fifth disc is particularly recommended, with Langlais' *Ave Mundi gloria* the only composition mentioned by name. (*See*: D18c)

B283. ORAISONS, TROIS (1973)

Rouger, Michel. "Création mondiale lundi à Cancale/Jean Langlais: 'La musique grégorienne m'a certainement influencé'." *Ouest-France*, August 10, 1973.
Interview and announcement of the premiere performance at Cancale on August 13. Langlais cites Gregorian chant, Palestrina, and Breton folklore as influences in his work.

B284. PAROLES (1946)

Clarendon [Bernard Gavoty, pseud.]. "Les concerts Milstein, Samson, François et Cie." *Figaro*, June 5, 1946.
Premiere review. These text settings are discrete, pertinent, and charming. Mlle. de Barbentane was exquisite, vocally and physically.

B285. PASSION, LA (1957)

B285a. Clarendon [Bernard Gavoty, pseud.]. "«La Passion» par Jean Langlais." *Figaro*, March 29, 1958.
Unlike some works which are made up of bits and pieces, this composition is a complete work. However, it leans toward a certain monotony. The vocal soloists were well chosen, but the reviewer grew tired of listening to the narrator's injured, emotional voice.

B285b. Davies, Margaret E. "The close of the season in Paris." *Musical Opinion* 81 (August 1958): 705.
This musical setting of the Passion has characteristics of Stravinsky and Messiaen, and echoes the simplicity of Masson's text. However, the music has "a certain monotony and lack of variety."

B285c. Facchinetti, Mario. "Premières auditions." *Guide du Concerts et du Disques* 38, no. 192 (April 18, 1958): 1085.
A truly original work, this oratorio lacks only a backdrop in order to be an opera. The conductor, singers, and orchestra were remarkable, with Giraudeau and Peyron outstanding for their diction and sensitivity.

B285d. "La Passion/Jean Langlais." *Guide du Concerts et du Disques* 38, no. 189 (March 21, 1958): 981.

Announcement of the premiere for March 27. The poetic text is of high quality, and the orchestral part emphasizes, rather than overburdens, the sacred drama.

B285e. Pendleton, Edmund J. "Music and musicians, twentieth-century French." *New York Herald,* Paris edition, April 4, 1958.
Here Langlais has used a more dramatic language than he usually employs. "Formless, the oratorio risks a certain monotony in spite of passages of tender and deep feeling expressed in linear, modal music. Following the crucifixion, a Gregorian-inspired hymn sings the glorification."

B285f. Queval, Jean. "Musique." *Mercure de France*, June 1958, 338-339.
Brief biography; this work ranks with the most remarkable productions of contemporary French religious music. The score is very expressive and clear, a very original work.

B285g. Rostand, Claude. "Création d'une 'Passion' de Jean Langlais." *Carrefour* (Paris) 707, April 2, 1958.
A work with strengths and weaknesses, austere and sincere. Its profound thought will adhere to those who don't pass by like hurrying tourists.

B285h. -----. "«La Passion» de Jean Langlais et Loÿs Masson." *Le Monde*, April 3, 1958.
The composer has not forgotten that the Passion narrative can be used by the church as sacred drama. Mystical elements of the poetry have been faithfully carried into the music with discretion and simplicity. Some influences of Stravinsky and Messiaen are noted. The static, flowing rhythmic lines have a certain monotony if one is not reading the text.

B285i. Sarnette, Eric. "Premières auditions." *Musique et Radio* 570 (Novembre 1958): 401.
French and English review of the first performances of works by Martinet, Langlais, Dandelot, and Trebinsky. Langlais' oratorio *La Passion* has an "extraordinary force of evocatory and descriptive character." The use of bells is particularly noted, as is "one of the best interpretations" of the National Orchestra under the conductorship of Manuel Rosenthal.

B285j. Vasa, Jacques. "La «Passion» de Jean Langlais." *La Nation Française*, Paris, April 9, 1958.
The high expectations which one has for Langlais' music were not quite met.

B286. PRIERES, TROIS (1949)

Sarnette, Eric. "Musique religieuse." *Musique et Radio*, November 1949.
The *Ave Verum* has an expressive melody line, idiomatic for the voice (rare in today's composers) and not difficult.

See also: B176.

B287. PSAUME 111, "BEATUS VIR QUI TIMET DOMINUM" (1977)

Dufourcq, Norbert. "Musique." *L'Orgue* 196 (October-December 1985): 24.
A great "motet à la française," energetic, forceful, and strong, with colorful harmonies.

B288. PSAUMES, DEUX (1937)

B288a. Altomont, Claude. *Le Ménestrel* (Paris), March 25, 1938.
Langlais' sensitivity and profound intuition result in music of grandeur,
solitude, and in *Psalm 58*, indignation.

B288b. C., E. "Deux œuvres nouvelles du compositeur rennais Jean
Langlais." *Ouest-Eclair*, 1938.
Dateline "Paris, 24 March (from our Parisian correspondent)." The French
setting of *Psalm 123* was easily understood, an admirable setting of the
text's unreserved trust, using quadruple vocal counterpoint against the
soloists' serene Gregorian psalmtone melody. The vehement indignation in
Psalm 58 was shown by willfully rude harmonies and a constant
fortissimo.

B288c. Capdeville, P. "Société Nationale." *Le Monde Musical*
(Paris), March 31, 1938.
The second *Psalm* did not lack accents (**"ne manque pas d'accents"**).

B288d. Demarquez, Suzanne. *L'Art Musical* (Paris), April 1,
1938.
The reviewer found that the choral voices were not well balanced, with
the soprano sound distressing, and their delivery rapid to the point of
being incomprehensible.

B288e. Schmitt, Florent. *Le Temps* (Paris), April 2, 1938.
Langlais is mentioned first in this review of concert premieres, and
Psalm 123 is classed as first-rate.

B289. SOLEMN MASS (1969)

B289a. Sears, Lawrence. "New Langlais mass filled with
grandeur." *The Evening Star* (Washington, D.C.), November 11, 1969,
B-7.
"Military pageantry, three organs, two brass choirs, several hundred
choristers, and at least two acres of bishops, archbishops and cardinals,
joined with a huge congregation at the National Shrine of the Immaculate
Conception last night for the first performance of the new "Solemn Mass
in English" by the French composer, Jean Langlais....Though the fabric of
his harmonies is threaded with anguish and torment, the final effect is
one of nobility and grandeur....Shrine music director Joseph Michaud and
his staff are to be congratulated on bringing this historic event to
Washington."

B289b. Sears, Lawrence. "Records: 4 top organists at the National
Shrine here." *The Evening Star* (Washington, D.C.), n.d. (1970).
Review of Vantage SLBT-1015 "Christ in Majesty." "Joseph Michaud, the
Shrine's music director, leads choral forces of 350 singers in a
performance of Langlais' new Solemn Mass in English, dedicated to
Michaud. Quite austere in comparison with his Messe Solennelle, it is
nevertheless an eloquent plea for peace." (*See*: D25)

B289c. Singer, Samuel L. "Mass by Langlais pleases all." *The
Philadelphia Inquirer*, December, 1970.
Christmas concert at the Cathedral of SS. Peter and Paul conducted by Dr.
Peter LaManna. The important organ part carries the more contemporary
aspect of the music. "The organ score, constantly moving and replete with
solid harmonies chromatic to the point of tone clusters, offers contrast
and support to the vocal lines, which are principally based on a Gregorian
Mass melody." The *Mass* received a "superior performance." The

principal chorus was the Collegiate Choir of the cathedral;   the congregational part was sung by the Cardinal O'Hara High School Chorale.

B290. TANTUM ERGO (1930)

"Tantum ergo." *La Musique Sacrée*, January-February 1933.
Reviewed and recommended to readers, this work for 3 mixed voices is original, colorful, yet simple, within the reach of the average choir.

VOIX DU VENT, LA (1934) *See*: B200.

ORGAN

B291. ADORATION (1968)

Sittler, René. "Dans le cadre des «Soirées de musique de chambre», Jean Langlais a donné un récital d'orgues à l'église St-Etienne." *Les Dernières Nouvelles d'Alsace* (Mulhouse), March 25, 1969.
First performance of *Adoration* in recital: "un court poème où chante la «voix humaine» en un récitatif plein de charme." (**a short poem where the "vox humana" sings a recitative full of charm.**)

B292. AMERICAN SUITE (1959-60)

B292a. Alderman, Hugh.   "Organist is superb at recital." *Times-Union*(Jacksonville, Florida), March 10, 1962.
At *Buffalo Bill's Grave* demonstrated that frequently the blind "'see' more than most of us who accept everything so casually, for Langlais had captured a spirit and melody in this work which was most revealing."

B292b. Berry, Ray. "Programme for the National Convention of the Royal Canadian College of Organists." *The American Organist* 44, no. 10 (October 1961): 11.
Langlais' recital on August 29 included the first performance of "Confirmation in Chicago" from *American Suite*.

B292c. Chamfray, Claude. "Premières auditions françaises." *Le Courrier Musical de France* 43 (1973): 101.
European first performance, given May 29, 1973 by Marie-Louise Jaquet, with note that the world premiere was in New York in 1970.

B292d. Sheridan, Jack. "French organist thrilling to appreciative audience." *Avalanche-Journal* (Lubbock, TX), March, 1967.
Langlais' recital in First Methodist Church before almost 1,000 persons included a dramatic and explosive performance of "Storm in Florida." "It is a graphic composition, vivid and frightening in its tonal description, the (s)torm lashing, fading, rising again (i)n greater strength, fading, coming ultimately to the full vortex of fulfillment. It is a work of savagery felt in the whirl of the angered elements."

B292e. Proskowetz, Pat. "Blind organist gives BR recital." *Morning Advocate* (Baton Rouge), March 13, 1962, 6-A. (*See*: B201)
"The tremendous range of both the performer and his instrument were evident in his transition to "Storm in Florida." As in many pieces of modern music, certain phrases bring to mind specific scenes, as the thunder and lightning the composer 'saw' perhaps more vividly with his ears and emotions than many persons see with their eyes. Electricity and drama filled the air during the presentation."

See also: B114, B119, B122, B147, B202, B229.

B293. B.A.C.H. (1985)

Vanmackelberg, Maurice. "La musique." *L'Orgue* 197 (January-March 1986): 28.
The six short pieces are described as a floral bouquet of hommage to the Leipzig Cantor; "ces six fleurettes composent un magnifique petit bouquet aux couleurs harmonieusement diversifiées, que met encore en valeur l'éclairage d'une registration précise."

B294. CHANTS DE BRETAGNE, HUIT (1974)

Bertault, Julien. "Le concert Jean Langlais à Luçon." *Le Nouveau Messager de la Vendée* (La Roche sur Tyon, France), May 7, 1976.
April 25 concert, Société des Amis de l'Orgue de Vendée. Langlais played the first, second, and eighth *Chants de Bretagne*. Professor Claude Dubois-Guyot sang the Breton melodies before each section.

See also: B106, B125, B134, B309j.

B295. CHARACTERISTIC PIECES, THREE (1957)

Noss, Luther. "Music reviews/organ music." *Notes* (Music Library Association) 18, no. 1 (December 1960): 132-33.
Reported as short but charming, simple, direct, and easy to play.

CHORALES, CINQ (1971) *See*: B241.

B296. CONCERTO "REACTION", TROISIEME (1971)

Metzler, Wolfgang. "Noten/Universal-Edition, Wien." *Ars Organi* 30, no. 4 (December 1982): 271.
Worthy of consideration, deserves many performances.

See also: B71, B238, B386.

B297. DOMINICA IN PALMIS [In die palmarum] (1954)

B297a. Bonfils, Jean, *L'Organiste Liturgique 8/Passion.*
Editions Schola Cantorum, 1954, preface. Translated by Scott Cantrell in "Editor's notes." *Music/The AGO-RCCO Magazine* 11, no. 3 (March 1977): 2.
Analysis of the composition, with chants identified.

B297b. Langlais, Jean. "Dominica in Palmis." *Music/The AGO-RCCO Magazine* 11, no. 3 (March 1977): 31-34.
Musical supplement in issue which commemorates Langlais' seventieth birthday. Previously printed in volume 8, *Passion*, of "L'Organiste Liturgique." (*See*: B297a)

See also: B122, B128.

B298. ESQUISSES GOTHIQUES, TROIS (1975)

B298a. Fauquet, Joël-Marie. *Musiques pour deux orgues* (Music for two organs). Translated by Charles Whitfield. Paris: Arion, 1979.
Booklet in French and English included with disc *Les orgues de Masevaux* (*see*: D34a). Program notes include the information that the

third *Sketch* is in the medieval form of an estampie.

B298b. Gay, Dom Claude. "Recensions." *Etudes grégoriennes* (Solesmes Abbey) 1981: 88.
The archaic modality of the six *Esquisses* is a reflection of the Middle Ages, the goal of the composer. The fluid paraphrase of the antiphon *Virgo Dei Genitrix* in the second *Gothic Sketch* is noted.

B298c. Himes, Douglas D. "A new wedding processional of Jean Langlais." *The Diapason* 69, no. 2 (January 1978): 1, 16.
Use of the first *Gothic Sketch* as a wedding processional (as at premiere), with analysis of plainchant themes.

B298d. Jaquet, Marie-Louise. "Jean Langlais/zu den werken." 1978.
Album notes for Motette M 10160 (*see*: D34c). The harmonic treatment of the *Gothic Sketches* is more modern than the previous *Romanesque Sketches*. Langlais seeks to renew interest in two organ literature, important in the 17th-18th centuries.

See also: B106, B241, B380.

B299. ESQUISSES ROMANES, TROIS (1975)

B299a. Dufourcq, Norbert. "Chroniques/musique." *L'Orgue* 173 (January-March 1980): 22.
The medieval influence in these pieces is accompanied by a spicy substratum which almost leads to polytonality.

B299b. Jaquet, Marie-Louise. "Jean Langlais/zu den werken." 1978.
Album notes for Motette M 10160 (*see*: D34c). The themes used were selected by the musicologist Jacques Chailley, and date from the 10th to 11th centuries. Langlais wishes to evoke the harmonic and rhythmic atmosphere of the medieval age. *Esquisse Romane No. 2* was inspired by the Romanesque basilica of St. Sernin of Toulouse, and by Pérotin.

See also: B106, B241, B380.

B300. ESSAI (1962)

B300a. Raver, Leonard. "Music for organ." *The American Organist* 47, no. 1 (January 1964): 6-7.
Found to be a provocative piece with "complex rhythmic structures and lightning-quick changes of registration. It's an atmospheric work with stark pauses which punctuate sharp jabs of sound contrasting with reflective passages of quiet beauty."

B300b. [Sarnette, Eric?] "Morceaux de Concours." *Musique et Radio* (1962): 264.
Not just a competition piece which is only accessible to highly trained virtuosi; this is a solid work of pure lines which does not employ technical difficulties foreign to the musical structure.

See also: B13, B195, B230.

B301. ETUDES DE CONCERT POUR PEDALE SEULE, SEPT (1983)

B301a. Bovet, Guy. "Nous avons reçu..." *La Tribune de l'Orgue* (Switzerland), December 1985.

A display piece. "On est quand même loin du Concerto pour la main gauche."
(In spite of all [the piece's qualities], we are far from the
[Ravel] Concerto for the left hand.)

B301b. Rochester, Marc. "New organ music." *The Musical Times*
127, no. 1727 (January 1987): 49.
Evaluated as a difficult technical study with interesting musical
references (plainsong, chorale) but slight musical substance.

B301c. Shuler, David. "Music reviews/keyboard music." *Notes*
(Music Library Association) 42, no. 4 (June 1986): 858.
Extensive review which finds that the composition transcends "virtuosity for its own sake." "Countrepoint I" and "Alternances" are the most
successful sections.

B301d. Voss, Peter L. "Universal orgel edition." *Musik und
Kirche* 55, no. 3 (May-June 1985): 144.
A pedagogical work of outstanding, virtuoso music.

B302. FOLKLORIC SUITE (1954)

"New works for the organ." *The Diapason* 45, no. 12 (November 1,
1954): 34.
For the organist with ordinary proficiency, an important set of pieces,
"not radically 'modern' either in harmony or rhythm."

See also: B125, B202.

B303. HOMAGE A JEAN-PHILIPPE RAMEAU (1962-64)

Cohn, Arthur. *Recorded Classical Music (A Critical Guide)*.
New York: Schirmer Books, Macmillan Co., 1981.
A review of "Evocation" (*see* : D39b) is on page 1033. "It has toccata
thrusts that explode in contrast to the very opposite of
chant-characterized passages. Excitingly colored, nicely fricative."

See also: B122, B195.

B304. HOMMAGE A FRESCOBALDI (1951)

B304a. Dufourcq, Norbert. "La musique d'orgue." *L'Orgue* 64
(July-September 1952): 93-94.
Langlais is to be thanked for writing these beautiful, not technically
difficult pieces. The "Epilogue" pedal solo has energy, fire, and fantasy.

B304b. Nicholas, Louis. "Pleasing organist draws full house."
The Nashville Tennessean, March 12, 1954, 40.
Concert given at Fisk University. "Epilogue," a prelude and fugue, "strikes
me as the best piece of music for pedals alone I have heard, though it is
not as flashy as some others."

B304c. Sarnette, Eric. "Orgue." *Musique et Radio* 497, 1952.
This suite refuses to follow the current musical tendency of bewilder-
ing, algebraic complexities.

See also: B44, B103, B118, B122, B167, B230.

B305. IMPLORATIONS, TROIS (1970)

Dufourcq, Norbert. "La musique." *L'Orgue* 140 (October-December 1971): 185.
The registration colors of the second *Imploration* are mentioned. The third *Imploration* is "very original and successful." The technical difficulties and "snares" of the first work were created especially for the concours d'orgue du Conservatoire national in 1970.

See also: B97.

B306. INCANTATION POUR UN JOUR SAINT (1949)

Dreisoerner, Charles. "The themes of Langlais' Incantation." *Music/The A.G.O.-R.C.C.O. Magazine* 6, no. 4 (April 1972): 41-44.
Thematic and theological analysis; one of Langlais' most popular works.

See also: B9, B42, B44, B122, B125, B230.

B307. LEICHTE STÜCKE, DREI [TROIS PIECES FACILES] (1986)

Busch, Hermann J. "Noten/Pro Organo, Leutkirch." *Ars Organi* 35, no. 1 (March 1987): 69.
Short pieces, a welcome addition for teaching and service-playing.

B308. LIVRE ŒCUMENIQUE (1968)

B308a. Denis, Pierre. "L'activité des «Amis de l'Orgue» saison 1967-1968." *L'Orgue* 128 (October-December 1968): 150-51.
Langlais' concert at Saint-Merry on June 19, 1968, sponsored by this French organization, included the first performance of the large part of the *Ecumenical Book.* "Ces belle pièces montrent l'auteur en plein renouvellement de son language, tout en restant fidèle à son esthétique coutumière." (These beautiful pieces show the author in full renewal of his language, always remaining faithful to his habitual aesthetic.)

B308b. Langlais, Jean. "Preface." *Livre Œcuménique.* Paris: Bornemann, 1968.
The composer's aim was to write music for teaching and service use.
"Roman Catholic organists will have no scruple in playing the commentaries on the chorals during the services or in recitals. May our brothers separate from us in religion but united with us in art, do the same for the pieces of gregorian inspiration."

B308c. Wasson, D. DeWitt. "Reviews/organ and harpsichord music." *Music/The AGO-RCCO Magazine* 11, no. 11 (November 1977): 15-16.
Useful service music in a "wide variety of styles." Eight of the twelve works are named as best of the volume.

See also: B103, B114, B122.

B309. MEDITATIONS SUR L'APOCALYPSE, CINQ (1972-73)

B309a. Busch, Hermann J. "Schallplatten." *Ars Organi* 52 (February 1977): 120.
Review of Arion recording by Marie-Louise Jaquet. (*See*: D43a)

B309b. Fauquet, Joël-Marie. *L'Apocalypse selon Jean Langlais* **(The Book of Revelation according to Jean Langlais).** Translated by Charles Whitfield. Paris: Arion, 1976.
French and English booklet included with disc ARN 38 312. (*See*: D43a) The musical analysis includes specific scriptural references with motifs.

B309c. Jaquet, Marie-Louise. "Une somme théologique et musicale." **(A theological and musical summation)** *L'Orgue* 154 (April-June 1975): 43-61.
A comparison and analysis of two long meditations on Christian mysteries, the organ works *Neuf méditations sur le Mystère de la Sainte-Trinité* of Olivier Messiaen (1974) and Langlais' *Cinq méditations sur l'Apocalypse"* (1973).

B309d. Lacas, Pierre-Paul. "Langlais Jean." *Diapason* 206 (April 1976).
Arion ARN 38 312. (*See*: D43a) "La forme de chaque pièce est nette bien que l'ensemble donne l'impression d'une série de vastes fresques libres." **(The form of each piece is very neatly written and the whole work gives the impression of a series of vast free frescos.)**

B309e. Le Dour, Patrig. "Jean Langlais: Cinq méditations sur l'Apocalypse." *Ouest-France* (Rennes), April 20, 1976.
Arion ARN 38 312. (*See*: D43a) The text inspires Celtic temperaments, and the setting is profoundly Breton, full of reflection.

B309f. Malary, Albert. "Cinq méditations sur l'Apocalypse, de Jean Langlais." *Medaille Miraculeuse*, November 1976.
Review of Arion ARN 38 312. (*See*: D43a) These mystical and difficult pages of music require reflection and study (as does the Apocalypse). They show the testimony of a "Cantor" whose great talent is completely at the service of an ardent faith.

B309g. Millet, Y. "Jean Langlais: Cinq méditations sur l'apocalypse." *La Voix Du Nord* (Lille), March 14, 1976.
A visionary work, with audacious harmonies, which communicate exhortation, prayer, consolation, and terror. It is both conservative and revolutionary. (*See*: D43a)

B309h. Reynolds, Gordon. "Instrumental." *Gramophone* 64, no. 762 (November 1986): 734.
John Scott's playing of the fifth trumpet section communicates the apocalyptic terror of this "mysterious, spine-chilling" piece. (*See*: D43b)

B309i. Rocas, Luis A. "Jean Langlais/organista y maestro." *El Universal* (Caracas, Venezuela), January 4, 1975.
On October 15, 1974 Langlais played the Five Meditations on the Apocalypse of St. John in the series "Les Heures Liturgiques et Musicales de Saint-Merry" in Paris. The reviewer was profoundly impressed with these musical paintings of eternity. (*See*: B332b for *Suite baroque*, same recital.)

B309j. Thomerson, Kathleen. "L'Apocalypse & Huit Chants de Bretagne by Jean Langlais." *Music/The AGO-RCCO Magazine* 11, no. 3 (March 1977): 37-39.
This 70th birthday tribute article included program notes and errata.

B309k. Wasson, D. DeWitt. "Reviews/organ and harpsichord music." *Music/The AGO-RCCO Magazine* 9, no. 8 (August 1975): 13.

Evaluated "a major contribution to organ literature!"

See also: B27, B84, B106, B122, B134.

B310. MEDITATIONS SUR LA SAINTE TRINITE, TROIS (1962)

Leonard Raver. "Music for organ." *The American Organist* 47, no. 1 (January 1964): 6.
"The Three Meditations on the Holy Trinity are not demanding technically; employing the same unifying thematic device found in Langlais' The Nativity."

See also: B128.

B311. METHODE D'ORGUE (1984) [with Marie-Louise Jaquet-Langlais]

B311a. Dufourcq, Norbert. "Musique." *L'Orgue* 196 (October-December 1985): 24.   Evaluated a short method, clear and useful.

B311b. Eifrig, W. F. "Book reviews." *The Diapason* 77, no. 12 (December 1986): 4.
Pedal exercises form the main part of this volume. Its value is in setting down "opinions and technical ideas that come out of a conservative musical and pedagogical tradition."

B311c. Smith, Rollin. "Reviews/organ music/methods." *The American Organist* 20, no. 1 (January 1986): 36.
Since the Langlaises assume a sufficient piano technique precedes organ study, they have put together "a book of 115 pedal exercises."

B312. MINIATURE (1958)

[Cunkle, Frank?] "New York Conclave proves rewarding." *The American Organist* 50, no. 3 (February 1, 1959): 14.
Marilyn Mason's premiere: "typical Langlais, and rather good Langlais, it seemed a little lacking in daring and exuberance in these surroundings."

B313. MOSAIQUE (1976-77)

B313a. Beechey, Gwilym. "Reviews/scores." *Musical Opinion* 102 (July 1979): 436.
The best piece of the first volume is *Stèle pour Gabriel Fauré*. The volume 2 *Salve Regina* "is a fine fantasia on plainsong themes in the manner of Tournemire."

B313b. Jaquet, Mariet-Louise. "Musique pour 2 organistes au même orgue." *Jeunesse et Orgue* 29 (1976): 9-12.
Survey of organ duet literature, including volume 1 *Double Fantaisie*.

See also: B27, 93, B106, B241, B380.

B314. NOELS AVEC VARIATIONS (1981)

Koch, Karl Hermann. "Noten/Universal Edition, Wien."
Ars Organi 30, no. 1 (March 1982): 63.
Langlais' personal style of music in the historic form of the French Noël.

See also: B106, B128, B238.

OFFERTOIRES POUR TOUS LES TEMPS, DEUX (1943) *See*: B122, B128.

OFFICE POUR LA SAINTE FAMILLE (1957) *See*: B118, 122.

B315. OFFRANDE A MARIE (1971)

Nalle, Billy. "Langlais in New York." *Music/The AGO-RCCO Magazine* 6, no. 11 (November 1972): 19.
The first New York performance of three of the six movements (#1, 3, 4) left the impression of "a cycle of earth to heaven and back to earth. It is not a major work in Langlais terms but it is beautiful and well crafted." (*See*: B191, same review.)

See also: B42, B122, B128.

B316. OFFRANDE A UNE AME, DIPTYQUE pour orgue (1979)

Labounsky, Ann. "Program notes for May 10, 1981."
Two pages, typescript, with explanation of the programmatic elements and identification of themes.

See also: B126, B131.

B317. ORGAN BOOK (1956)

B317a. Bingham, Seth. "Bingham considers new Langlais Book of notable value." *The Diapason* 48, no. 12 (November 1, 1957): 44.
These are easy pieces, yet vary in mood and treatment. "They have originality, distinction and expressive power--qualities utterly lacking in hundreds of worthless attempts by 'short and easy' writers."

B317b. Hoyt, Stuart E. "Music world at fingertips." *Milwaukee Journal*, Jan. 19, 1959.
Langlais is an imaginative and sophisticated composer. "Easiest to take on first hearing was a light 'Pasticcio,' from his 'Organ Book,'...with rapid, clear modulations from key to key. The finale from his 'First Symphony' published in 1944 was brilliant in color and strong in developments."

See also: B128, B259, B336f.

ORGAN POSTLUDE ON THE *DEO GRATIAS* (1958) *See*: B122.

B318. PARAPHRASES GREGORIENNES, TROIS (1933-34)

B318a. Banta, Lorene. "André Marchal teaches French music." *The American Organist* 21, no. 1 (January 1987): 56-60.
Includes performance notes on the "Te Deum" on page 60.

B318b. Messiaen, Olivier. *Le Monde Musical*, March 31, 1938.
The "Ave Maria, Ave maris stella" is written on two plainchant themes, hymns to the Holy Virgin. A beautiful organ piece, very poetic and well written, which should be in the repertoire of all organists.

B318c. Jacques-Lerta, Hélène. "Jean Langlais a joué sur l'orgue du Sacré-Cœur." *La Liberté* (Clermont-Ferrand), October 20, 1951.
Review of recital October 18. "Son *Te Deum* est d'une majesté triomphante qui se clôture en brillants arpèges et dans tout l'éclat des accords." (His *Te Deum* is of triumphant majesty which encloses itself in brilliant arpeggios and in exploding chords.)

See also: B4, B6, B42, B44, B64, B122, B125.

PETITES PIECES, DOUZE (1960, 1962) *See*: B122, B128.

PIECES, NEUF (1942-43) *See*: B9, B44, B103, B114, B122, B125, B195, B202.

B319. PIECES, VINGT-QUATRE, pour harmonium ou orgue (1933-39)

B319a. Bousquet, R. "A l'église St-Amans (24 septembre)." *Journal de l'Aveyron,* October 1, 1933.
Langlais played the premiere of *Arabesque*, not yet published, in this recital. "M. Jean Langlais est un grand, un très grand artiste."

B319b. "24 Pièces pour orgue ou harmonium." *Union* (Paris), November 1946.
The four sources of inspiration for these works are folk melodies, Gregorian chant, medieval polyphony, and the rich harmonic language of the symphonic organists, Vierne in particular.

See also: B122, B127, B170.

PIECES BREVES, DEUX (1983) *See*: B128.

B320. PIECES MODALES, HUIT (1957)

B320a. Bingham, Seth. "The modal writing of Langlais." *The American Organist* 41, no. 7 (July 1958): 252.
Recommended as an excellent introduction for those unfamiliar with Langlais' music, they show "certain facets of his art: poetic imagery, harmonic freshness, rhythmic freedom. With the greatest of ease the musical sections pass from one tonal center to another."

B320b. Dufourcq, Norbert. "Jean Langlais, huit pièces modales." *L'Orgue* 84 (October-December 1957).
Traditional writing, rich in invention, yet a language often audacious.

B320c. Raver, Leonard. "Music for organ." *The American Organist* 47, no. 6 (June 1964): 8.
"Given this composer's imagination, the results are not dry academic studies in modality but rather music of charm and inventiveness as one has come to expect from this leading French composer."

See also: B259.

B321. POEMES EVANGELIQUES (1932)

B321a. Case, Del Williams. "A study and performance of three organ works by Langlais, Dupré and Messiaen." D.M.A. diss., University of Southern California, 1973. iii-130.
Three twentieth century French programmatic-liturgical works are studied: *Poèmes Evangéliques, Le Chemin de la Croix,* and *L'Ascension.*

B321b. Rayfield, Robert. "Jean Langlais' *La Nativité.*" *Clavier* 18, no. 8 (November 1979): 18-24.
One of Langlais' former students teaches a lesson on this work, giving details of dynamics, registration, phrasing, legato, rubato, and programmatic themes. The score is printed, with suggested fingering and notes of added duration marked.

See also: B5, B44, B64, B195, B262.

B322. POEM OF HAPPINESS (1966)

B322a. Blanchard, Robert. "Reviews." *Sacred Music* 95, no. 1 (Spring 1968): 52.
Brief appearance of the Gregorian *Gaudeamus* and *Gaudete*, but this happy piece is primarily non-chant writing. Characteristic is "a melodic treatment of diminished triads followed by leaps of 6ths and 7ths."

B322b. Noss, Luther. "Organ music/an annual survey/original comtemporary compositions." *Notes* (Music Library Association) 24, no. 4 (June 1968): 819.
"An exuberantly joyful toccata," this is a substantial, rewarding work.

See also : B114, B128.

B323. POEM OF LIFE (1965)

Bingham, Seth. "Marie-Claire Alain." *The American Organist* 50, no. 11 (November 1967): 10.
Review of Alain's recital in New York City which included this work dedicated to her. Program notes called it "a grand sonorous fresco re-tracing the joys and sorrows of mankind." The reviewer believes it presents an exciting experience for virtuoso organists.

See also: B128.

B324. POEM OF PEACE (1966)

B324a. Blanchard, Robert I. "Reviews." *Sacred Music* 95, no. 1 (Spring 1968): 52.
A work built on "plainsong themes on peace: invocation *Regina Pacis* from the Litany, the *Pax Comini sit semper vobiscum* and its response *Et cum spiritu tuo*, and the entire antiphon for peace, *Da pacem*. It is a masterful little piece and not difficult."

B324b. Noss, Luther. "Organ music/an annual survey/original comtemporary compositions." *Notes* (Music Library Association) 24, no. 4 (June 1968): 819.
Not hard; "appropriately quiet, sustained, and irenic."

See also: B128, B220.

B325. POSTLUDES, FOUR (1950)

B325a. Lester, William. "New music for the organ." *The Diapason* 43, no. 12 (November 1952): 23.
"couched in the acrid idiom of the presentday leaders of French organ writing." High marks in musical content and expertness of writing.

B325b. Noss, Luther. "Keyboard music." *Notes* (Music Library Association) 9, no. 4 (September 1952): 658.
"Each is a brief flourish, highly improvisatory in character, sharp in its impact, and stunning in its effect. Perhaps no high musical purpose is served, but all organists will appreciate their value."

B325c. Rosalie, Sister, O.P. "Other music." *Caecilia* 87, no. 2 (Summer 1960): 93- 95.

"Worthwhile additions to any organist's repertoire," these pieces are not yet generally known. Langlais has suggested them for use at weddings.

PRELUDE A LA MESSE "ORBIS FACTOR" (1956)   *See*: B127.

B326. PRELUDE ON *CORONATION* (1963)

Peeters, Flor. "Boekbespreking." *De Praestant* 17, no. 2 (April 1968): 46.   A short free fantasy in the typical French style of Langlais.

B327. PRELUDES, HUIT (1983-84)

Grondsma, Folkert. "Besprekingen." *Eredienstvaardig*(Holland) 1, no. 2 (1985): 92.
Review with special attention given to the last prelude to be performed by two organists, *Troisième Fantaisie pour 2 Organistes.* The *Préludes,* useful for both church and teaching situations, have separate technical problems, and great musical imagination.

See also: B127.

B328. PRELUDES, SIX (1929)

B328a. C., J. "Courrier artistique/deux concerts d'orgue." n.p., n.d. (Toulouse, France, August 1930.)
This August 10 concert given by Langlais, shortly after winning his *premier prix* in the organ class of the Paris Conservatory, included two of the *Préludes* : *Adoration des bergers* (with its primitive cantilena) and *Chant héraldique* (so harmonious under the Gothic arches of Sacré-Cœur Church in Toulouse).

B328b. Dufourcq, Norbert. "Chroniques et notes/les concerts/premières auditions d'œuvres pour grand orgue." *La Revue Musicale* 116 (June 1931): 58-59.
First performance of two of the *Préludes. Lamentation* is a long crescendo on the eight foot foundation stops; *Images* is an elusive sketch on the 1, 2, and 4 foot stops. These two short pages denote a delicate sensitivity, a particular predilection for tone color, with use of pure timbre and contrasting colors. "C'est un peintre... et Jean Langlais est aveugle." (**He's a painter...and Jean Langlais is blind.**)

See also: B127.

Première Symphonie, *see* Symphonie, Première, B336.

B329. PROGRESSION (1978)

Dufourcq, Norbert. "Chroniques/musique." *L'Orgue* 173 (January-March 1980): 22.
The last piece, *Fugue et Continuo,* is a muscular conclusion, full of spirit and unexpectedly rough vigor.

See also: B127, B131.

ROSACE (1980)   *See*: B238.

B330. SOLEILS, CINQ (1983)

Schmidt, Dennis. "New organ music." *The Diapason* 78, no. 5 (May

1987): 9.
Five impressionistic pictures of the sun. "The interesting themes and harmonies used in these pieces make this collection a fine addition to the organ works of Langlais."

B331. SONATE EN TRIO (1967)

B331a. de Lisle, Christiane. "A entendu." *Guide du Concert*, October 12, 1968, 12.
Account of the organ examinations at the Paris Conservatory where the *Trio Sonata* was performed by each of the ten candidates.

B331b. Dufourcq, Norbert. "La musique/1. Musique française." *L'Orgue* 128 (October–December 1968): 158.
Langlais' musical language shows a coarseness and an amusing directness in this trio.

B332. SUITE BAROQUE (1973)

B332a. Mona, Joseph. "Au temple Saint-Jean: Jean Langlais/création de sa «Suite baroque»." *L'Alsace* (Mulhouse), December 4, 1973.
Premiere played by the composer on the organ for which it was written, a new Silbermann-style instrument. The recreation of a Baroque organ inspired a contemporary "classic" suite with a touch of malice. Langlais writes music of astonishing vitality while being humorous about an 18th century organ in the 20th century. The concert was recorded by the ORTF and Langlais gave an interview.

B332b. Rocas, Luis A. "Jean Langlais/organista y maestro." *El Universal* (Caracas, Venezuela), January 4, 1975.
In very flowery, poetic language the critic reports that the composer tried to write an ironic work, but was unable to do so because of his great talent; instead he places ancient reminiscences in new contexts. (*See*: B309i for the other work on the recital program.)

See also: B84, B106, B126.

B333. SUITE BREVE (1947)

B333a. Farmer, Archibald. "New organ music." *The Musical Times* 90 (June 1949): 195.
"For those who can use the dissonant manner.... I find little to be said for the 'Grands Jeux' and 'Dialogue sur les Mixtures', where the wilful eccentricity of the writing verges on cacography."

B333b. de Nys, Carl. "Kynaston Nicolas, orgue." *Diapason* 147 (May 1970): 36–37.
Review of Philips 65 28 001. (*See*: D67d) Jehan Alain and Langlais are discussed as representatives, with Messiaen, of those who have not abandoned the traditional concept of melody, unlike Ligeti.

B333c. Dufourcq, Norbert. "Chroniques et mélanges/musique d'orgue." *L'Orgue* 46 (January–March 1948): 23.
This work is welcome because it is not necessary to possess the technique of a virtuoso to be able to play it. The character of the movements vary from strongly majestic, to pastoral, to heart-rending echoes, to a virile march.

See also: B125, B179, B336e.

B334. SUITE FRANÇAISE (1948)

B334a. Farmer, Archibald. "New music." *Musical Times* 90 (December 1949): 447.
"Surely the *voix céleste* has never before been made to sound so dyspeptic as in the movement so named, nor the *nazard* so much like a wet Sunday in Wales. In all this there is nevertheless an interesting technique."

B334b. Lester, William. "New music for the organ." *The Diapason* 41, no. 1 (December 1, 1949): 28.
"One of the most interesting and appealing of the newer French publications for organ." Langlais' "tangy" idiom, clever effects, imagination, and creative ability are praised.

B334c. S., R. [Sabin, Robert?] *Musical America* 69, no. 11 (September 1949): 34.
"His musical ideas, stemming from the Guilmant-Widor-Bonnet school of thought, are tasteful, expertly framed, and uniformly ingratiating."

B334d. Selby, Norman L. "Langlais fingerings." *The American Organist* 21, no. 7 (July 1987): 15.
Suggestions for successful finger patterns in "Arabesque sur les flûtes."

B334e. Sheridan, Jack. "French organist thrilling to appreciative audience." *Avalanche-Journal* (Lubbock, TX), March, 1967.
In "Arabesque sur les flûtes" the organ flutes play a "moth-and-flame caprice over the manuals. Again, Langlais' gleaming sense of musical joyousness and humor was underscored throughout."

See also: B126, B195, B229.

B335. SUITE MEDIEVALE (1947)

B335a. Alain, Olivier. *Le Conservatoire* (Paris), October 1950.
Pieces with a certain rhapsodic aspect; "Tiento" is the most successful.

B335b. Beechey, Gwilym. "Jean Langlais' 'Suite Médiévale' en forme de Messe Basse." *Musical Opinion* 106 (September 1983): 381.
"The most striking feature of the work as a whole is the suppleness and freedom of Langlais' rhythmic invention." Characteristics of the individual movements are given, with chant themes identified.

B335c. Coci, Claire. "The Suite Medievale." *Choir Guide* 4, no. 8 (November 1951): 40-41.
Introductory remarks for Suite Medievale as a Low Mass. The pedal part of the "Elevation" symbolizes the eternity of the Word.

B335d. Noss, Luther. "Organ music." *Notes* (Music Library Association) 2d ser. 7, no. 3 (June 1950): 447.
The increasing use of Langlais' organ pieces in America is noted. Well-written, usually not too difficult, they "are always interesting and colorful in their romantically dissonant way."

B335e. Reynolds, Gordon. "Instrumental." *Gramophone* 58, no. 692 (January 1981): 972.
The fusion of Langlais' modern harmonies with the timeless chants "produces a fire varying in intensity from the small candle flame of the Communion Meditation to the scorching heat of the sun in the Acclamantions." (*See*: D69n)

B335f. Sarnette, Eric. "Orgue/Jean Langlais." *Musique et Radio* (Paris), October 1950.
Reviewed shortly after publication, this work shows the "richness of color" which is "one of the most captivating marks" of Langlais' music.

B335g. -----. "Revue de l'édition musicale." *Musique et Radio*, February 1963.
In French and English, slightly updated version of 1950 review (*see*: B335f). Level of difficulty for performer not great, yet profound musicial meaning. "In pieces like the *Suite Medievale*, we guess the long ripening of a creative thought (in the most complete sense of the word)."

See also: B42, B44, B103, B118, B122, B126, B195.

SUPPLICATION (1972) *See*: B128.

SYMPHONIE, DEUXIEME, "ALLA WEBERN" (1976-77) *See*: B106, B183, B241.

B336. SYMPHONIE, PREMIERE (1941-42)

B336a. B., P. *Paris-Soir*, June 26, 1943.
Favorable review of the premiere played by the composer in Paris.

B336b. Bernard, Robert. *Les Nouveaux Temps* (Paris), June 25-26, 1943.
The premiere was played by the composer at the Palais de Chaillot. The composition disclosed the true nature of a poet.

B336c. Berry, Ray. "Reviews." *The American Organist* 42, no. 8 (August 1959): 282.
Langlais' recital at Central Presbyterian Church, New York City, March 17, 1959, included the last movement, "Final," "a brilliant *tour de force* played as the fine work it is."

B336d. Jones, Celia Grasty. "The French organ symphony from Franck to Langlais." D.M.A. diss., University of Rochester, Eastman School of Music, 1979, ix-151.
A survey of twenty organ symphonies. Chapter 8 has eleven pages of discussion and analysis of the *Première Symphonie*, rating it as not innovative, with conservative harmonic language.

B336e. Sarnette, Eric. "Revue de l'édition musicale/Orgue." *Musique et Radio* (Paris), November 1947.
Review praising Langlais' work, particularly the "monumental" *Symphonie pour orgue* and *Suite brève*.

B336f. Sasonkin, Manus. "Recital on organ by Jean Langlais." *The St. Louis Post-Dispatch*, January 19, 1959.
Langlais' own compositions "displayed a wide range of mood, from the whimsical Scherzando, out of the Organ Book, to the more dramatic and turbulent Final of the First Symphony. In general, I found the shorter pieces, four altogether, rather more satisfactory than the symphony movement, which struck me as being somewhat overly sectional and lacking in cohesiveness."

See also: B13, B64, B183, B195, B211.

SYMPHONIE, TROISIEME (1979) *See*: B183, B238.

B337. TRIPTYQUE (1956)

B337a. Gay, Harry W. "Music for organ." *The American Organist* 41, no. 10 (October 1958): 388.
Representative of a facile technique, "leaves much to be desired in real musical composition." The *Trio* section is clever, but awkward, and the *Final* resembles a Vierne scherzo, "utterly predictable and sometimes stagnantly impressive."

B337b. Ramsey, Basil. "Royal Festival Hall recitals." *The Musical Times* 99 (April 1958): 218.
Langlais' recital of February 19 included this newly composed work, "a delightful exploration of three distinct moods." (*See also*: B359)

B337c. [Swinyard, Laurence?] "Organ and church music reviews." *Musical Opinion* 81 (July 1958): 671.
Langlais is usually associated with two trends in French organ music, plainsong basis, or portrayal of biblical scenes. This work, however, is in concert style. "A brilliant, colourful suite that will delight the proficient recitalist."

See also: B114, B202, B223, B230.

B338. TRIPTYQUE GREGORIEN (1978)

Sutherland, Donald S. "Music reviews/keyboard music." *Notes* (Music Library Association) 37, no. 3 (March 1981): 695.
The reviewer feels that the work is lacking in rhythmic vitality due to its being based on Gregorian chant, "causing the work to wander about without much sense of direction."

See also: B126, B131.

B339. VOLUNTARIES, THREE (1969)

B339a. Chamfray, Claude. "Premières auditions françaises." *Le Courrier Musical de France* 37 (1972): 16.
First performance on November 9, 1971, by Michelle Leclerc.

B339b. Vos, Wesley. "Organ music." *The Diapason* 62, no. 1 (December 1970): 20.
Extended compositions in differing styles, with high technical demands.

See also: B127, B174.

ORGAN AND INSTRUMENTS

B340. CORTEGE (1969)

"A Bitschwiller-lès-Thann: une œuvre de Jean Langlais en première audition." *L'Alsace* (Mulhouse), May 25, 1976.
Announcement that the brass ensemble of the Collegium musicum of the University of Marburg, Germany will join organist Marie Louise Jaquet in the premiere of the *Cortège* on May 27.

CONCERTO, TROISIEME (1971) *See*: B296.

B341. PIECE IN FREE FORM (1935)

B341a. Bingham, Seth. "Recitals and concerts/Jean Langlais."
The American Organist 45, no. 3 (March 1962): 24.
Performance by Langlais at the Church of the Heavenly Rest, New York
City, January 28, 1962, with the Galimir Quartet. "This very personal
work...dedicated to the composer's wife, gains with each hearing. Its
warm humanity and sensitive approach is that of a true tonal poet; it is
surely one of Langlais' finest creations."

B341b. -----. "New Langlais work for organ, strings discussed."
The Diapason 52, no. 3 (February 1, 1961): 6.
The reviewer heard the first American performance, by the Guilet Quartet
with Hugh Giles, organist. He finds the work highly original.

B341c. "«Les Amis de l'Orgue».--Mme Mairot-Jacquot et M. Porte."
n.d. [Clipping in collection of Jean Langlais, Paris.]
In the first concert of "Les Amis" 1936-37 season Mlle. Noëlie Pierront
premiered Langlais' *Quintette*. This work in free form and modal
character expresses two feelings, one ecstatic, the other opening out in
poignant cries of deep humanity.

Trumpet and Organ   *See*: B344-47.

PIANO AND INSTRUMENTS

B342. FANTAISIE (1935) string quartet and piano

B342a. Altomont, Claude. "Société Nationale de Musique." *Le
Ménestrel*, February 12, 1937.
The reviewer hears a poignant resignation in the music, the heroic debate
of a soul refused light. Langlais creates his own light through sound, as a
visionary composer.

B342b. *Musique & Instruments* (Paris), March 1, 1937.
Unsigned review of the premiere: "...est l'émouvante expression d'une
douleur vrai." (...is a moving expression of true sorrow.)

PIANO

B343. SUITE AMORICAINE (1938)

B343a. Le Guével, Firmin. *Poésia* (Paris) 16 (May 1939).
Performance by the composer of this nostalgic suite.

B343b. "Societe Nationale." *L'Art Musical*, April 28, 1939.
Premiere performance by Ida Périn, dedicatee of the last movement . This
Movement Perpétuel reflects the incessant and eternal movement of
the sea. All movements are inspired by the sea in Brittany.

BRASS

BRASS CHOIR: CORTEGE *See*: B340.

TWO TRUMPETS

B344. PASTORALE AND RONDO (1982)

B344a. Haas, Wolfgang G., trans. Richard A. Lister. 1983.
Album insert notes for *Trompete und orgel Köln*, Motette M 2011. This
composition was written at the request of the ensemble "Trumpet and
organ, Cologne." Premiere information is given, and additional program
notes. (*See*: D81)

B344b. Nelson, Leon. "Organ music/music for organ &
instruments." *The Diapason* 75, no. 6 (June, 1984): 17.
Described as highly unusual, effective, and exciting; the Rondo being an
elaborated version of *Pasticcio* of 1957.

B344c. Ogasapian, John. "Reviews/Records." *The American
Organist* 20, no. 5 (May 1986): 29.
Motette 2011. Although the reviewer is "not especially a fan of most of
Langlais's music," he finds the *Pastorale* " quite captivating" and the
Rondo "generally successful." (*See*: D81)

TRUMPET

B345. CHORALS, SEPT (1972)

Mona, Joseph. "Une nouvelle création de Jean Langlais au Temple
Saint-Jean." *L'Alsace*, January 15, 1974, 23.
Recital which included the premiere given in Mulhouse by Marie-Louise
Jaquet, organ, and André Bernard, trumpet, before an enthusiastic
audience.

B346. PIECE POUR TROMPETTE (1971)

B346a. Malettra, Françoise. 1975. Album notes for *Trompette &
orgue/Quatre compositeurs français contemporains*, Decca QS
7.315).
The organ and trumpet parts do not follow a solo with accompaniment
pattern, but rather a dialogue, seen as a struggle: "... a combat carried out
according to an intelligent strategy: violence of the discourse in a first
phase; discussion in the form of a truce, putting into action every
possible means of persuasion, even of seduction, in a second phase; total
engagement of the two partners in the final struggle where there is
neither a victory, nor a defeat, but a just appraisement of the forces in
view of each other." (*See*: D82a)

B346b. Mannoni, Gérard. "Trompette et orgue." *Harmonie*
(Boulogne) 115 (March 1976): 101.
Review of Decca QS 7.315. Langlais' writing for the trumpet is not avant-
garde style at its most audacious, and will not shock anyone. (*See*: D82a)

B347. SONATINE (1976)

Reynolds, Gordon. "Chamber Music." *Gramophone* 60, no. 716
(January 1983): 841.
Vista VPS 1107, "...a musical surprise packet. Brilliant playing here, a
witty performance." (*See*: D83d)

See also: B93, B241.

REVIEWS AND ARTICLES ON LANGLAIS' IMPROVISATIONS

B348. Arnatt, Ronald. "In our opinion...Reviews/recitals and concerts." *The American Organist* 42, no. 7 (July 1959): 247-48.
Langlais' recital at Graham Chapel, Washington University, St. Louis, January 19, with discussion of his strengths as a composer and improviser, his consistency of style while improvising, and his inventive treatment of themes.

B349. Bret, Gustave. "Musique. Le concours des Amis de l'orgue." *L'Intransigeant,* July 28, 1931.
This organ competition won by Langlais was in two parts, improvisation and memorized performance. The requirements were so difficult that only two competitors played. Langlais' rare personality was shown from the first measures of his improvisation on l'*Ave Maris Stella*.

B350. Bertault, Julien. "Le récital Jean Langlais à Radio-France." *Le Nouveau Messager de la Vendee* (La Roche sur Tyon, France), December 24, 1976.
The recital broadcast from Sainte-Clotilde concluded with an improvisation on "Veni Creator." The melody started in a calm manner, then expanded and animated gradually until it reached a dazzling toccata.

B351. Dodane, Charles. "Jean Langlais aux grandes orgues de St-Jean." *La Depeche du Midi* 1961. (Besançon recital.)
The reviewer found listening to a Langlais improvisation on the *Veni Creator* to be better than a fireworks display; it was a work of religious art, taking on the aspect of a prayer.

B352. Fisher, Jack. "Recitals and concerts." *The American Organist* 39, no. 4 (April 1956): 127-28.
Langlais' recital, February 18, 1956, Northrop Auditorium, University of Minnesota, Minneapolis. "M. Langlais told us in his after-dinner speech that improvisation and composition are two different animals, and he offered no tricks in improvisation. He stated that one has to love music and love to play music for people in order to improvise. He improvised on three submitted themes, one a Gregorian Kyrie, which he wove into a ten minute piece, sonata form, one of the most musical feats I have heard."

B353. Galard, Jean. "Disques." *L'Orgue* 200 (October-December 1986): 26-27.
Review of Medias Music MEM 009FC45, two Langlais improvisations. Total recording time was 50 minutes, two twenty-five minute periods; a true account of what one would hear at a church service or concert where the 80-year-old Langlais was improvising. "What an astonishing man." (*See*: D86, D97b)

B354. Goldsworthy, William A. "Jean Langlais recital." *The American Organist* 35, no. 4 (April 1952): 123-24.
Review of the recital at Central Presbyterian Church, New York, April 22, 1952, on Langlais' first American tour. "...primarily his playing is that of the head, not too much of the emotions. It was in his improvisation he proved himself, for here was one of the best we have heard. He worked out the theme in a remarkable manner with real ideas and registration, using little of the so-called Conservatoire Padding; he made an improvisation of dignified length, but not too wordy (as most are); Mr. Bingham, who submitted the theme, must have been pleased."

B355. Hollander, Harrison. "Bach Festival musical success." *Winter Park Herald* (Florida), March 5, 1959.
Langlais' all-Bach program opened the 24th annual Bach Festival.
"Just before the beginning of his recital Mr. Langlais was given the theme of one of the chorales from the "St. Matthew Passion" on which to improvise, and it was with this improvisation that he closed the program. Begun simply and quietly, it was gradually built up into a massive contrapuntal edifice that culminated in a powerful climax. The members of the audience, deeply impressed by Mr. Langlais' performance, gave him a standing ovation at its conclusion."

B356. Huff, Serge. "Blind organist overcomes difficulties." *The Phoenix Gazette*, February 20, 1967.
"Just prior to the recital here, ASU resident organist Charles Brown played original themes of his own as well as several by Professor Grant Fletcher, also of the university's music department. The soloist then selected one from each composer, wrote the melody line in braille then ... transformed these themes into an extemporaneous study of musical forms and devices climaxing with a tumultuous fugato and sequential passage which superimposed the rhythmic Brown theme over the free-flowing Fletcher melody now in the bass pedals."

B357. Humphreys, Henry S. "Fabulous improvisateur." *The Cincinnati Enquirer*, November – [Concert of November 1], 1964, 47.
"Listening to this **Cesar Franck Redivivus**--"Franck Come To Life Again"--improvise on the chorale "A Mighty Fortress Is Our God" ... I would have given anything to descend into the mystical grotto of Langlais' tonal - imagery just at the moment this fantasia reached the height of its clashing, writhing, now-ecstatic, now-frantic descant!"

B358. Labounsky, Ann. "Improvising on chant themes." *The American Organist* 17, no. 12 (December 1983): 26-27.
Former student of Langlais describes his improvisation class at the Schola Cantorum.

B359. Ramsey, Basil. "Royal Festival Hall recitals." *The Musical Times* 99 (April 1958): 218.
Langlais' recital of February 19 concluded with an improvisation on a theme submitted by Benjamin Britten. "...it became the subject of a whirlwind display that picked haphazardly at almost every contrapuntal device known to man. A *tour de force* that showed the amazing vitality, and occasional vulgarity, of the modern French school."

B360. Raymond, Jean. "Le récital d'orgue de Jean Langlais a ouvert en beauté le cycle des concerts des Amis de la musique sacrée."
Le Midi-Libre (Nimes), November 11, 1966.
Langlais' concluding improvisation depicted the scene at the tomb of Jesus. Sorrow, suffering, surprise, dialogues, and ultimately the resurrection exultation, all were represented.

B361. Reinthaler, Joan. "Blind organist performs here." *The Washington Post*, January 16, 1967, B9.
Recital concluded with an improvisation on "O Tod" from the Brahms *Vier Ernste Gesange*. "This provided the most exciting moments of the evening. Langlais wove increasingly complex and intense lines around this fine theme with a decisiveness of direction which can only come from a complete original concept. To those used to the kind of aimless wanderings which often accompany the taking of a collection on Sundays all over the world, this must be quite a revelation."

B362. Salabert, Nicole. "Jean Langlais: Un musicien de grand talent." *La Marseillaise* (Marseille), Feb. 19, 1971.
Recital given at the church of Saint-Joseph concluded with an improvisation on a Noël provençal. Langlais' careful treatment of the inner voices and his colorful use of dissonances were highlights.

B363. Sasonkin, Manus. "Recital on organ by Jean Langlais." *The St. Louis Post-Dispatch*, January 19, 1959.
"M. Langlais's improvisation on a theme submitted apparently anonymously, was a marvel of ingenuity and resourcefulness and served to demonstrate that even a mediocre theme—and make no mistake, this one was mediocre—is not a deterrent to a composer with imagination and technical skill." (This review also entered as B336f; another review of same recital is B348.)

B364. Sears, Lawrence. "Langlais' improvisations crown organ concert." *The Evening Star and Daily News*, Washington, D.C., August 21, 1972, D-8.
"It was like being present while Chaucer wrote, DaVinci painted, Michelangelo sculpted, or Franck, Pierne, Tournemire or Bonnal played."

B365. Tripp, Ruth. "French organist gives recital at Sayles Hall." *The Providence Journal* (Rhode Island), October 14, 1964, 24.
"A final display of musicianship came with the improvisation which was played on two themes submitted a few moments before the program by Dr. Ron Nelson, chairman of the department of music at Brown University. The first resembled the call of a wood thrush and the second seemed to be an inversion of the first theme. What we heard was a marvelous display of skill in an art which is practiced to perfection in France."

B367. Williams, Martyn. "Organ recitals." *The Musical Times* 125 (January 1984): 51.
Recital of October 26, 1983 before a capacity audience in Royal Festival Hall concluded with "a cunningly free-ranging improvisation on a theme provided by Nicholas Danby. The major-minor dichotomy gave a piquant colouring to a *moto perpetuo* movement before realizing its true identity in a stylized toccata, firmly anchored on G: a remarkable performance."

See also: B148, B163, B222, B227, B230, B249, B388.

REVIEWS OF RECORDINGS MADE BY LANGLAIS

Arion ARN 36 331. *8 chants de Bretagne et improvisation.* **1976.** (*See*: B134)

B368. Arion ARN 336 008. *César Franck à Sainte-Clotilde.* **1975.**

Busch, Hermann J. "Schallplatten." *Ars Organi* 52 (February 1977): 120.
Langlais' records are a challenging lesson in Franck's musical language.

B369. Ducretet-Thomson LAG-1017. *César Franck: pièces d'orgue.* **1953.**

B369a. Affelder, Paul. "Franck, César." *Records in Review, 1957.* Joan Griffiths, ed. Great Barrington, Mass.: Wyeth Press, 1957.
Entry on page 85 comments on "a reverent tribute."

B369b. Hamon, Jean. "Sur votre pick-up/Quelques disques d'orgue."
Combat (Paris), Edition A, October 24, 1953.
Engineering of the disk is superb, and the atmosphere of Sainte- Clotilde
is captured. The *Prière* is a poignant meditation where Langlais shows
the measure of his personality as an organist.

B369c. Rostand, Claude. "Chronique des nouveaux disques/Franck."
Disques (Paris) 58: 467.
Highly complimentary review; superb style and sound, brilliant execution.

B370. Ducretet-Thomson 270 C 003. *Messiaen/Langlais.* 1954.

Rostand, Claude. "Messiaen et Langlais: œuvres pour voix et orgue."
Disques 66 (Summer 1954): 464.
Langlais' recording of three Messiaen works is highly recommended, with
the comment that this is the first French LP of Messiaen's works. Only
78's exist, and LP's recorded outside France. "Incroyable, sans doute,
mais tristement vrai!" **(Unbelievable, no doubt, but sadly true!)**
Langlais' *Missa « In Simplicitate »* is evaluated as "one of the most
remarkable realizations in the field of contemporary religious music."

See also: B251, B279.

Studio SM 33-74. *Cantiques et messe brève.* 1960. (*See*: B275a, b)

B371. Studio SM 45-87. *Cinq motets de Jean Langlais.* 1962.

P., F. "Discographie." *Musique et Liturgie* 90 (November-
December 1962): 15 (31).
The freshness of execution and purity of inspiration are equal.

See also: B282a.

B372. Erato EFM 42.035. *Récital Jean Langlais.* 1957.

B372a. Tricou, Paul. "Les Disques." *Journal du Soir* (Lyon),
April 24, 1953.
Contrasting styles of four composers were well represented; the regis-
tration of the Pachelbel *Magnificat Versets* was particularly pleasing.

B372b. Valois, Jean de. "Discographie." *Musique et Liturgie* 62
(March-April 1958): 31.
Langlais' virtuosity and sense of tempo is praised, with some
reservations about a few registrations.

Erato LDE 3023. *Missa « Salve Regina ».* 1955. (*See*: B281b, h, i, m, n, q) Reissued as Erato STU 70358. 1967. (*See*: B176, B279d)

B373. Erato LDE 3024. *Œuvres modernes pour orgue.* 1955.

Sarnette, Eric. *Musique et Radio* 548 (January 1957): 29.
"Belonging to the same generation, having studied at the same school,
these two musicians **(Alain, Langlais)** do not hesitate to draw their
inspiration from sources of the far-away past while nevertheless keeping
their own personality."

B374. Erato LDE 3049. *Œuvres pour orgue d'inspiration grégorienne.* 1960.

B374a. Demarquez, Suzanne. "Œuvres pour orgue d'inspiration grégorienne." *Disques,* 1961.
Outstanding qualities of Langlais are his sincerity and lyricism.

B374b. Martin, V. "Récital Jean Langlais, orgue." *Guide du Concert et du Disque,* January 20, 1961.
Excellent review. Langlais gives a magnificient reading of the Tournemire works, as well as his own.

B374c. P., J. [Pagot, J.?] "Discographie." *Musique et Liturgie* 81 (May-June 1961): 15.
The music and Langlais' interpretations are praised.

B375. Erato LDEU 2024. *La Chorale de L'Institution Nationale des Jeunes Aveugles chante Noël.*

P., J. [Pagot, J.?] "Discographie." *Musique et Liturgie* 81 (May-June 1961): 16 (48).
The choir's diction is not quite captured, but the overall quality of this record and its picturesque Noels is good.

B376. Gregorian Institute of America 108-10, 208-10. *The Complete organ works of César Franck.* **1964.**

B376a. Bingham, Seth. "Cesar Franck: complete organ works." *Caecilia* 91, no. 2 (Summer 1964): 80-82.
The performance of each of the twelve pieces is discussed, and Langlais is judged "an ideal interpreter."

B376b. "Franck played at Basilique Sainte-Clotilde." *Le Guide du Concert* 450 (March 13, 1965): 11.

B376c. Van Bronkhorst, Charles. "New records." *The American Organist* 47, no. 7 (July 1964): 6.
Review praises the "authentic reproductions of Franck's musical intentions" through use of the composer's own registrations.

Medias MEM 0009F, 009FC45. *Jean Langlais improvise à Sainte Clotilde.* **1986.** (*See*: B237, B353)

B377. Motette M 1023. *Jean Langlais spielt französische orgelmusik in der Abteikirche Marienstatt.* **1979.**

B377a. Reynolds, Gordon. "The Critics' Choice -- 1982." *Gramophone* 60, no. 715 (December 1982): 696.
Reviewers chose the outstanding records of the year. This disc of French organ music and "two brilliant improvisations on plainsong hymns" is mentioned second in the list of four organ choices. Langlais is the only non-English organist selected.

B377b. -----. "Instrumental." *Gramophone* 59, no. 706 (March 1982): 1274.
"What a pleasure it is to hear such youthful confident playing from a man in his seventies."

B377c. Urwin, Ray W. "Reviews." *The American Organist* 14, no. 2 (February 1980): 12.
The *Te Deum* and two Vierne pieces receive "an excellent performance." The two improvisations are "beautiful and marvelous."

B378. Motette M 1037. *An der Cavaillé-Coll-Orgel von Ste. Clotilde-Paris: JEAN LANGLAIS.* **1981.**

    B378a. Gotwals, Vernon. "Reviews/records." *The American Organist* 17, no. 7 (July 1983): 21.
An important document showing the organist-composer at home.

    B378b. Reynolds, Gordon. "Instrumental." *Gramophone* 60, no. 716 (January 1983): 846.
Comments on the various organ sounds. Recommended as a young person's guide to the organ, "this box of delights filled with mysterious shapes and colours by a very great magician."

B379. Motette M 1066. *Orgelwerke von Joh. Seb. Bach/Jean Langlais an der orgel der Abtei Marienstatt.*

    Mardirosian, Haig. "Records/Bach: organ works." *The American Organist* 17, no. 9 (September 1983): 23-24.
Langlais' Bach style as recorded on Marienstatt's Rieger organ is "greatly Gallic, proudly romantic, deeply insightful."

B380. Motette M 10160. *Six esquisses pour deux orgues.* **1978.**

    B380a. Berger, Günter. "Schallplatten/Motette Ursina, Wiesbaden." *Ars Organi* 60 (September 1979): 604.   Excellent performances.

    B380b. Gotwals, Vernon. "Reviews." *The American Organist* 13, no. 7 (July 1979): 10.
An exciting sense of dialogue "is not clear from this recording."

    B380c. Mardirosian, Haig. "Langlais: Six esquisses pour deux orgues." *Fanfare* 9, no. 5 (May/June 1986): 167-68.
The reviewer notes "chromaticism and subtle drama" in these works, "somewhat understated" by the performers, yet with musical warmth.

    B380d. Reynolds, Gordon. "Organs and choirs." *Gramophone* 63, no. 751 (December 1985): 847-48.
The well-defined music has grandeur "studded with sharp-edged discords."

B381. Solstice SOL 1. *Langlais joue Langlais.* **1976.**

    Noisette de Crauzat, Claude. "Jean Langlais." *Harmonie* 138 (June-August 1978).
It is fascinating to hear a composer play his own works, here those from 1935-1970. The album interview gives real insight into Langlais' personality.

IN PREPARATION

B382. Jaquet-Langlais, Marie-Louise. "La vie et l'œuvre de Jean Langlais." Doctoral dissertation in musicology, University de Paris, [Sorbonne].

B383. Labounsky, Ann. "Jean Langlais: the man and his works." Ph.D. diss., University of Pittsburgh, scheduled for summer 1988.

B384. Sligting, Amelia C. "The eight organ duets of Jean Langlais." D.M.A. diss., American Conservatory of Music, Chicago, scheduled for 1988.

NONPRINT

FILM/VIDEO CASSETTE

B385. Vytvar, Vaclav. *The singing organ* (*Die singende orgel, L'Orgue chantant*). Filmed in Britanny, Paris, and Germany, 1983.
Excellent documentary film on Jean Langlais. Musical excerpts include the choral *Psaume Solennel 3* and organ works *Méditations sur l'Apocalypse* and *Double Fantaisie pour 2 organistes* played by Langlais and his wife. Available in English, German, French, or Dutch.

Two versions: a 16 mm. 40-minute film, and 26-minute video cassette, the latter currently available. European address: Vytvar Productions, Gutenbergstr. 18, D-4200 Oberhausen 1, West Germany.   American distributor: Cantus Productions Ltd., 156 Woburn Ave., Toronto, Ontario, M5M 1K7, Canada.

Premiere February 15, 1984, the Cathedral of Bonn, Germany, presented by Vaclav Vytvar, sponsored by the French Institute of Bonn and the Bonn Cathedral Musical Assocation.
Other performances February, 1984, Düsseldorf.
May 17, 1987, French television, channel 2.
July 22, 1987, Keynes Hall, King's College, Cambridge, England, during the International Congress of Organists. Shown as "a tribute to the French composer and organ virtuoso during the year of his 80th birthday." (p. 49, *Souvenir Handbook,* ICO 1987.)

B386. *Concert videotapes*. In files at universities and stations, *e.g.*:
Troisième Concerto: Réaction and *Messe Solennelle* filmed at the Crane School of Music, SUNY, Potsdam, New York, March 2, 1978, televised on PBS; 1987 Messiaen-Langlais dialogue and Paris concert mentioned in "Interview," page 19.

TAPE RECORDINGS

Many private copies exist, also interviews and concerts were recorded for radio. Some examples:

B387. *Labounsky collection*.   41 items on tapes made from 1972-85; interviews, masterclasses, improvisations, recitals, interpretations of his works for Musical Heritage Society recording project.

B388. *Messe Solennelle*. Concert at Boston Symphony Hall, March 27, 1954, recorded by Station WGBH-FM; Jean Langlais, organist, Theodore Marier, chorus director. Presented by Archbishop Richard J. Cushing in cooperation with the Boston Chapter of the American Guild of Organists. Program included Langlais' recital: works by K.P.E. Bach, J. S. Bach, Litaize, Vierne, four of his own compositions, and a four-movement improvised symphony on chant themes.

B389. *Passion, La*. Langlais has a tape of the 1958 French radio broadcast.

B390. *Pipedreams*. Produced by Michael Barone and the Minnesota Public Radio (St. Paul), distributed to affiliated stations of the American Public Radio Network.
February 1987, Program #8706, "Vive Langlais!" An 80th-birthday tribute

using recorded performances by Langlais with comments from Ann Labounsky.

B391. *Recital, St. George's Hall,* Liverpool, England. Langlais' program recorded in 1960 by Douglas R. Carrington.

B392. *Thomerson collection.* 8 tapes; interviews, improvisations, Paris concerts, lessons. 1976-86.

See also: B19, Station WQED-FM, Pittsburgh.

ARCHIVE COLLECTIONS

B393. *Labounsky, Ann.* Pittsburgh, PA, USA.
Copies of all Langlais' manuscripts made for doctoral research. Printed scores of almost all the published compositions, many European and American recordings.

B394. *Langlais, Jean.* Paris, France.
Manuscripts and scrapbooks of programs and press reviews are in Langlais' apartment.

B395. *Organ Library at Boston University School of Theology,* Boston, MA, USA.
In 1987 Karen McFarlane of Murtagh/McFarlane Artists Inc., Cleveland, Ohio, deposited her files of Langlais press reviews and correspondence. The material dates back to 1951 from the files of Langlais' previous managers, Colbert-LaBerge Concert Management, New York City, and Lilian Murtagh Concert Management, Canaan, Conn. The Organ Library, opened in November 1985, is a project of the Boston Chapter, American Guild of Organists, and is housed in a room of the Theology Library of Boston University. Inquiries may be addressed to the Organ Library, Boston University School of Theology, 745 Commonwealth Ave., Boston, MA 02215.

B396. *Thomerson, Kathleen.* Collinsville, IL, USA.
Copies of all articles and press reviews indexed in the present volume. 125 printed scores, 65 records, including 18 discs recorded by Langlais.

ADDENDA

Two articles were received after the bibliography was compiled and numbered:

B397. Jaquet-Langlais, Marie-Louise. "Anniversaire." *Bretagne et Orgue* 1, 1986.
The 40th anniversary celebration of Jean Langlais as titular organist at the Basilica of Sainte-Clotilde, 13-18 November 1985.

B398. -----. "Jean Langlais/L'Histoire d'une nomination mouvementée."
La Tribune de l'Orgue (Switzerland) 3, September 1987.
The story of the appointments of Ermend-Bonnal as *l'organiste
titulaire* at Sainte-Clotilde in 1942, and that of Langlais in 1945.
Includes letters written to Langlais in 1941 and 1942 by the parish
priest, the *Curé de Sainte-Clotilde*.

Appendix

This list is a catalog made by Marie-Louise Jaquet-Langlais as part of her dissertation work, presently in progress. The opus numbers are assigned with the composer's permission and approval. Sources used include a catalog written by Jeannette Langlais, the manuscripts, and published dates of first performances. Opus numbers from the earlier catalog are given here in brackets, for comparison. Compositions with a dash in brackets, [--] , are not found in the first catalog. The date when it was compiled is not known, though it appears to date from the 1950's, as those manuscripts lost during World War II are not listed. By 1958 the entries seem to be contemporary. After Jeannette Langlais' death the entries were made by Marie-Louise Jaquet-Langlais until early 1984, when she realized that revision was needed and started a new catalog. Some manuscripts of exercises from Paris Conservatory days exist, such as fugues written for the class of Noël Gallon. They have not been given an opus number as Jean Langlais regards them as study assignments. Many scores have been dated by the transcriber, making it possible to know the chronological order of such a large body of work. Unless otherwise designated, works are for organ solo. "Choir" indicates a choral work without independent accompaniment.

Opus	Date	Work
1	1927	Prélude et Fugue, W179 [1bis]
2	1929	Adoration des Bergers, W121 (from Six Préludes, W184) [1]
3		Prélude sur une antienne, later placed in W167, Opus 40 [--]
4		Thème Libre, W200 [--]
5	1930	Tantum Ergo, W70 [choir] [--]
6	1931	Deux Chansons de Clément Marot, W25 (printed as Opus 1) [choir] [2]
7	1932	Poèmes Evangéliques, W171 (printed as Opus 2) [3]
8	1932/42	Cinq Motets, W47 (printed as Opus 3) [choir, organ] [4]
9	1933/34	Trois Paraphrases grégoriennes, W162 (printed as Opus 5) [5]

10 1933/39 Vingt-quatre Pièces pour harmonium ou orgue, W166
              (printed as Opus 6) Vol. I, 12 pieces; Vol. 2, 12 pieces [6]
11   1934 La Voix du Vent, Hymne, W76 [choir, orchestra] [8]
12   Une dentelle s'abolit, W89 [vocal solo, piano] [--]
13   Suite pour piano à quatre mains, W219 [piano duet] [7]
14a   1935 Essai sur l'Evangile de Noël, W4
14b   Hymne d'Action de grâces, W5
             [versions for orchestra and organ] [11]
15   Trio, W230 [flute, violin, viola] (Suite Brève) [12]
16   Cloches de deuil, W1 [flutes, oboe, clarinet, bassoon,
                strings]   24 measure manuscript, with attached
             Minuet [same instrumentation] 27 meas., repeated [--]
17   Humilis, 6 mélodies, W94 [vocal solo, piano] [9]
18   Piece in Free Form, W212 [strings and organ] [14]
19   Messe pour 2 voix et harmonium, W41 [--]
20   1936 Suite Concertante, W10   (ms. marked   Opus 13)
             [violoncello, orchestra] [18]
21   Symphonie Concertante, W11 [piano, orchestra] [19]
22   Mélodies, W98 (ms. marked Opus 14, completed 1938) [vocal
             solo, piano] [13]
23   Mouvement perpètuel, W215 [piano] [17]
24   1937 Lègende de St. Nicolas, in W137 [20]
25   Ligne, W232 [violoncello solo, optional piano] [15]
26   Deux Psaumes, W61 (ms. marked Opus 17) [choir, organ/
             piano/orchestra] [21]
27   Thème, Variations et Final, W12 [strings, brass, and
             organ] [23]
28a   Choral Médiéval, W207 [3 trumpets,3 trombones, organ] [--]
29   Pièce symphonique, W7 [brass, strings, and organ; 3 move-
             ments: Opus 18, 28a, 27 of the present list] [23]
30   Prélude et Fugue, W218 [piano] [10]
31   1938 Suite armoricaine, W220 (printed as Opus 20) [piano] [22]
32   Parfums, W110 [vocal solo and piano] [--]
28b   Choral Médiéval, expanded version of W207 [3 trumpets,
             3 trombones, organ] [--]
33   Suite Bretonne, W231 [string ensemble] [--]
34   1940 Tantum Ergo, W71 [choir]   [24]
35   Quatre Mélodies, W101 [vocal solo, piano] [25]
36   1941 O Salutaris, W54 [choir, organ] [--]
--   O Bone Jesu, in W47, see Opus 8
37   Première Symphonie, W197 (completed 1942) [26]
38   Histoire vraie pour une Môn, W214 [piano] [--]
--   1942 Chant Litanique, in W47, see Opus 8

39   1942 Deux Pièces, W239   [flute, piano] [16]

40   1942-43 Neuf Pièces pour orgue, W165 [28]

41   1943 Mystère du Vendredi Saint, W49 [choir,organ(orchestra)][30]

42   Deux Offertoires pour tous les temps, W155 [29]

43   Suite concertante, W234 [violin, violoncello]
                original title: Duo [27]

44a, b   Pie Jesu, W114 [choir and vocal solo with violin, 'cello,
                and organ, optional harp] [--]

45   Trois Motets, W106 [1 or 2 voices, organ(orchestra)] [31]

46   1944 Trois Danses, W2 [woodwinds, piano] [32]

47   Suite pour clavecin, W221 [harpsichord] [33]

48   1946 Paroles, W111 [vocal solo, piano] [34]

49   Cantate à St. Vincent, W17 [choir, string orchestra] [35]

50   Le Diable qui n'est à personne, W3 [orchestra] [36]

51   Fête, W136 [37]

52   Pour Cécile, W115 [vocal solo, piano] [--]

53   1947 Cantate en l'honneur de Saint Louis-Marie de Montfort, W19
                [treble choir, organ, and optional trumpets] [38]

54   Suite brève, W192 [39]

55   La Ville d'Is (d'Ys), W75 [choir] [39b]

56   Suite médiévale, W194 [40]

57   Au pied du Calvaire, W80 [vocal solo, piano/organ] [41]

58   Lègende de St. Julien l'Hospitalier, W6 [orchestra] [42]

59   1948 Suite française, W193 [43]

60   Passe-temps de l'homme et des oiseaux, W112 [vocal solo,
                piano] [44]

61   Libera Me, Domine, W37 [choir, organ] [45]

62   Cantiques dans *Gloire au Seigneur*, W84 (1948-1952)
                [unison choir/soloist, organ/harmonium] [60]

63   1949 Premier Concerto pour orgue ou clavecin et orchestre, W210
                [47]

64   Incantation pour un jour Saint, W141 [46]

65   Trois Prières, W116 [vocal solo, organ] [48]

66   Trois Mélodies, W102 [vocal solo, piano] [49]

67   Messe Solennelle, W42 [choir] [50]

67a   [version with two organ accompaniment]

67b   [version with orchestral accompaniment]

68   1950 Le Soleil se lève sur Assise, W9 [orchestra] [51]

69   Four Postludes, W175 [52]

70   1951 Hommage à Frescobaldi, W139 [53]

71   My Heart's in the Highlands, W107 [vocal solo, piano] [54]

72   Pièces pour violon, W233 [violin, piano] [55]

73   Cantate de Noël, W18 [choir, orchestra] [56]

74	1952	Mass in Ancient Style, W39 [choir] [57]
75		Hommage à Louis Braille, W92 [vocal solo, piano] [58]
76		Missa "in simplicitate", W105 [vocal solo, organ] [59]
77		Folkloric Suite, W137 [61]
78		Armor, W79 [vocal solo, piano] [62]
79		Advent the promise, W13 [choir] [63]
80	1953	Caritas Christi, W24 (from the 1946 *Cantate à St. Vincent,* W17) [choir] [--]
81		Chants pour la Messe, W86 [unison choir/soloist, congregation, organ or harmonium] [64]
82	1954	Saint Clèment, W118 [vocal solo, piano or organ] [65]
83		Dominica in palmis, W130 (In die palmarum) [66]
84		Trois Chansons Populaires Bretonnes, W26 [treble choir] [67]
85		Missa Salve Regina, W44 [choir, congregation, organs, brass] [68]
86		Cinq Mélodies, W99 [vocal solo, piano] [69]
87	1955	Lauda Jerusalem Dominum, W36 [choir, congregation, organ] [70]
88		Antiennes, W15 (Antiphons, Gelineau Psalms) [choir] [--]
89	1956	Prélude, Fugue et Chaconne, W56 [choir] [71]
90		Huit Pièces Modales, W168 [72]
91		Organ Book, W160 [73]
92		Cantique Eucharistique, W83 [unison choir/solo,organ] [74]
93		Dieu, nous avons vu ta gloire, W31 [congregational hymn] [75]
--		Edition of *Six Sonatas for Organ* of C.P.E. Bach, in two volumes, no W* (cataloged by Jeannette Langlais as [76])
94		Prélude à la messe "*Orbis factor*", W176 [77]
95		Triptyque, W201 [78]
96	1957	Three Characteristic Pieces, W128 [79]
97		Office pour la Sainte Famille, W157 [80]
98		Office de la Sainte Trinitè, W156 [88]
99		La Passion, W55 [soloists, choir, large orchestra] [81]
100		Le Mystère du Christ, W48 [soloists, choir, orchestra] [82]
101	1958	Regina Caeli, W65 [treble choir, organ] [83]
102		Cantate "En ovale comme un jet d'eau", W20 [choir] [84]
103a		Psalm 150, "Praise Ye the Lord," W57 [male choir, organ] [85]
104		Motet "Venite et audite," W74 [choir] [86]
105		Missa Misericordiae Domini, W43 [choir, organ] [87]
106		Organ Postlude on the *Deo Gratias*, W161 [89]
107		Miniature, W149 [90]

108	1959	Sacerdos et Pontifex, W117 [unison choir, organ, brass][91]
109a		Trois Noëls, W50 [version for mixed choir] [92]
109b		Trois Noëls, W50 [version for male choir] [93]
110		American Suite, W123 [94]
111		L'Errante, W90 [vocal solo, piano] [95]
112	1960	Rhapsodie savoyarde, W187 [96]
--		Pièces pour la *Nouvelle Méthode de Clavier*, W169 [--]
113		Deux petites pièces dans le style médiéval, W169 [97]
114		Deux versets du 7e ton, W169 [--]
115		Noëls populaires anciens, W51 [choir, organ/piano] [98]
116		Neuf Chansons folkloriques françaises, W85 [unison choir, piano] [99]
117		Motet pour un temps de pénitence, W46 [choir] [100]
118	1961	Nouveaux chants français pour la messe, W108 [unison choir, organ] [101]
119		Sonnerie, W223 [brass choir] [102]
120		Europa, Hymne, W91 [vocal solo] [103]
121		Deuxième Concerto, W209 [organ, string orchestra] [104]
122		Ave Maris Stella, W16 [choir] [105]
123		O God, our father, W53 [choir, organ] [106]
103b		Psalm 150, "Praise the Lord," W57 [a. 1958 version for male choir, organ] [85] [b. 1961 version for mixed choir, organ, brass] [107]
124		Deux Chansons Populaires de Haute-Bretagne, W27 [choir] [108]
125		A la claire fontaine, W14 [choir] [108bis]
126	1962	Trois Méditations sur la Sainte Trinite, W147 [109]
127		Dix versets dans les modes grégoriens (includes the Deux versets, Opus 114), combined with Deux petites pièces (Opus 113); title: Douze petites pièces, W163 [110]
128		Essai (Trial), W133 [111]
129		Offertoire pour l'office de Ste. Claire, W52 [choir] [112]
130		Douze Cantiques Bibliques, W23 [113]
130a		[version for unison choir]
130b		[version for mixed choir]
131		Missa "Dona nobis pacem," W104 [unison choir, organ][116]
132a		Homage to Jean-Philippe Rameau, W138 (first version) [114]
133		MacKenzie, W95 [vocal solo, piano] [117]
134		Psaume Solennel no. 1, "Laudate Dominum in Sanctis ejus" (Ps. 150), W62 [choirs, organ, brass, timpani] [115]
135	1963	Prelude on *Coronation*, W181 [118]
136		Chants pour la Pentecôte, "Ouvron nos cœurs à l'Esprit," W87 [unison choir, organ/harmonium] [119]

132b 1963 Homage to Jean-Philippe Rameau, W138 (final version) [120]
137   Deux mélodies, W100 [vocal solo, piano] [121]
138   Psaume Solennel no. 2, "Miserere Mei Deus" (Ps. 50), W63
              [choirs, organ, brass, timpani] [122]
139 1964 Chants pour les dimanches de l'Avent, W88 [unison choir,
              organ/harmonium] [123]
140   Psaume Solennel no. 3, "Laudate Dominum de caelis"
              (Ps. 148), W64 [choirs, organ, brass, timpani] [124]
141   Mass "God have Mercy," W96 [unison choir, organ] [125]
142 1965 Messe "Dieu, prends pitié," W40 [126]
142a   [version for mixed choir, congregation, organ]
142b   [version for unison choir, congregation, organ]
143   Chant d'entrée pour la fête de Saint-Vincent, W28 [mixed or
              unison choir, congregation, accompaniment] [127]
144   Poem of Life, W173 [128]
145   Mass "On earth peace," W97 [unison choir, organ] [129]
146   The Canticle of the Sun, W22 [130]
146a   [version for choir, organ/piano]
146b   [version for choir, strings, organ/piano]
147   Elegie, W229 [flute, oboe, clarinet, French horn,
              bassoon, string quintet] [131]
148   Pater Noster, W113 [definitive French translation, unison
              choir] [132]
149   Messe "Joie sur Terre," W103 (final version of Chants pour la
              Messe, W86, Opus 81, with revisions and Credo) [unison
              choir/soloist, congregation, organ/harmonium] [--]
150 1966 Poem of Peace, W174 [133]
151   Poem of Happiness, W172 [134]
152 1967 Carillons, W222 [handbells] [135]
153   Sonate en Trio, W190 [136]
154   Rèpons pour une Messe de Funèrailles, W67 [mixed choir or
              vocal solo, organ] [137]
155 1968 Livre Œcumènique, W144 [138]
156   Prélude dans le Style ancien, W177 [139a]
157   Adoration, W120 [139b]
158   Psaume 120, "Des montées," W60 [choir, organ] [140]
159 1969 Solemn Mass, W69 [choir, congregation, organ, brass][141]
160   Festival Alleluia, W32 [choir, organ] [142]
161   Cortége, W208 [2 organs, 8 brass, timpani] [143]
162   Three Voluntaries, W205 [144]
163 1970 Cantate "Le Prince de la Paix," W21 [choir, organ] [145]
164   Trois Implorations, W140 [146]

165   1971 Troisième Concerto: Réaction, W211   [organ, string
            orchestra, timpani] [147]
166   Cinq Chorals (Choralvorspiele), W129 [148]
167   Pièce pour trompette, W226   [trumpet/oboe/flute,
            organ/piano accompaniment] [149]
168   Offrande à Marie, W158 [150]
169   1972 Supplication, W195 [151]
170   Sept Chorals pour trompette, W225   [trumpet/oboe/flute,
            organ/piano/harpsichord accompaniment] [152]
171   1973 Hymn of Praise "Te Deum Laudamus," W35   [choir,
            congregation, organ, trumpets, timpani] [153]
172   Trois Oraisons, W109 [unison choir/solo, flute, organ]
            [154]
173   Cinq Méditations sur l'Apocalypse, W146 [155]
174   Suite baroque, W191 [156]
175   1974 Rèpons Liturgiques Protestants, W66   [choir, organ] [157]
176   Plein Jeu à la française, W170 [158]
177   Diptyque pour piano et orgue, W213 [piano-organ duet] [159]
178   Cinq Pièces, W238 [flute/violin, piano/organ/harpsichord]
            [160]
179   Huit Chants de Bretagne, W127 [161]
180   Vocalise, W119 [vocal solo, piano] [162]
181   1975 Cèlèbration, W126 [163]
182   Hommage à Louis Braille, W93   [vocal solo, piano] [164]
183   Quatre Préludes, W183 [165]
184   Trois Esquisses Romanes, W132 [166]
185   Trois Esquisses Gothiques, W131 [167]
186   Gloire à toi Marie, W33   [noted as (60), placed between 167
            and 168]
            [a. version for unison voices, in W84, Opus 62]
            [b. version for 3 treble voices, W33, arr. 1975]
            [c. version for mixed choir, 4 parts, W33, arr. 1975]
187   1976 Mosaïque I, W151 [174-75]
            Stèle pour Gabriel Fauré [174] [arr. from Opus 8, no.2]
            Double Fantaisie [175]   (The other two pieces in the
            volume are from W123, Opus 110)
188   Six petites pièces, W164 (Organ Method A. Hobbs) [168-73]
189   Mosaïque II, W152 [179]
190   Sonatine, W228 [trumpet, piano/organ] [176]
191   Cantique en l'honneur d'Anne de Bretagne, W82 [unison choir,
            organ] [173bis]
192   Psaume 116, "Laudate Dominum omnes gentes," W59 [choir,
            organ, 3 trumpets] [177bis]

193   1976 Deuxième Symphonie "alla Webern," W196 (Completed January
          11, 1977) [177]
194   1977 Mosaïque III, W153
              Parfum [180] ;   Lumière [181] ;   Printemps, thème danois
              (Danish theme) [182] ; Thèmes [184] ;   Double Fantaisie,
              2ème [185] ; Pax [186]
195   Ave Maris Stella, Choral pour orgue, W124 [178]
196   Psaume 111, "Beatus vir qui timet Dominum," W58 [choir,
              organ] [183]
197   1978 Triptyque Grégorien, W202 [187]
198   Three Short Anthems, W68 [choir, organ] [189]
199   Progression, W186 [188]
200   1979 La Prière pour les Marins, W240 [choir] [--]
201   Mass "Grant Us Thy Peace," W38 [choir, organ] [194]
202   Noëls avec variations, W154 [191]
203   Prelude Grégorien, W180 [190]
204   Offrande à une âme, Diptyque, W159 [192]
205   Troisième Symphonie, W198 [198]
206   Corpus Christi, W30 [choir, organ] [193]
207   Marienstatt Chorals, W145 [organ preludes, also organ/
              choir harmonizations] [195]
208   1980 Réminiscences, W8 [strings, 2 flutes/trumpets, timpani,
              harpsichord] [196]
209   Rosace, W188 [197]
210a 1981 Chant des Bergers, W121 ([1] reprinted) [199]
210b   Prière des Mages, W185 (arranged for organ from W211, Opus
              165) [199]
211   A la Vierge Marie, W77 [vocal solo, organ/piano] [200]
212   1982 Pastorale et Rondo, W224 [2 trumpets, organ] [201]
213   Prélude et Allégro, W178 [202]
214   Alleluia-Amen, W78 [unison choir/solo, organ] [203]
215   Deux Chants Choral, W29 [choir, optional organ] [--]
1   Prélude et Fugue, W179 ([1bis] of 1927, entered again at
              time of publication) [204]
216   1983 Cinq Soleils, W189 [205]
217   Sept Etudes de Concert pour pédale seule, W134 [206]
218   Deux Pièces Brèves, W167 [207]
219   Petite Rhapsodie, W237 [flute, piano] [208]
220   Huit Préludes, W182 [--]
221   1984 Méthode d'Orgue, W148 (with Marie-Louise Jaquet-Langlais)
              [--]
222   Miniature II, W150 [--]
223   Hymne du Soir, W34 [choir] [209]

224   1985 Talitah Koum (Résurrection), W199
225   Drei leichte Stücke für Orgel/Trois Pièces faciles pour
              orgue/Three easy pieces for organ, W143
226   Hymntune, "A Morning Hymn," W45 [choir, organ]
227   Hymntune, "The Threefold Truth," W72 [choir, organ]
228   B.A.C.H., Six Pièces pour orgue, W125
229   1986 American Folk-Hymn Settings, W122
230   In Memoriam, W142
231   Petite Suite, W217 [piano]
232   Ubi Caritas, W73 [choir, organ]
233   Neuf Pièces, W227 [trumpet, organ]
234   Douze Versets pour orgue, W204
235   15 Elevations, W206 (Title changed, combined with 15 short
              pieces by Naji Hakim, probable new title: Expressions)
236   Fantasy on Two Scottish Themes, W135
132c   1987 Hommage à Rameau, W138 (Three pieces reprinted: Ostinato,
              Meditation, and Evocation, from the out-of-print *Homage
              to Jean-Philippe Rameau*)
237   Trumpet Tune, W203
238   Mouvement pour flute et clavier, W236 [flute, keyboard]
239   Noël Breton, W216 [piano]
240   Pièce pour clarinette et piano, W235   [clarinet, piano]

DATE NOT KNOWN, UNCATALOGED, NO OPUS NUMBER:
              Ave Maria, W81   [voice, organ, violin, violoncello,
              manuscript of 20 measures is not dated; uncataloged;
              not copyrighted; no performance recorded; possibly
              written as funeral solo, *see* W114, Pie Jesu] [--]

Index of Works

Page numbers, *e.g.,* p. 5, refer to pages in the "Biography" section. Numbers preceded by a "W" refer to the "Works and Performances" section, numbers preceded by a "D" to the "Discography," and numbers preceded by a "B" to the "Bibliography." Capitalization follows the form found on printed scores or on manuscripts. Alphabetization is the letter-by-letter system; "Organ Postlude" precedes "O Salutaris."

Index of Authors and Translators

Authors with additional entries are designated by "GI" for "General Index." All "B" numbers refer to the "Bibliography." Page numbers, *e.g.*, p. 5, refer to pages in the "Biography" section.

A., A., B269a
Abel, Jean, B1
Affelder, Paul, B369a
Alain, Olivier, B2, B335a
Alderman, Hugh, B292a
Allan, Gilbert, B281b
Alston, Vernon, B3
Altomont, Claude, B288a, B342a
Anderson, Roy, B278a
Arnatt, Ronald, B348
Arnold, A. N., B4
Arnold, Denis, B278b
Assistant, Un, B5
Aubert, Louis, B264a, GI

B., P., B336a
Banta, Lorene, B318a
Barber, Clarence H., B7
Barnard, L. S., B8
Barrett, Gavin, B9
Barrillon, Raymond, B10
Beckley, Paul V., B12
Beechey, Gwilym, B13, B313a, B335b
Berens, Fritz, B14
Bernard, Robert, B336b
Berry, Ray, B15, B281c, B292b, B336c
Bertault, Julien, B16, B294, B350, GI
Bertho, Hervé, B17
Biba, Otto, B18
Billings, David, p. 16n.8, B19, B20
Bingham, Seth, p. 16n.9, B21–25, B317a, B320a, B323, B341a–b, B376a, GI
Birkby, Arthur, B26

Birley, Margaret, B27
Blanchard, Robert I., B322a, B324a
Blanchard, Roger, B279a
Bloch, Catherine, B28
Boeglin, Paul, B29
Bonfils, Jean, B297a, GI
Boros, Ethel, B30
Bousquet, R., B319a
Bovet, Guy, B301a
Bret, Gustave, B349
Brierre, Anne, B32
Brousse, J. J., B33
Bruyr, José, B275a, B281e
Burns, Richard C., B34
Busch, Hermann J., B307, B309a, B368
Butcher, Harold, B35

C., E., B288b
C., J., B328a
Cantrell, Scott, B37, B297a
Capdeville, Pierre, B288c, GI
Carbou, François, p. 6, B38, GI
Case, Del Williams, B321a
Caylot, A. M., B266–67a
Chailley, Jacques, B279b, GI
Chamfray, Claude, B292c, B339a
Chasse, Charles, B39
Chatellard, Francis, B40
Ciccone, Louis, B41
Clarendon, B284, B285a
Coci, Claire, B335c, GI
Cogen, Pierre, B42, GI
Cohn, Arthur, B43, B278c, B303
Cooksey, Steven Lee, B44
Coqueux-Le Boel, Pierre, B46
Craig, Dale, B47

General Index

The letter-by-letter system of alphabetizing is used; "St. John's College" precedes "St. John Seminary Choir." Page numbers, *e.g.*, p. 3, refer to pages in the "Biography," "Interviews," or "Appendix" sections. Numbers preceded by a "W" refer to the "Works and Performances" section, numbers preceded by a "D" to the "Discography," and numbers preceded by a "B" to the "Bibliography." "IAT" indicates additional listings are found in the "Index of Authors and Translators."

About the Author

Organist Kathleen Thomerson, Music Director of University United Methodist Church in St. Louis, Missouri, teaches organ at Southern Illinois University, Edwardsville, and the St. Louis Conservatory of Music. She holds the certificates of Fellow and Choirmaster from the American Guild of Organists, and is a past member of the National Council of the AGO. Mrs. Thomerson received a Master of Music degree with Performance Award Diploma from the University of Texas, and studied in Europe at the Flemish Royal Conservatory in Antwerp with Flor Peeters, and privately in Paris with Jean Langlais. In addition to recitals in the United States, she has played in Coventry Cathedral, England; Paisley Abbey, Scotland; the Basilica of Sainte-Clotilde, Paris; the Abbey of Tongerlo, Belgium; and most recently, August 1987, in the Cathedral of Notre-Dame de Paris.